HOW KENTUCKY
BECAME SOUTHERN

HOW KENTUCKY BECAME SOUTHERN

a tale of **OUTLAWS, HORSE THIEVES, GAMBLERS,** *and* **BREEDERS**

Maryjean Wall

THE UNIVERSITY PRESS OF KENTUCKY

Scholarly publisher for the Commonwealth,
serving Bellarmine University, Berea College, Centre
College of Kentucky, Eastern Kentucky University,
The Filson Historical Society, Georgetown College,
Kentucky Historical Society, Kentucky State University,
Morehead State University, Murray State University,
Northern Kentucky University, Transylvania University,
University of Kentucky, University of Louisville,
and Western Kentucky University.
All rights reserved.

Editorial and Sales Offices: The University Press of Kentucky
663 South Limestone Street, Lexington, Kentucky 40508-4008
www.kentuckypress.com

14 13 12 11 10   5 4 3 2 1

Library of Congress Cataloging-in-Publication Data

Wall, Maryjean.
  How Kentucky became southern : a tale of outlaws, horse thieves,
gamblers, and breeders / Maryjean Wall.
       p.   cm.
  Includes bibliographical references and index.
  ISBN 978-0-8131-2605-0 (hardcover : alk. paper)
  1. Horse racing—Kentucky—History—19th century. 2. Horse
industry—Kentucky—History—19th century. 3. Kentucky—Social
life and customs—19th century. I. Title.
  SF335.U6K66 2010
  798.409769'09034—dc22

                              2010020664

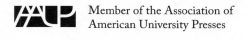

To my parents,
John and Mary Wall,
who believed in education

Contents

The Kentucky colonel is often associated with the traditions and history of Thoroughbred racing in Kentucky. (1917 postcard from the author's collection.)

Introduction

Kentucky, racehorses, and Southern colonels just seem to go together naturally. Whether picturing Bluegrass horse farms or their close relative, the Kentucky Derby, many of us cannot summon one of those images without calling up all three. The goateed colonel holds the dominant position in the landscape of imagination that defines this central portion of Kentucky. Place the colonel on the colonnaded plaza of a grand mansion, surround him with guests and family sipping juleps served on silver trays, indulge him in his telling of tall tales about fast horses, and the image evokes Kentucky horse country.

This picture has been stamped so indelibly on notions of Bluegrass Thoroughbred culture that not even Kentuckians seem aware that horse country did not historically fit this image. To borrow a phrase from Michael Kammen, who argues that memory is reconstructed as history, the "mystic chords of memory" have failed to serve Bluegrass history in any faithful way. True, the mineral-rich soil, water, and bluegrass, the latter known scientifically as *Poa pratensis,* did spawn a significant racehorse business during the antebellum period. However, this business as it stood in Kentucky rocked precariously on the edge of decline during the first forty or fifty postbellum years. True, Thoroughbred horse racing experienced an explosive growth in popularity during this era. However, at the same time, Kentucky lost its dominant position as the locus for the breeding of racehorses. Modern new farms were arising in New Jersey and New York, fragmenting the business among multiple states.[1]

A generation would pass before Bluegrass Kentuckians managed to return the center of the Thoroughbred breeding world to their region. This mattered greatly to them, primarily because of the direct and residual income that a Bluegrass-centered industry could bring to the state. We all know how the story turned out: that horse breeding became the commonwealth's signature agricultural industry, bringing worldwide respect and recognition to the state. Today, the Kentucky horse industry has an economic impact that is estimated to be $4 billion, not to mention the $8.8 billion in associated tourism that it brings in. Had the story turned out differently, the commonwealth might never have realized the wealth in modern times that horses have brought to it. The victory was hard-won.[2]

Many are unaware that, for decades, Kentucky horsemen engaged in a power struggle with the new money in the sport—those industrialists and capitalists of New York who were spending money at unprecedented levels to develop horse farms in the Northeast. The architecture and design of these new horse-breeding operations in New Jersey and New York outshone anything existent in Kentucky, even the famed Woodburn Farm. The latter, a premier breeding operation located in Woodford County and known throughout the United States even before the Civil War, stood the leading stallions in the United States at stud. However, Woodburn Farm could not boast of the fancy appointments of these nouveau racehorse operations rising in the Northeast. The agricultural wealth of Kentuckians simply could not compete with the vast array of industrial wealth in the Northeast. Only one among Kentucky's horse breeders, Robert Aitcheson Alexander, who owned Woodburn Farm, possessed a fortune founded in industry. The numerous industrialists from the Northeast who were getting into the sport outnumbered him. And it was to the Northeast that the center of the sport had swung, with the new men of the turf breeding their own mares to their own stallions far removed from traditional horse country.

Permanent loss of this business would have affected the Bluegrass region in myriad ways, beginning with the physical landscape that has become iconic to horse country; this iconography helps draw tourism and other business. The physical landscape that marks central Kentucky as horse country includes the multitude of manicured farms, such as Calumet, that exist close to the city and can be seen without having to travel too far from downtown Lexington. The regional iconography extends to the miles of board fences signifying horses, the architecturally astounding horse barns, and the emerald-green pastures populated with bloodstock that is valued in the multimillions of dollars. As for the economic impact, earnings from horse farms ripple through the regional and state economy in numerous directions, ranging from veterinary services and hay and feed suppliers to grocery stores, office supply companies, automobile dealerships, insurance companies, and shopping malls, bringing a better lifestyle to residents regardless of whether they are directly involved in the horse economy. If the story behind the making of Kentucky's horse business provides a usable past, it is the cautionary tale of how integral this business remains to the state's economy—and how, without protection, it could easily be snatched away by other states eager to grab the wealth.

The overarching theme behind this struggle to build a Kentucky horse industry was the realization among the region's horsemen that they could not begin to do so without luring the big money from outside capitalists into central Kentucky. And it is my contention in this book that the money began to flow into Bluegrass Kentucky only after both locals and outsiders embraced a popular plantation myth that gave the region a neo-Southern identity. Ironically, this occurred some thirty-five to forty years after the end of the Civil War and the disappearance of the Old South. Bluegrass Kentucky's new identity had fortunate economic consequences, as it negated the region's notorious reputation for violence and lawlessness, thus bringing business to horse country. But, at the same time, this altered identity excluded African Americans from participation in the new horse industry. The new identity also rewrote the region's history, for it ignored the role the commonwealth had played as a loyal part of the United States during the Civil War. A mistaken notion grew that Kentucky had remained neutral throughout the war.

The neo-Southern image was a cleverly crafted picture, situating the Bluegrass within an Eden of smoothly operating plantations where the horses ran fast, the living seemed ideal, and all African Americans occupied servile positions of offering juleps to the colonels as the white folk relaxed in the shade of columned mansions. This picture grew in direct contrast to the highly visible sphere that blacks had occupied as

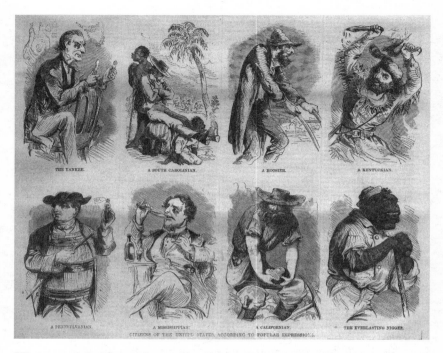

"Citizens of the United States according to Popular Impressions." Although highly offensive to modern sensibilities, this illustration depicts stereotypes associated in 1867 with a variety of Americans. The popular image of Kentuckians retained the old notions of the Western frontier: a wild, uncivilized character in coonskin cap with a hunting knife in one hand and a recently taken scalp in the other. Bluegrass Kentucky would not begin to acquire its civilized and highly polished Southern identity until decades later. (*Harper's Weekly*, January 12, 1867, 29.)

star athletes of the sport, some, like the jockey Isaac Murphy, becoming wealthy in the generation following freedom.

Today, some persons might argue that, as a slaveholding state, Kentucky shared a common ideology and common characteristics with the seceded South even if it had remained loyal to the United States. Commonly shared interests did exist; however, Americans of that era did not readily view Kentucky as Southern. Neither did all Kentuckians, who were notoriously divided on who and what they were. Kentucky was a state of multiple regions, each with its own identity. The state's overall identity was imprecise and vague.

We've all heard the story that Kentucky did not secede from the Union—until after the war was over. Arguably, the state's central region, the Bluegrass horse country, did not begin to associate with a Confederate identity until sometime after the Civil War. The historian Anne Marshall has pointed out that this turn appeared quite strange indeed, given that it brought Kentuckians to embrace the war's losing side when in reality Kentucky had fought on the winning side. Historians are beginning to show how and why this notion expanded within the regional consciousness.[3]

Generations of Kentuckians once explained away this change of mind as pure resentment over atrocities that the U.S. Army committed while stationed in the commonwealth. E. Merton Coulter had promulgated this theory in his history of Kentucky after the Civil War. As a Southern man of his times—the 1920s and 1930s—he had viewed the Kentucky conundrum through a racist and neo-Confederate prism. According to his analysis, Kentuckians turned their backs on the federal government and wished, in retrospect, that they had fought on the side of the Confederate states. They made their feelings clear when they assimilated a Confederate identity after the war was over. Revisionists have effectively argued against Coulter's thesis. But, until recently, little work had been done to explain whether and why, if Coulter's theory no longer held up, Kentucky had actually gone over to the side that had lost.[4]

More recent historians of Kentucky generally have agreed that, following the war, those Kentuckians living at least in the central portion of the state—the Bluegrass—increasingly identified with the Southern states. However, they do not agree specifically on when, how, or why this turn occurred. For example, Marshall has argued that white Kentuckians came to imagine their state as Confederate by embracing racial violence, Democratic rallies, and the myth of the Lost Cause, all of which suggested a Southern and Confederate identity. Luke Edward Harlow has connected a proslavery theology in the politics of Kentuckians—following the demise of slavery—as a link to a Confederate identity. In his argument, Kentuckians reconfigured white religious understandings of slavery from before the war into a justification for Jim Crow practices long after the war.[5]

I argue in this study that Bluegrass horsemen joined with outsiders in assigning a Southern identity to their region early in the twentieth century, when doing so suited the nostalgic needs of white Americans generally and the economic needs of Bluegrass horsemen specifically.

Americans at the turn of the twentieth century felt beleaguered. They longed for a more wholesome and orderly lifestyle that they believed might have existed in the past. A postwar, industrialized age that people had hoped would create an easier lifestyle for all was accomplishing the opposite: creating angst because machines replaced traditional craftsmen, because large corporations devoured family businesses, and because industrialists, capitalists, and the financial speculators on Wall Street had cornered the majority of American wealth. These wealthy folk might have seemed to inhabit an ideal sphere, given their magnificent mansions, their elegant parties, and their showy stables of racehorses. But not even the very rich could escape the rising angst of the times. They lived in a world fraught with violent labor strikes directed against their industries, with race riots in their city streets, and with servant problems in the private sphere of their homes.

Small wonder, then, that the upper class as well as the middle class found an escape in novels and nonfiction idealizing the past. This past came popularly to life as an imagined antebellum Southern lifestyle. As depicted on the printed page, this antebellum world appeared as quite the opposite of the impersonal world that Americans knew at the turn of the twentieth century. The Southern cavalier ruled his plantation with a fatherly kindness that benefited both his family and his servants. The only turmoil to be found in this imagined world might have been a daughter's love affair with a Yankee, a love affair that crossed taboo geographic lines. As it happened, the Bluegrass region of Kentucky became associated with this cavalier South thanks to a group of esteemed and highly popular writers whose work pictured central Kentucky in these terms. Outsiders and regional inhabitants alike began to picture horse country in a new and different way that brought a great economic boom to the region's equine business. This boom turned the Bluegrass into the horse capital of the world.

Bluegrass horse and business interests had been trying since the Civil War to attract outside capital to the region. But they never were successful, largely owing to the violence and lawlessness that kept this capital away. Not until Bluegrass Kentucky evolved as Southern in the popular imagination did those outsiders with big money change their

Iconic to Bluegrass Kentucky are images of well-bred horses, well-bred women, and Southern mansions. (Undated postcard from the collection of the author.)

minds about buying into the region's horse-farm land. When the outsiders began buying up Bluegrass land, they helped create a horse-farm iconography with the lavish improvements they made to the land. The mining king James Ben Ali Haggin at Elmendorf Farm and the Wall Street wizard James Keene at Castleton Farm, both of these Thoroughbred operations, and the Standard Oil heir Lamon Harkness, who created a trotting-horse estate at Walnut Hall Farm, came first. More soon followed. As this study will show, an imagined construct of plantation life that quickly morphed into reality enabled the Bluegrass to acquire unusual cachet, thus regaining the power in the horse world that it had lost after the Civil War.

Chapter 1 shows how Kentucky racehorse breeders got left behind in the new expansion of the sport even before the Civil War had ended. Racing shifted to the Northeast, Bluegrass breeders lost valuable horses to both armies as well as to guerrillas and outlaws, and the only plan of action for a productive future resided with Robert Aitcheson Alexander, the owner of Woodburn Farm, and his handpicked associates. However, not even Alexander could foresee the future faultlessly. He forfeited an opportunity to immediately align the interests of Kentucky horsemen with those in the Northeast when he ignored their requests to send his brilliant racehorse Asteroid to Saratoga Race Course. This apparent snub of the outsiders, new to Thoroughbred racing, turned out to haunt Kentucky's breeding business. The New Yorkers eventually retired their brilliant racehorse, called Kentucky, to stand in New York. This portended a shift in horse breeding to the Northeast, following the sport of racing.

Chapter 2 describes the competition that breeders in central Kentucky faced in trying to join the expansion of Thoroughbred racing. Lavish, ultramodern horse farms began arising in New York and New Jersey. As well, Tennessee horse breeders quickly reestablished their business, giving Kentucky competition from the South. Bluegrass horsemen also faced major labor shortages after the war. Had they not found a way to lure labor back to the farms—by creating rural hamlets for the labor force—the horse business might never have progressed. The greatest assist to Kentucky's horsemen, however, was in the voice they acquired in the publishing world of New York through Alexander's associates, Sanders and Benjamin Bruce. The two brothers initiated marketing techniques that helped bring attention to Bluegrass farm country. These two set about trying to show how the natural advantages in Kentucky Bluegrass soil and water resulted in superior racehorses. However much attention their marketing efforts brought to the Bluegrass, these efforts still failed to bring the capitalists. The reputation for violence in the Bluegrass had stamped the region as too unstable for capital investment.

Chapter 3 demonstrates how the culture of violence and lawlessness made the Bluegrass region as unsafe for the wealthy landowner as it was for all others, including African Americans. It also reveals how even the wealthy landowners manipulated the culture of violence, going outside the law when it suited their purposes. The gentry class in the Bluegrass manipulated the Ku Klux Klan, according to the New York press. Events at Nantura Farm in Woodford County, adjacent to the famed Woodburn Farm, demonstrated the extent to which landowners went in following or mimicking KKK practices. Every lawless event, however, stacked up against the Bluegrass, making it that much harder for the region to regain its central position in horse breeding.

Chapter 4 brings to light the success and accomplishments of the African American horsemen who, in turn, brought recognition to Kentucky's horse business. Recognition boosted the fragmented reputation of Kentucky as the cradle of the racehorse. African American jockeys and horse trainers were iconic to Kentucky's horse country, and some of the most talented competed successfully against white riders in the Northeast. Black horsemen appeared to live protected lives apart from the violence raging against blacks in Kentucky. The most talented black jockey, Isaac Murphy, lived a lifestyle parallel to that of whites in Lexington and entertained with elaborate parties given at his mansion. But the recognition of their talent and way with horses given to black jockeys and trainers was never enough to bring the big money to the Bluegrass and to centralize the growing industry in the commonwealth. The business remained fragmented, with the majority of the largest, most productive farms lost to the Bluegrass.

Chapter 5 illuminates the tensions arising between Northeastern and Kentucky racing interests at the very time the sport underwent a nationwide expansion. This power struggle further fragmented the sport, with racing leaders in New York doing whatever they pleased to minimize the significance of competing interests in Kentucky. Nonetheless, the face of the sport was changing from the small sphere of the New York banker August Belmont and his acquaintances from industry and Wall Street. The sport had grown far beyond the vision they had held, to draw in mining kings and railroad industrialists of the West and Midwest. This expansion began to see increasing numbers of horse owners reaching down into the Bluegrass for stock to replenish their

racing stables. Their object was to find a winning edge over an expanding competition base. However, with violence continuing unabated in
the Bluegrass, none of these wealthy men moved their operations to the
region. Consequently, only a few of the most fortunate Bluegrass horse
breeders experienced financial wealth; the industry remained fragmented throughout a variety of states. A critical turn was August Belmont's
decision to move his breeding operation from Long Island to Lexington. Kentucky's reputation for violence shone an unflattering spotlight
on this move, for Belmont's manager arrived in Lexington fully armed.
With the reputation and the reality of violence continuing unabated in
central Kentucky, Belmont's move failed to initiate a run of capitalists
on Bluegrass land.

Chapter 6 illuminates how the campaign of social reformers to
shut down Thoroughbred racing throughout the United States would
eventually tie in to Kentucky helping save and centralize the industry by
manipulating the Southern myth. By the 1890s, the expansion of racing had brought fraudulent practices to the sport, drawing the attention
of antigambling forces. By the early twentieth century, social reformers
had persuaded various state legislatures to shut down racing in many
jurisdictions, most notably in New York. A number of the wealthiest
in racing sent their stables to Europe to race. But some held out the
possibility that racing might return to New York. One was a Bluegrass
entrepreneur named John Madden, whose life story was partly Horatio
Alger and partly that of the physically fit, natural man that President
Theodore Roosevelt believed was the only type that could return order
and supremacy to white America. Madden began to draw the interest of
wealthy men in racing. He sold them horses at fantastic prices, gaining
their trust, not only because of his expert horsemanship, but also because
he represented the pristine, natural, white American. He projected this
popular image onto the Bluegrass region, helping create a notion that
vied successfully with the debilitating picture that the antigambling forces had projected onto the sport. The image Madden projected also might
have diminished somewhat the lawless reputation of the Bluegrass.

Chapter 7 concludes this study by demonstrating how the rising
popularity of the plantation myth created a Southern identity for the
Bluegrass; this new identity elevated Kentucky horse country into a
place that America's wealthy desired to own. Consequently, the wealthy

bought Kentucky farms, and the industry became centered in the Bluegrass. Madden, Murphy, and others had laid the building blocks; the plantation myth corralled the free-floating images these men had evoked into a nostalgic notion of the antebellum South that white Americans now were eager to embrace. Wealthy capitalists began purchasing Bluegrass horse farms, bringing into the region the big money that enabled the industry to grow. The plantation myth caused these capitalists to overlook and ignore the ongoing violence and lawlessness that continued in the region. It also dashed all future possibilities for African American jockeys and horse trainers in the sport. They simply disappeared even though they had once been iconic to Kentucky racing. However, Northeastern turfmen who now were combining with Bluegrass interests to change the identity of the region looked on African Americans with repugnance. In this instance, big money trumped racial possibilities. A lily-white sport emerged even as the Bluegrass regained its centrality to racehorse breeding. The stamp of approval was the Confederate memorial to General John Hunt Morgan erected at the courthouse in Lexington with major help from families in the horse business.

This story is not told in the published histories of the sport. The narratives popular in Thoroughbred racing generally have assumed that Bluegrass Kentucky was the cradle of the American racehorse and always has been, and always will be, central to the horse racing industry. Not told was the power struggle over where the locus of horse breeding was to be in the postbellum world that engaged Kentucky with the Northeast. Resentments and rivalries spilled over from Civil War battlefields onto the racecourse in the postwar turf. The economic future of the Bluegrass lay at risk.

Kentucky's horsemen spent a generation attempting to swing the business back their way. When they stumbled on the winning formula, they unexpectedly found willing partners among those outside capitalists who had ignored them in the past. A nationwide need among white Americans for nostalgia, working in tandem with a rising racism throughout the United States, solidified into plantation imagery as the balm to soothe the nation's soul. The imagery settled on Bluegrass Kentucky, and only then did the horse business in the commonwealth begin to attract the big money needed to grow and support the infrastructure for an equine and tourism industry.

The Kentucky colonel, the columned mansion, and the imagined construct of Bluegrass horse country as representing the Old South cannot be underestimated in securing the Thoroughbred industry its locus in the commonwealth. What follows is the story of how the Bluegrass became Southern.

chapter **ONE**

The Fast Track into the Future

July 1865 found some of New York's wealthiest citizens joining an eclectic collection of gamblers, horsemen, and social hangers-on in the daily rounds of mineral baths and Thoroughbred racing at Saratoga Springs, New York. The Civil War had ended only three months previously, and most of those visiting this Adirondack resort sought to put all lingering thoughts of the war behind them. If they had entertained any thoughts at all of this late war, they had viewed it as an opportunity to make vast sums of money or, at worst, as a period of unpleasant news reports. Saratoga visitors quickly turned their thoughts to much more pleasant prospects lying ahead. What lay most immediately ahead was a showdown between two outstanding Thoroughbreds, one called Kentucky and the other Asteroid.

Kentucky's color was a rich and lustrous bay. His mahogany-hued body shone with a dark glean, in striking contrast to the white hair extending upward from his hoof halfway to the knee on his right front leg. A white stripe ran the length of his face, narrowing toward his nose. His tail had been cropped straight across in the English fashion, about four inches above the hock. He had two white marks on his back caused by wear from the saddle. Kentucky stood not hugely tall at only fifteen and a half hands—a little more than five feet at the withers where his shoulder blades came together. But people weren't looking at his height when they studied the fire in his eye and the strength in his limbs.[1]

A son of the prolific Lexington, a breeding stallion who reigned

Kentucky was of a rich bay color, one in a triumvirate of talented sons of
Lexington, all foaled in 1861 in the Bluegrass. Kentucky's dam was Magnolia,
a daughter of the imported sire Glencoe. John Clay, a son of Henry Clay, bred
Kentucky. Magnolia was among the highly prized Thoroughbreds that once
belonged to Henry Clay. (W. S. Vosburgh, *Racing in America, 1866–1921*
[New York: Scribner Press, 1922], facing 70.)

as the most successful sire of American Thoroughbreds, Kentucky had
come into the hands of a triumvirate of wealthy men in the Northeast
soon after his Bluegrass breeder, John Clay, took the colt to the track at
Paterson, New Jersey, to sell in 1863. The track at Paterson had opened
its gates for the first time that year and stood at the forefront of a revival
of racing in the North, a revival that undoubtedly delighted wealthy
sportsmen of New York. Interest among them in Thoroughbred horse
racing had reignited with a spark that by the end of the war would erupt
into a roaring flame. This represented a huge change in the future course
of racing in the North. For close to twenty years, the Northeast had
existed without any Thoroughbred racing, at least without any racing of
consequence organized by jockey clubs. Melvin Adelman has written
in a history of New York sports: "By 1845 horse racing in New York

was in a state of virtual collapse. . . . For the next twenty years the sport floundered." Men whose fortunes had expanded exponentially during the war were among those eager to take up the sport, in a desire to show off their new wealth.[2]

Clay, taking racehorses with him to Paterson to sell in 1863, was among a vast number of Kentuckians who had chosen not to fight in the war. Throughout the war, he lent his energies to his business, which was the breeding, raising, racing, and selling of Thoroughbreds. Choosing not to enlist did not mean that he remained unaffected by wartime strife, however. On account of the war, the amount of horse racing declined throughout the South and in the border state of Kentucky, and, thus, Clay would have faced a greatly diminished market for the sale of his racing stock. He had three options. The first was to stay home and race the colt called Kentucky in Lexington, where the sport managed to stumble along throughout the war. The only occasion when the club in Lexington did not hold a race meet during the spring of 1861, when racing shut down after the first day owing to military maneuvers held close by. The second option was to take his horses to New Orleans to race, if he thought the journey safe, which it probably was not. The final option was the choice a number of Kentuckians had made: take their stables to race in the North, where they would, it was presumed, be safer from wartime hostilities.[3]

The Kentuckians Zeb Ward, Clay, Captain T. G. Moore, and Dr. J. W. Weldon campaigned their racing stables in Pennsylvania and on Long Island at New York's old Union Course in 1862. They also raced in Boston. Back in the Bluegrass, Kentuckians who had not shipped their horses to the Northeast were beginning to see them impressed for army duty or stolen by guerrillas and outlaws. Bluegrass breeders lost untold numbers of bloodstock this way, for this war that began in an effort to save the Union and wound up as a war to end slavery "did much to interfere both with breeding and racing in Kentucky," as the *Kentucky Farmer and Breeder* observed. Edward Hotaling likewise has observed: "Kentucky [horsemen] had to look northward for buyers, tracks, and safe havens for their stables. The scene was bleak."[4]

However bleak the racing outlook might have appeared throughout the South and in Kentucky, interest in sports was on the rise in New Jersey and New York. Northern racing experienced a rebirth during

John Clay, a Bluegrass horse trainer and breeder, was a son of Henry Clay, whose exemplary career in politics earned him the nickname the Great Compromiser. John Clay inherited his father's Thoroughbred breeding operations and continued them on a portion of Ashland, the family estate in Lexington. (*Turf, Field and Farm* 66, no. 11 [March 18, 1898]: 345.)

these war years, just as other modern sports also began to attract urban crowds. In fact, it was not unusual for New Yorkers to attend athletic events as spectators despite the war, even when the war entered their midst. This happened around the time of the draft riots in Manhattan in 1863. Some 105 persons, many of them Irish, rioted over four days in mid-July of that year because they resented the fact that they could not buy their way out of military service as the wealthy could. However, some five thousand New Yorkers had forgotten the riots by July 22. They boarded ferries to attend a championship baseball game at Elysian Fields at Hoboken in New Jersey. New York lost the game to Brooklyn, 10–9.[5]

During that same summer, from July 1 through July 3, the Battle of Gettysburg took place in the nearby state of Pennsylvania. Some forty-six to fifty-one thousand Americans died over three days of fighting in and surrounding this small town, ending the South's second invasion of the North under General Robert E. Lee. Gettysburg, in fact, acquired notoriety as the battle having the greatest number of Civil War casualties. Four and a half months later, in November, President Abraham Lincoln redefined the purpose of the war with his Gettysburg Address, shaping its new framework into a mission to end slavery. Despite the battles, despite the redefined purpose of the war, nothing was stopping the rebirth of racing in the Northeast. A month following the Battle of Gettysburg, Northern sportsmen inaugurated Thoroughbred racing at Saratoga Springs. "Where did anyone ever get the idea that racing had stopped at Saratoga in wartime?" Landon Manning asked rhetorically when writing his history of trotting and Thoroughbred racing at Saratoga Springs. The answer stood the same as it did downstate, when New Yorkers boarded ferries to watch the baseball game at Elysian Fields.[6]

By the time of the inaugural race meet at Saratoga Springs, Clay had raced and won with his colt Kentucky at the Paterson track in New Jersey. This caught the attention of the well-regarded sportsman John F. Purdy. Purdy was a wine dealer, a "gentleman" jockey (which meant that he did not pursue a living riding racehorses), and a man whose advice people in racing held in high regard. He promptly bought the colt for $6,000, taking him in a package deal with a filly named Arcola. Clay had insisted that Purdy purchase Arcola as part of the sale, but Purdy's interest had been entirely in Kentucky.[7]

Purdy pronounced Kentucky the most magnificent two-year-old colt he had ever seen. As well, he announced that he was buying Kentucky, not for himself, but for all New York, a development that indicated the rising interest in horse racing in that state. What Purdy really might have meant to say was that he was acting as a sales agent for wealthy buyers. The next time Kentucky appeared on the racecourse, which was the following spring (1864), when he was three years old, he raced under the colors of an elite group that included William R. Travers, John Hunter, and George Osgood. This group brought much attention to itself that same year for being among the founders of a new racecourse at Saratoga Springs. The group had assumed control of racing at Saratoga in 1863 and opened a new grandstand and racecourse across the road from the primitive racing grounds where the inaugural 1863 meet had raced. Purdy served as the new Saratoga track's vice president and Travers as its president.[8]

Travers and Hunter were well known beyond the racecourse at Saratoga Springs. In fact, they were better known as Wall Street speculators who had realized remarkable success with buying and selling equities. Under the firm name of Travers and Jerome, Travers and his

William R. Travers served as the first president of the new Saratoga Race Course, opened in 1864. He also was a partner in the ownership of the horse Kentucky, purchased from John Clay of Lexington. (Courtesy of the New York Public Library.)

Wall Street partner, Leonard Jerome (the latter destined to be Winston Churchill's grandfather), had notoriously run up a $50,000 capital investment in 1856 to a sum larger than $1 million three years later. This seems even more remarkable for the clear profit it produced, as the partners had pulled off their financial coup during an era when personal income tax did not exist. By 1864, Travers and Jerome had expanded their involvement in horse racing into building racecourses, beginning in 1864 with Saratoga Springs. Jerome would open a course in 1867 with much more lavish facilities in Westchester County, closer to the city of New York. He called his swank new track Jerome Park.[9]

Two years later, by the summer of 1865, when the war was over, Kentucky had run up a remarkable record. Although he had suffered his only career loss in 1864 in the Jersey Derby at Paterson (where he ran third—fourth according to some reports—behind another son of Lexington called Norfolk), Kentucky had strung together a winning streak that included the Jersey St. Leger Stakes, the Sequel Stakes, and a match race—a one-on-one contest against one other horse. All that remained for him to do if he were to secure a place as champion over all other American racehorses was to race against the third member of Lexington's great sons who were all born in 1861. This was the colt named Asteroid, who, like Kentucky and Norfolk, was bred in the Bluegrass.

Asteroid was also bay. He and Kentucky both were four years old, born the year the Civil War broke out. Asteroid, unlike Kentucky, had never known defeat on the racecourse. This might have seemed to make him the champion of American racehorses, for Kentucky, his only equal, had lost one race. Later, at the close of his career, Kentucky would also lose a race against the clock when he attempted to beat the timed record of his sire, Lexington. But Asteroid had accumulated an unblemished record, even if he had raced entirely in Ohio and the border states of Kentucky and Missouri, a geographic happenstance that New Yorkers imperiously viewed as parochial.

Asteroid had also proved his speed and endurance in quite another way. He had survived a devil of a gallop at the hands of outlaws disguised as Union soldiers who had taken him during a raid on Woodburn Farm, in the heart of horse country. "Mr. Alexander and his family were just sitting down to dinner . . . when an old negro woman came running in with the news that there was a great commotion at the stables, a party of men being engaged in seizing and carrying off the horses," read one account. The theft had occurred quite brazenly, in the middle of the day.[10]

The theft took place during the autumn of 1864, six months before the war ended. The outlaw riding Asteroid had forced him to swim across the Kentucky River under a hail of bullets fired their way. Asteroid wound up ransomed for Woodburn Farm and was back at the races

Asteroid, another of Lexington's famous offspring (his dam was Nebula, a daughter of the imported Glencoe), raced for his owner, Robert Aitcheson Alexander, of Woodburn Farm in Woodford County, Kentucky. Outlaws stole the horse during the Civil War. Alexander's friends ransomed him and returned him to Alexander. Asteroid then resumed his racing career. He was undefeated on the racetrack, winning twelve races and a total of $12,800. (Courtesy of the New York Public Library.)

in the spring of 1865, with people in the Northeast calling for him to race against Kentucky. This challenge certainly was taking everyone's mind off the late war, as the prospect of a widely anticipated race between the two posed all kinds of intriguing possibilities.

With Asteroid having defeated all his competition west of the Allegheny Mountains, it seemed a shame to many patrons of the sport that he had never gone east to race against Kentucky. As people in the Northeast saw it, a showdown of this sort would settle the matter of which colt was the better of the two and, therefore, the fastest racehorse in the United States. But people also looked for something more than a horse race in this challenge issued to Asteroid. Sectional rivalries lingered after the war, and these two horses had acquired the status of sectional rivals. General Ulysses Grant and his Confederate counterpart, General Robert E. Lee, had barely signed the terms of peace in April 1865 at Appomattox Courthouse in Virginia when New York's wealthy sportsmen had begun to anticipate still another sectional confrontation, this one to occur on the racecourse. There seemed no better way to reassert the North's victory in the war.

None could hide their feelings about this event: the rivalry between these two horses stirred up "a little unpleasant feeling between men of different sections," according to the recollections of the era's turf authority, Hamilton Busbey. This highly anticipated showdown was "marked with much feeling, and the names of the two horses were daily in the mouths of thousands," Busbey wrote. Ironically, although these horses represented sectional rivalries, their coming together on the racecourse was also expected to signal sectional healing. Busbey suggested that the sport of horse racing had already demonstrated healing qualities because "men who, a few months before, had faced each other on the battle-field, stood side by side on the race-course, enthusiastically applauding the silken-coated thoroughbreds."[11]

Sportsmen sensed another irony in the challenge. They might have seen this confrontation not so much as between North and South, as the war had been fought, as between West and East, the latter being where the locus of power in horse racing had shifted immediately after the Civil War. The West, during this era, meant Kentucky—and every other place on the map to the left of the Allegheny Mountains. While the power in racing had, indeed, shifted east, Kentucky no more than Virginia or Pennsylvania actually occupied a geographic position that could be described as *in the West*. This geographic designation, though it held ominous meaning for horse racing, was at the same time misleading.

Kentucky's historic moment at the edge of the Western frontier had passed decades earlier in the relentless push Americans had made from the East Coast toward the Pacific Ocean. Nonetheless, sporting men of New York continued until the twentieth century, almost one hundred years later, to refer to Kentucky horse racing as situated in *the West*. They had their reasons, which might have been mostly chauvinistic. New York viewed itself as superior to a rough-and-ready Kentucky situated on the fringes of American society. The terms *East* and *West* denoted power, and for decades after the war, a power struggle ensued between New Yorkers and Kentuckians over control of Thoroughbred racing. For reasons not quite clear, however, Kentuckians placidly accepted the characterization of their racing as Western and unfolding on a mythical frontier. Never during the latter part of the nineteenth century did Bluegrass Kentuckians attempt to discourage the use of this designation by insisting that their racing was Southern. So it remained Western. The Kentucky Derby, in the years following its 1875 inauguration, became known as the great race of the Western states.

Any sectional showdown between Kentucky and Asteroid consequently would carry the weight of this social and political divide. The way Northeastern patrons of horse racing regarded Asteroid illustrated precisely how they considered their side of the divide superior to the West. Although racing's patrons in New York and New Jersey acknowledged Asteroid as the "bright star of the West," never did they accord him the recognition they probably should have. Never did they call him the bright star of *all the turf.* They had planned to bestow that kingly moniker on Kentucky.[12]

Northeastern patrons had placed all their support with their horse, despite the irony that he bore the name of his home state, Kentucky, the same place Asteroid came from. And how they loved to watch their horse race. *Wilkes' Spirit of the Times,* published in New York, paid homage to Kentucky as though this Thoroughbred were king of the animal kingdom. *Wilkes' Spirit* and the public had fallen so deeply under his spell that they overlooked the nagging fact that he had a blemished race record while Asteroid's record remained perfect. Obscuring reality, they thought of Kentucky as though he were the champion, when the two horses had never met.

The attention paid Kentucky by *Wilkes' Spirit of the Times* was going far in boosting his popularity in the Northeast. The magazine's editor, George Wilkes, weighted his news columns in favor of Kentucky, giving scant coverage to Asteroid. Wilkes was pro-Unionist, anti-Southern, and a chauvinistic New Yorker of the boldest stripe, all of which translated to a man suspicious of the state of Kentucky, which, although officially loyal to the United States, had sent soldiers to both sides during the war. Wilkes had more than a political ax swinging in favor of the horse Kentucky. He and Kentucky's owners wanted to see the highly anticipated showdown between the two colts take place nowhere else but at that summer place of decadence, Saratoga Springs.[13]

Pleasure seekers had been coming to Saratoga Springs for decades, fondly referring to this little village as "the queen of watering places." Since the Battle of Burgoyne during the Revolutionary War, Americans

John Morrissey introduced Thoroughbred racing to Saratoga Springs in 1863. The following year, William R. Travers led the group of capitalists that opened a new racecourse, the Saratoga Race Course, across the road from the old. Racing continues on that site to this day. (*Harper's Weekly* 9, no. 557 [August 24, 1867]: 541.)

had recognized this fancy watering hole for its mineral springs, which were believed beneficial to one's health. Saratoga Springs also proved popular for quite another reason, however, as the scene of wide-open gambling, a favorite pastime of the elite class of visitors. This elite class had turned Saratoga Springs into the social centerpiece of the summer season, deeming it the proper place for an annual reunion of the wealthy and the famous. The village was *the* place to see and be seen, as gamblers and social and political leaders all realized. From 1863 on, Saratoga Springs also developed into the summertime place to thrill to the sight of fast Thoroughbreds competing on the racecourse. The racetrack scenes and those along the main thoroughfare of the village stood out as ostentatious demonstrations of excessive wealth.[14]

"Saratoga's Broadway was a canyon flanked by magnificent elms and gargantuan hotels and jammed with men in expensive black broadcloth and women in the latest fashions," writes Edward Hotaling, describing the nightly promenades through the heart of the village. New Yorkers who participated in this annual migration upstate by steamboat or rail brought their servants, their children, their fancy dogs, and their racing stables to escape the oppressive heat and foul odors that they had no wish to endure in the sweltering city of New York. As these folk saw it, Saratoga existed as their private garden, their escape from the worrisome burdens of urban life.[15]

The carefree lifestyle in Saratoga reflected the prevailing mood among the Springs's summer residents during those months when the United States emerged from its civil war. No longer obliged to consider even remotely the dour topic of battles fought and Americans dying, summer visitors in 1865 turned their full attention to the training progress of Kentucky and Asteroid. Although the intended race was not to occur until August, advance betting had begun at the Cincinnati, Ohio, races in June.[16]

The race for the Saratoga Cup decidedly was building into much more than a showdown between these horses. As June turned into July, the event did, indeed, appear to be turning into a power struggle between New Yorkers and the old guard of rural Bluegrass Kentucky. A racing periodical would editorialize two years later that "the American turf—at least so far as New York, the capital, is concerned—has ceased to be provincial and has become metropolitan." Contemporaries could see this beginning to unfold in 1865. The result would greatly affect the position of the Bluegrass in the new, postwar world of horse racing, for it compromised the stranglehold that Kentucky landowners once had held over the sport.[17]

The war years had altered much about power relations in the United States, and now, it seemed, horse racing was poised to take its turn at this wheel of change. Racing in the Northeastern cities was experiencing a resurgence because men of old money along with those whose wealth had grown exponentially during the Civil War had taken control of the sport. They did so by default, the sport having collapsed in much of the South. And they did so simply by exerting the power of their wealth, building their own racecourses in New York. People referred deferentially to this elite class as "the substantial men of the day . . . some of the most respectable men," as though paying obeisance to their wealth and social standing.[18]

The wheel of change did not stop at the new racecourses constructed in the Northeast. In a short while, horse breeders in New York and New Jersey would challenge the claim of Bluegrass Kentucky as the cradle of the racehorse. Hanging in the balance was the livelihood of Bluegrass horsemen and, with this, the economy of central Kentucky. If the breeding of racehorses no longer centered in full strength on the Bluegrass, Kentuckians would lose the full potential of this livelihood, and all in the local community would feel the effects. And horse breeding was emerging as a livelihood: few breeders in Kentucky possessed the wealth of Robert Aitcheson Alexander, owner of Woodburn Farm. Alexander alone could stand on a par with the new money coming into the sport because he was not dependent on farming or horse breeding for a living. Like many in the Northeast, his money came from outside the realm of agriculture, from his ironworks in Scotland and Kentucky.[19]

The power struggle emerging in Thoroughbred racing did, in fact, mirror the shifts in power occurring at all levels of American economy and life. More people were moving to the Northern cities. More immigrants were arriving on American shores. Increasing industrialization was bringing expanded wealth to the elite class among industrialists and financial brokers living in these Northern cities. Industrialization was creating a sea change in demographics because the major portion of wealth no longer lay in the South or in agricultural pursuits, including the breeding and raising of racehorses.

But, for this particular moment during the summer of 1865 at Saratoga Springs, the question of shifting economics and power narrowed down to which group was to control the breeding and racing of fast horses. Was the future to lie with the old guard in Kentucky (and also in Tennessee, where a class of gentry landowners pursued horse breeding on a smaller but highly successful scale) or with the new moguls of industry and finance in the Northeast? The power struggle to ensue would cut across a wide swath of American demographics, from wealthy New York capitalists to Bluegrass landowners, while also touching peripherally on the mountain folk of eastern Kentucky, who would constitute a convenient contrast to these other groups. The power struggle also would involve Kentucky's African American community: the once dominant numbers of black jockeys and trainers who rode and trained many of these fast horses in Kentucky and also in New York.

This was a critical time for the future of Thoroughbred racing. The shift of power in the sport represented no small achievement to those New Yorkers who had lent their support to Thoroughbred racing, for the breeding industry had collapsed in that state following the economic Panic of 1837. New York's breeding and racing activities had not recovered prior to the Civil War. The sport had been virtually dead in New York, stomped into oblivion first by the financial crisis and then by public sentiment opposed to gambling and racing. The Union Course on

Long Island, once the site of well-attended races that brought together horses from the North and the South, had fallen into a disreputable state in which mule racing coexisted with what little Thoroughbred sport remained. One Thanksgiving Day, mules raced for a $50 purse that saw "eight of the obstinate brutes . . . brought to the starting point, . . . only four [of which] could be induced . . . to go anyhow." Without a horse-breeding industry, racing in New York could not exist. The new, Northeastern turf moguls relied on Southerners to supply their sport with horses during the middle years of the Civil War until the resurgence of the sport in New York. New York sportsmen even had problems persuading the most reputable of their society to join in supporting the return of Thoroughbred racing, for the sport remained tainted with the unpopular specter of gambling.[20]

For at least ten years before the war, men of solid reputation in the Northeast had severed any connection they once might have had with the turf, owing to the sport's disreputable notoriety. During this decade, individuals deemed unworthy by the elite class operated the tracks located in and around New York. Rather than see their names connected with these questionable entrepreneurs, wealthy sportsmen spurned racehorses and took up yachting.

Following the Panic of 1837, a second economic disaster occurred in 1857; this one affected not only the general welfare of Americans but also the health of the turf. The 1857 Panic exacerbated the decline of the turf because numbers of men who could afford to own racing stables experienced financial ruin. A nineteenth-century author, Lyman Weeks, observed that, on the eve of the Civil War, racing flourished only in Kentucky. Everywhere else, he wrote, the situation was grim: "Public interest in the turf had become reduced to a low point and the final clash of arms gave the sport what was feared at the time would be its death blow."[21]

Thus, a handful of wealthy New Yorkers accomplished the near impossible when, partway through the war, they initiated a revival of Northern racing on bringing their good names and social reputations to the sport. Joining Travers, Hunter, Osgood, Jerome, and a few others in this effort was August Belmont, a titan of Fifth Avenue society and the founder of a bank in New York. Belmont was wealthy beyond the imaginings of the average Bluegrass horseman. He represented the archetypal capitalist of the Northeast—writ large. He took control of New York racing and soon become the virtual dictator of the American turf. His close friend Leonard Jerome, who made his money selling short in the stock market during the 1857 Panic, was already planning his elaborate racecourse, Jerome Park, on 250 acres known as the Bathgate estate that he had purchased in 1865 for $250,000 at Fordham, north of Manhattan. Belmont agreed to serve as the first president of the track.[22]

Powerful Northern men like these took Thoroughbred racing from regional popularity in the South to prominence as a national and commercialized sport. They made many changes, with the most radical being the way they converted a diversion of the Southern rural gentry into a major urban sport. They also changed the manner in which races were run. They followed the more recent English custom, replacing the old-style multiple heat racing with "dash" races in which a single trip around the track (or, perhaps, only a portion of the track) was all it took to determine the outcome of a race.

Heat racing, in which the horses returned to the track perhaps three more times following their first run to determine the outcome of an event, took all day to determine a winner. As Americans became more hurried in their lives, this change proved highly popular and helped boost the sport's popularity in this country. No one, especially the new moguls of the business world, had time to while away an entire day waiting for horses to race one another into the ground over multiple heats to decide a race. That languid side of life had slipped away with the antebellum South.

Men like Belmont and Jerome were in a hurry, no different than other Americans. They were building fortunes and dynasties in their private lives. On the public front, they founded and ruled over lavish racecourses meant to complement the opulent breeding farms they were building in New York. These men determined the locations of the new racecourses, choosing places conveniently close to the city of New York, where they lived and worked. With lifestyles that differed so remarkably from the slower tempo of those of the antebellum planters of the South, these men were reshaping the sport to move to an upbeat pace.

These men might never have had the opportunity to seize this power had not the wartime interruption of racing and breeding in the slaveholding states forced the latter to surrender control of Thorough-bred racing and breeding. Control of the sport had swung back and forth between North and South in a cyclic pattern almost from the time racing began in the seventeenth century in the New World. However, the outcome of the Civil War left no doubt that the Northeast had regained the control that it had lost during the 1840s. This situation coincided with the rapidly rising popularity of this sport among men of means in New York: men like Travers and his group, which owned the racehorse Kentucky.

This showdown at Saratoga, then, really constituted more than a race between two horses. The cry that went up to see the horses race against each other appeared more like powerful New Yorkers stepping up to dictate where and how the sport should operate in this new world that emerged after the war. The race was looking more like an occasion for these new men in racing to show Bluegrass horsemen a thing or two about the sport that the Bluegrass and the South had so recently con-trolled. The rivalry between Asteroid and Kentucky fueled this power struggle and contributed directly to the revival of the sport in the North. "The fever spread, and the glory of the turf was revived in the North," as one early history of Thoroughbred racing puts it.[23]

Before the war, Kentucky-bred horses had ruled the turf, sent via steamboats down the Ohio River to the Metairie course at New Or-leans, where the greatest of them all, the horse named Lexington, had settled a regional rivalry on the racetrack. He had defeated his Mis-sissippi rival, Lecomte, in a sectional contest on a par with any of the famous North-South contests held before the war in New York and the southern Atlantic states. Lexington retired from the track to a new career as a breeding stallion and, during the mid-1850s, came into the hands of the wealthiest breeder in Kentucky, Alexander, the squire of Woodburn Farm.

Here was a man who, despite living a solitary life in the country, never would have been mistaken for an individual of unsophisticated ways or means. A lifelong bachelor, Alexander was Kentucky born but a Cambridge-educated member of the British aristocracy who chose to return home to the Bluegrass. He also was the owner of Asteroid. Alex-ander had raised Asteroid on his grand estate in Kentucky's Woodford

County. As an agriculturist, he lived for the thrill and pride of breeding racehorses of Asteroid's caliber. He could afford to pay a then-record $15,000 for Lexington to stand at stud at Woodburn because he possessed a fortune founded in industry and divested into agriculture and livestock breeding. Before the war, he had held more power than anyone in Kentucky breeding circles. If he felt this power in danger of slipping away soon after the war, he did not disclose this in any overt way. He seemed determined not to bow to the dictates of the new money emerging on the turf in the Northeast. Consequently, his initial reaction to challenges for a race against Kentucky was to ignore them.

Alexander's disinterest in sending Asteroid to Saratoga began to come clear to Kentucky's owners after their colt arrived at Saratoga—and Asteroid did not show up. Their reasons for insisting that the race take place at Saratoga and not farther west no doubt reflected the sense of power and control this group had begun to flex on the turf. Asteroid would have had to make a long journey by rail if Alexander were to send him to Saratoga. "Only he who has traveled with horses on a freight train can fully realize [the difficulties]," a *Turf, Field and Farm* contributor wrote during those years. "Journeys which require a day's time on a passenger run, are of a week's duration, and the jerkings of the inevitable stoppages and starts are enough to make every joint and muscle so sore that weeks are required to remedy the bad effects. . . . The animals are frequently thrown down or severely strained by their efforts to resist the shock." Asteroid had raced in June at Cincinnati, winning twice, but no word had been heard of him since. Alexander remained aloof and silent, even as *Wilkes' Spirit of the Times* initiated an assault in print on the squire of Woodburn for failing to put his horse on the train.[24]

The fiery and opinionated George Wilkes was as eager as Kentucky's owners to see this race take place. He relied on all the power of his printing press to try to persuade Alexander to send Asteroid to Saratoga. Easterners had so highly anticipated this encounter that the Saratoga Race Course had sent a representative to Cincinnati during the races there in June to take advance wagers on the race. Kentucky's owners had to save face, and in his editorials Wilkes revealed how closely aligned his interests were with these men. He began to goad, cajoling at first, then stepping up the tempo as the weeks went on.

Wilkes appealed to Alexander's chivalry in trying to persuade him to put Asteroid on a train. "We should not like to be in Mr. Alexander's shoes," he wrote, "so far at least as the indignation of the ladies is concerned, if he should fail to bring his horse." Wilkes might have intended his gentle nudge to sting more deeply than, at first glance, it would appear to, given that Alexander lived in a state bordering the South, where chivalry toward the ladies greatly mattered. Whatever his intentions, however, Wilkes failed to elicit a response from Alexander.[25]

Wilkes ramped up the tenor of his attack in a later edition, suggesting that Alexander "shirks the only opportunity he has ever had of measuring Asteroid against a horse of known merits and first-class reputation." This statement might have stung even more deeply than the chivalric barb, for Western racing enthusiasts believed Asteroid to be the horse with the first-class reputation. He had never experienced defeat, while Kentucky had lost one race. So the question would have reverted to one of why Kentucky did not take a train west for a race.[26]

The barb with the greatest sting might have been the editor's suggestion that Alexander simply was afraid to race Asteroid against Kentucky. Wilkes wrote that a man worth "millions of dollars, and who seems to believe in his horse should not have turned his back upon such an offer." He added: "This is not the way to support the interests of the turf." Alexander had profited from purchases that breeders made from his Woodburn Farm, according to *Wilkes' Spirit,* and now, in turn, those breeders "are entitled to know which of these two rival stallions should be preferred as the stock horse of the future." Wilkes was arguing that Alexander owed a debt of responsibility to the sport and, thus, needed to send Asteroid to Saratoga to meet Kentucky. By declining to race, Alexander was revealing his real intention: "to contribute nothing to racing in the North."[27]

Late in July, Alexander found his voice. He sent a telegram directly to John Hunter, one of the triumvirate of Kentucky's owners, agreeing to send out Asteroid against Kentucky—as long as Kentucky came west for two races: the first at Cincinnati and the second at Louisville, where Alexander was the leading force behind the Woodlawn Course. Like Kentucky's owners, who operated the Saratoga course, Alexander shrewdly saw the effect on track attendance that this match would have. Thus, he insisted that one of these races take place at the track he supported, Woodlawn. He even offered to pay Kentucky's travel expenses. "I think our tracks are as good as those in the east," he wrote, adding: "A horse owned east of the Alleghenies will be as great a curiosity on a course in this section of country as one of my entries would be were he to appear to run for the Jersey Derby, St. Leger or Saratoga Cup." He gave Kentucky's owners until August 7 to respond.[28]

Hunter failed to respond directly, which irritated Alexander. "No doubt, he preferred to receive a proposition direct from Mr. Hunter," remarked Alexander's acquaintance, Sanders Bruce. Hunter's spokesman had expressed continuing interest in this showdown taking place—although not at Louisville. A race held September 25 at Cincinnati would be acceptable—if Alexander agreed to race his colt again the following summer at Saratoga. Wilkes had not forfeited an opportunity during this time to stir the pot of controversy a little more. He suggested that Alexander's disdain of Saratoga revealed an ugly "portion of a plan to contribute nothing to racing in the North." Here was a barb that revealed the tension between the old and the new centers of power in the racing world as well as one playing on four years of ill feeling that had existed between North and South with Kentucky caught in the middle. Alexander's response, sent through his intermediary, consisted of six words: "The propositions do not suit Alexander."[29]

Shortly afterward, Alexander relented and agreed to the terms of Cincinnati during 1865 and Saratoga during 1866. Too much ill feeling had arisen by this time, however, and Wilkes had not helped with his ranting to keep feelings on either side on an even tone. At one point Wilkes had written: "It is plain, therefore, that Mr. Alexander will have the proposed match his own way, or he will not have it at all." The controversy matched the old gentry against new money, and readers undoubtedly loved reading every word about this confrontation. But the central question remained: Why had Kentucky's owners assumed that Asteroid would need to race in the Northeast to settle the championship? One of Alexander's supporters in the Bluegrass asked: "Is the case to be made different to the East of the Alleghenies?"[30]

Perhaps Alexander had not wished to see nouveau money in the Northeast push him to the wall with demands for a showdown between Kentucky and Asteroid. Or perhaps, as his acquaintance explained in a lengthy letter to the sympathetic *Turf, Field and Farm*, he had been too preoccupied with reestablishing his own stable after the war to plan for a trip east with Asteroid. "It was Mr. Alexander's intention to have taken his horses North this summer had they done well," according to the letter writer, who signed his name Fair Play, "but owing to the outrages committed on him by guerillas, entailing a loss over sixty thousand dollars in stock, some that cannot be replaced, among them Nebula, the dam of Asteroid, and his own life and safety jeopardized, he had to remove all his stock from Kentucky, upwards of three hundred head, including stallions, broodmares, colts, and trotting stock. . . . When he got through his western engagements he had but one horse—Asteroid—fit to travel with." The writer went on to explain that, Alexander having but one horse trainer to put in charge of all his horses, his interests would have suffered if he had sent that trainer to Saratoga with Asteroid. For those in Kentucky who had endured guerrilla raids and the theft of their horses, this explanation would have seemed quite reasonable. Apparently, it did not seem so to the new titans of the Northeastern turf.[31]

Sectional interests and rivalries had entered this controversy at every turn, and Bluegrass horsemen expressed their disgust with the Northeast by threatening to withdraw their subscriptions from the New York–based *Wilkes' Spirit of the Times.* The editor responded, calling the Bluegrass folk "narrow-minded" persons who viewed this and other racing matters in terms that were "sectional between the West and East." Fine, Wilkes said in his own defense. If readers wished to withdraw their subscriptions, so be it; the *Spirit* would survive on the patronage of "true patrons of this paper." However, this did not relieve Alexander of his responsibility to race Asteroid, according to Wilkes. Because Alexander possessed the finest breeding stallion in the United States— the sire named Lexington—people in the North believed that he was able to manipulate bloodstock prices nationwide with this one horse. Therefore, he owed the sport an opportunity to see Asteroid race against Kentucky. "The side we represent," the editor intoned in his chauvinistic vein, "desires to promote the interests of the turf, by having the colt Asteroid come on and run; the other side, which seems to be composed mainly of those who are the natural followers of close rich men, have sprung forward to defend Mr. Alexander's personal right to keep his colt to himself, though the general interest should suffer." East versus

West, folks were lining up in opposition. It seemed so long ago, not just four months, that the lineup had been North versus South.[32]

The summer's outcome disappointed all. The Saratoga Cup went off as scheduled but without Asteroid. With the talented Irishman Gilbert Patrick, better known by his nickname, Gilpatrick, riding Kentucky, that colt easily defeated the only other two horses to start: Captain Moore, who finished second, and a horse from the Bluegrass named Rhinodyne. The renowned Abe Hawkins, the dean of black jockeys and a former slave whose riding fame would span the antebellum and postwar eras, rode Rhinodyne. The horses raced in the new style, going a lengthy two and a quarter miles but not returning for multiple heats.

A breezy, sunny day greeted the crowd of spectators for the Saratoga Cup, a good number of them women wearing the latest fashions, a touch that added a pleasant aspect to the spectacle. "No clouds gathered to darken the blue of the sky," reads a report of the race. The same could not be said of Alexander's standing with the Northeastern racing community, which had longed to see Asteroid in this race. Alexander's aloofness had cost him respect in the Northeast. Clouds of a similar nature were beginning to darken the relevance of Bluegrass horse country and its place at the center of power in Thoroughbred racing. Folks in the Northeast were no longer looking to the Bluegrass for leadership in this sport. They were making over the sport to suit themselves whether or not Alexander chose to participate.[33]

So much had changed since the late 1850s, when New Yorkers had looked to Bluegrass Kentuckians as Thoroughbred racing's leaders, seeking their help in resurrecting the sport in the Northeast. That situation, too, had represented quite a change from previous decades, when New York racing had been quite in vogue. But Thoroughbred racing had operated cyclically for so long in New York, depending on whether antiracing interests held power, that no one there could breed and raise Thoroughbreds with any assurance that there would be tracks where these horses could race.

From 1821 to the later 1830s, New York racing had existed as the epicenter of Thoroughbred racing and had hosted widely anticipated match races between Northern and Southern horses like Eclipse and Sir Henry. These races, some fifty of them, had taken on national import in the 1820s and especially in the 1830s following the Missouri Compromise. Adelman has suggested that these races assumed symbolic connotations for their Northern and Southern audiences, given the hardening feelings between North and South. Despite the increasing sectional animosities and the difficulty of travel, Southerners had brought their best horses north for these showdowns, which took place at the Union Course on Long Island. New York, with its large population base, provided the largest audiences and the greatest number of wagering opportunities, with the betting playing a significant role in these races. Some sixty thousand persons might have witnessed the Eclipse–Sir Henry match in 1823, although these estimates taken from contemporary press accounts may have been exaggerated. Eclipse defeated Sir Henry. The North and New York won that round.[34]

The economic collapse of 1837 hit the gentry class of horse breeders hard, particularly in New York, where the financial base of elites was grounded in industry and commerce, both sectors that were suffering in the depression. The final North-South race of any consequence was the Fashion-Peytona match in 1843; quality racing was in a free fall and virtually died out in New York by middecade. New York racing had hit the bottom again in another of those seemingly endless cycles that witnessed the sport rise and fall in this state through the decades.

The sport had been banned entirely in New York in 1802 with an antiracing law brought on by social reformers who disliked the gambling aspect; it had returned only two years prior to the Eclipse–Sir Henry match of 1823 after legislators changed the 1802 law. Eclipse's owner brought the horse out of retirement on the legislative change—he had been at stud and would be nine years old by the time of his race with Sir Henry, the Southern horse he defeated.

Two decades later, following the Fashion-Peytona match in 1843, sectional feelings between North and South had become so hardened that no further matches of consequence in New York occurred, although match races of similar import were taking place in New Orleans among horses representing various Southern states. Meanwhile, the Union Course in New York suffered from the twin blows of depressed economic times and mismanagement. Trotting horses and racing mules soon replaced the Thoroughbreds. Both were less expensive to maintain than the sleek racehorses that had formerly thrilled huge audiences.[35]

Economics aside, John Dizikes has suggested that cycles of expansion and contraction in New York horse racing paralleled periods of unrestrained gambling and fraud followed by social revulsion and alarm, the latter resulting in periods of prohibition of gambling. In hindsight, these cyclic swings throughout the nineteenth century foretold the future for racing in New York when Progressive reformers managed to shut down racing once more in the state, from 1910 to 1912: a situation that greatly affected the Bluegrass. With each waning cycle of the sport on the racecourse came a parallel decline in the breeding of Thoroughbreds in New York, to the point at which only a single Thoroughbred stallion stood at stud on Long Island prior to the Civil War. At the same time that New Yorkers sought the aid of Bluegrass breeders in the late 1850s to revive their sport, the *Spirit of the Times* equated the paucity of breeding in New York to the poor quality and insufficient number of horses racing on the track, a situation obvious to everyone "because we had no horses in this section of the Union fit to contend with even second- or third-rate Virginia horses."[36]

The *Spirit* described the situation as deplorable, noting: "Our Race course has fallen into disuse from want of Northern horses to compete successfully for the prizes, and we have witnessed numerous attempts to revive racing before the public in our vicinity were prepared for it, all of which have failed." The solution seemed to be to invite the racing men of Kentucky—"the Dukes, Vileys, Alexanders, Richards, Hamptons, Bradleys, Hunters, and Clays"—to combine with wealthy Northern sportsmen in rebuilding the sport in New York. As this sporting periodical made its case, it reminded Bluegrass horsemen than they would be able to expand the market for their horses this way since, of 1,200 Thoroughbreds born annually in the United States, "Kentucky alone contributed 450 thoroughbred foals this year." The New Yorkers realized that they could not interest Kentuckians simply with an altruistic motive; they would have to appeal to their business needs.[37]

No record can be found of what the Dukes, the Vileys, Alexander, or John Clay thought of this plea for help. But some of the better-known Kentucky horsemen had accompanied their racing stables to Philadelphia in 1862, the second year of the Civil War, to compete on a circuit that temporarily sprang up between that city, New York, and Boston. Zeb Ward and Captain T. Moore were the first to arrive; expected within a short time were the stables of Dr. Weldon, John Clay, and R. A. Alexander. The organizers acknowledged the superiority of Kentucky horses and advised that, for the opening race at Philadelphia, "horses that have won in Kentucky, at the Spring meeting, will be excluded from starting for this purse." Another race at Philadelphia was open only to white riders mounted on saddle horses. This meant that black (slave) jockeys brought up from Kentucky were to be excluded from this race with its prize of a gold watch inlaid with diamonds. The "gentlemen" entering their saddle horses for this race were required to pledge that, if they won the watch, they intended to make it a present to a "lady," a subtle suggestion that the presence of women at the racecourse was an integral part of the spectacle. New York planned to offer a similar gold watch, made by Tiffany, with the winner again sworn to present the watch to some lucky "lady." Ten stables of racehorses had assembled for these short meets, with the *New York Times* concluding that this gave "an assurance of the best racing ever seen in the North." The Kentuckians undoubtedly arrived pleased to find a place to race their horses, for, other than the track at Lexington, racing in the South lacked continuity during the war years.[38]

By 1859, New York remained without racing, although some twenty-five men were raising Thoroughbreds in New York, New Jersey, Massachusetts, Connecticut, and New Hampshire. Perhaps they had planned to race these horses in the South. Or perhaps they bred them merely for the pleasure of owning them, albeit without any decent place in the Northeast to race them. These men included William Astor (destined with his brother, John Jacob Astor, to inherit an estate of some $100 million), John Hunter (an eventual partner with Travers and Osgood in the horse Kentucky), Francis Morris (whose family's racing silks were the oldest in use in the United States), and William Bathgate (the owner of the Fordham, New York, estate that later would become Jerome Park). Belmont, Jerome, and Travers were not yet among this group but soon would be. When these three took up racing as a sport, the progress of the Northeastern turf would charge forward on a fast track.[39]

Despite the interest of these wealthy men, racing still had not returned to the mainstream of New York culture. In 1859, the editor of the *Spirit* lamented how Thoroughbred racing had slipped into such oblivion that even the rich were unfamiliar with the sport. "Very few of these gentlemen are acquainted with the details of racing, and the public have in a great measure lost their former love of it from the scarcity of close contests and repeated disappointments," he opined. He spoke of the need of education about the sport among both breeders, "in order to resuscitate in old patrons of the Turf their almost dormant love of racing," and the public, especially "the young," who "must be taught to appreciate it." Far from anticipating the sectional divisions that would come with the Civil War—and the disunity that followed—the *Spirit of the Times* suggested that stock certificates in a racecourse near New York be sold not only in the Northeast but also in the West and the South. The *Spirit* estimated that the New Yorkers would need some $60,000–$70,000 to build such a racecourse.[40]

Nothing came of this proposal. Whether Alexander and other Bluegrass horsemen received a direct request for help is not known. But the fact that Northerners had seen them as leaders in the sport and in the practice of breeding Thoroughbreds in 1859 was telling, given the change of perspective that New Yorkers had adopted by the end of the war. In the minds of the new breed of racehorse owners in the Northeast in 1865, the relevance of horse country had faded. Northern men felt secure in the notion that they had released the South's stranglehold on the sport and shifted the center of Thoroughbred racing back to New York.

The war had brought changes North and South, among these a 43 percent decline in Southern wealth. Along with the closing of numerous Southern racecourses, this did not portend a strong market for racehorses in that section of the country. In contrast, new, Northern fortunes had emerged during wartime from industry and Wall Street speculation. Families flush with new money placed their wealth and status on display in a variety of ostentatious ways, not the least of which was the ownership of fabulous racing stables.[41]

Social leaders like Belmont were raising the profile of the sport in the Northeast, lending horse racing a cachet of legitimacy it had not known there in decades. Men of Belmont's group also brought to the sport in the Northeast a set of practices that revealed how they planned to change the appearances of Thoroughbred racing. For example, instead of riding on horseback or traveling in buggies to the races, as Kentuckians generally had, these men arrived in magnificent heavy coaches

August Belmont played perhaps the most significant role in the revival of Thoroughbred racing in
New York after the Civil War. He founded the
Nursery Stud on Long Island, eventually moving
his breeding operation to the Bluegrass in 1885.
His son, August Belmont II, was the breeder of
Man o' War, foaled at Nursery Stud in Lexington,
and arguably the greatest of American Thoroughbreds. (Courtesy of the Keeneland Association.)

pulled by teams of four well-matched horses. In this practice, they mimicked traditions borrowed from England.

Belmont and Jerome both were skilled coaching men who drove
their own four-in-hands, a team of four look-alike horses trained to

pull these heavy, English-looking rigs. Liveried servants and guests accompanied their hosts, the guests seated inside and atop the coaches, with all appearing to enjoy a jolly good time. On reaching the racecourse, the servants pulled from each coach's boot a well-packed, fancy picnic, in keeping with the English coaching tradition. The Coaching Club American Oaks is a Thoroughbred race in New York named in honor of the organization that Belmont and his peers supported. Quite overnight, it seemed, the rich were adding their own socially conscious, English touches to this increasingly fashionable sport.

The ownership of racehorses appeared to be the perfect choice for wealthy men and their expansive egos. Nothing bespoke the wonders of a bottomless fortune quite like a stable of sleek, fast horses that were expensive to buy, beautiful to look at, and costly to maintain. Racehorses always have served as signifiers of wealth and status. The timing also was perfect for the sport to reemerge in the Northeast: this was precisely the time when increasing numbers of men successful in the worlds of business and industry were looking for ways to spend their fortunes. These highly competitive businessmen were discovering in racing a new arena where they could transfer their rivalries from the business and social worlds. Racing was proving to be a great game of one-upmanship. Expansive egos drove these men to racing and would bring them to spend vast amounts of money in this highly expensive sport even when they had little or no hope of making their racehorses pay for themselves. The purses were not large enough to pay for the upkeep of their stables.

Typically, the majority of these powerful new men in Thoroughbred racing lived in the city of New York. This demographic marked a clear break from the antebellum status quo in the Bluegrass, where the major landowners and an elite class of moderately wealthy gentlemen farmers had ruled the sport. The ownership of the racehorse Kentucky revealed just how clearly the sport that was reviving itself in the Northeast had shifted away from previous ownership patterns: Travers, Hunter, and Osgood all were urbanites and residents of New York. Their social and business interests were centered almost entirely on the city, except when they summered at the village of Saratoga Springs, where Travers served as president of the racecourse. They had not even traveled to the Bluegrass to purchase Kentucky. John Clay, the breeder, had brought the colt to the Northeast to sell.

Travers, a lawyer who had made a fortune on Wall Street, was the most recent of the three partners to take up Thoroughbred racing. He was a dapper sort who fully appreciated life's pleasures, taking up membership in twenty-seven social clubs. Friends and acquaintances overlooked an unfortunate impediment in his speech: he had a slight stutter. They did, however, appreciate his quick sense of humor. He loved to poke fun at everyone, even his own kind—the men of Wall Street. Once, when he and a companion passed by Manhattan's Union Club, the companion asked him whether the men sitting in chairs by the windows were habitués of the private club. "No," Travers replied, "some are s-s-sons of habitués."[42]

On acquiring the racehorse Kentucky, Travers experienced enormous beginner's luck. For the $6,000 it cost to purchase the horse, Travers wound up striking gold. Many more owners of racehorses have spent a lifetime throwing good money after bad horses while never acquiring a horse of this quality. Yet, just as he had on Wall Street, Travers once again exhibited his Midas touch. He could afford to spend whatever he wished to acquire any horse he wanted, but in this case he did not have to spend a fortune. He just spent more than most men could afford.

Some New Yorkers had amassed fabulous fortunes: the retailer Alexander T. Stewart had made more than $1 million during the year 1863. Seventy-nine residents of New York earned more than $100,000 that same year. Two years previously, when the Civil War had begun, the estimated number of millionaires residing in New York was 115. The rich were growing richer, with a growing number of them turning to horse racing for sport.[43]

Kentucky's owners, like other New Yorkers entering Thoroughbred racing, found themselves in good company with Belmont in the sport. Belmont was a smoothly polished urbane sort who exemplified elite society, showing the way to others in his class with the fascination he had developed for fast horses. Paradoxically, he was a self-made man. He began his working years sweeping floors in Germany for the money-lending Rothschilds financial empire and had advanced to a position as its American representative. He also owned his own bank. As a society leader, he had no peer. New Yorkers regarded him as the symbolic ruler of Fifth Avenue, and rightly so. He had shown so many of them how to live and enjoy the good life.

Thoroughbred racing at Jerome Park, which opened in 1866, drew New York society leaders as well as Bluegrass horsemen, who brought their stables to the Northeast. Jerome Park, with August Belmont serving as its first president, almost overnight became the leading racecourse in the United States. This new racecourse assumed the preeminent position in the sport, which Southern racecourses, in particular the Metairie track in New Orleans, had held before the Civil War. (Courtesy of the New York Public Library.)

Leonard Jerome, a lawyer like Travers and also a financial wizard on Wall Street, was soon to become the founder of several racetracks in the Northeast. To his dismay, he had missed the inaugural meet of Saratoga racing in 1863 because he was otherwise occupied, manning a Gatling gun from a window of the building housing the *New York Times*. He was a major stockholder in the newspaper and was intent on protecting his investment. To that end, he had aimed his gun on the masses, many of them Irish, who were rampaging through the streets in riots that broke out in 1863 over the army draft. Jerome made up for lost time, however, and was in attendance at Saratoga in 1864 and 1865.

In 1865, Jerome changed American racing forever. That year he founded the American Jockey Club, and, by 1866, the club opened the most modern, lavish, and elite racetrack yet seen in North America. The track was situated northeast of the city in Westchester County on the old Bathgate estate. The American Jockey Club members, quite an exclusive set, named their racecourse Jerome Park. Belmont served as the initial president. Jerome, like the others, grew only wealthier. He invested in railway companies and enjoyed yachting with William K. Vanderbilt. He also partnered with Commodore Cornelius Vanderbilt in railroad deals. Much later, following his death in 1891, he gained additional status as the grandfather of Sir Winston Churchill.[44]

Jerome's friend Cornelius Vanderbilt did not participate in Thoroughbred racing, favoring instead the trotting matches that also were popular at this time. This had not stopped the commodore from throwing his considerable support behind Travers and others in founding the Saratoga Racing Association. He patronized racing and the other gambling activities of the Saratoga summerfest, as did multimillionaires like William B. Astor, said to be the richest man in the world with his fortune of $61 million. With Astor, the commodore, and Jerome joining Travers, Hunter, and Osgood at Saratoga Springs during summer, the season must have been awe inspiring, one multimillionaire after another strolling down the village avenues.[45]

Alexander, the owner of Asteroid, also owned a sizable fortune. Contemporary accounts identified him as the second-wealthiest man in Kentucky, behind his close friend and fellow horse breeder Alexander Keene Richards of Georgetown in Scott County, Kentucky. But that was before the war; Alexander might have surpassed him. The friendship between these two men was such that they oversaw the care of each other's slaves and horses when necessity arose. Unlike Kentucky's owners, Alexander had passed nearly all his life in rural regions. Yet he was anything but a country rube.

He had graduated from Trinity College at Cambridge University in England after spending much of his youth on his uncle's Airdrie estate in Scotland. In fact, Alexander was quite the man of the world. He had inherited his uncle's title and wealth, which included a highly productive mining and refining operation in Scotland called the Airdrie Iron Works. Alexander returned to the United States to live in 1849, bringing with him expansive ideas gleaned from his travels in Europe: visions of the way an ideal livestock breeding operation should be de-

Robert Aitcheson Alexander, the owner of
Woodburn Farm in Woodford County, Kentucky, was a sportsman, an agriculturist, and a
visionary who stood the famed sire Lexington
at stud. He also was recognized for the premier
trotting horses he bred and stood at stud. His
contributions to the progress of the sport were
immeasurable. (Courtesy of Woodburn Farm.)

signed, grounded in the notion that ideas promulgated in England or on
the European continent were the goals that Americans should strive for.
He bought up portions of the family's Woodburn Farm that had been
divided among his siblings on their father's death. He set about planning and designing the layout of a farm that his contemporaries began
to view not only as mammoth but also as a model that they would be
wise to copy. "The breeding establishment at Woodburn is modeled on
the most approved English plan," the *Kentucky Gazette* noted in 1866
with an approving nod. The stables for horses and cattle were vast and

made of cut stone; the dairy houses, also built of cut stone, were managed by Scottish dairymaids.[46]

New Yorkers sometimes mistook Alexander for an Englishman, an understandable error since Kentuckians frequently called him Lord Alexander; it is even possible that he spoke with a slight British accent after spending his youth in Scotland and England. New Yorkers clearly saw him as set apart from the average person traveling up from Kentucky, for Kentuckians still bore somewhat of a frontier appearance in the minds of Easterners. Illustrative of this was one story told from the racecourse after reporters observed Alexander kneeling so that women standing behind him could have a better view of the track. One reporter remarked how this expression of good manners surely must be English. Another corrected him, writing: "[Alexander] was born in Woodford County, Kentucky, and lives on the home place of his father." Yet he did seem more English and less like a Kentuckian, the latter a type that *Harper's* magazine had characterized as a knife-wielding frontiersman.[47]

In manners, wealth, and social customs, Alexander assuredly came from the upper class. His father, Robert Alexander, was a native of Scotland who had received his education in France and become acquainted with Benjamin Franklin, at that time serving as the U.S. ambassador to France. The senior Alexander followed Franklin to the United States, later moved to Kentucky, acquired the property he named Woodburn, and became president of the Bank of Kentucky in Frankfort. He built a log cabin on Woodburn but never lived on the farm. The son who took up residency at Woodburn was Lord Robert Aitcheson Alexander, following his college years spent in the British Isles. He moved into the log house his father had built, expanding it to a sizable residence while maintaining the log porch exterior at one end.[48]

While some thought him English in his manners, Alexander also evoked popular notions of the archetypal plantation owner. His vast Woodburn Farm was sufficiently large, between three and four thousand acres, to pose the picture of a small plantation to those Northern writers who visited before and after the Civil War. Taking full advantage of the slave labor available in Kentucky, the younger Alexander developed his vast livestock cattle and horse-breeding operation into a model farming enterprise renowned throughout the United States prior to the Civil War. He owned several excellent trotting and Thoroughbred stallions, including Lexington, sire of that renowned triumvirate of excellent racehorses all born in 1861: Asteroid, Kentucky, and Norfolk. Alexander had sold Norfolk for a record $15,001 (exceeding by $1 the record $15,000 he had paid for the sire, Lexington) to a mining and transportation mogul in California named Theodore Winters. But he was to state many times over that he believed Asteroid to be the best of the three.[49]

Alexander was justifiably proud of Asteroid. In this horse more than any other, he saw his theories and agricultural practices approach as close as possible to perfection. He had set out to breed livestock in a highly organized manner according to those proved crosses of blood-lines that were known to result in success. He practiced this method during an era when some horse owners persisted in the old ways, breeding their mares to whatever stallions were closest to their farms, simply because this was more practical. Mares had to be walked or ridden or shipped to the breeding stallions via unreliable railroad transportation; this was difficult and, in many cases, impossible if one lived in a truly remote area.

Alexander had divided Woodburn Farm into well-organized sections so that the trotting horses were relegated to one area with their own exercise track close by and the Thoroughbreds had stabling quarters in another section with their track close to their stables. Everything Alexander did with his livestock he carried out with great planning and organization. He maintained journals and breeding records. He expressed particular interest in bringing order to the disarrayed state of American pedigrees in Thoroughbreds and trotting horses.

To Alexander's thinking, American horse pedigrees existed in such a state of disorganization that no one could know for certain which bloodlines would cross most profitably. Moreover, no one could be certain whether the stated pedigree of any mare or stallion was correct—or whether it was fabricated, something Kentuckians were frequently accused of. Alexander had vowed to bring order to the confusing state of American Thoroughbred pedigrees. He asked anyone sending a mare to the stallions at Woodburn to also send a written record of her family history, believing that all would tell the truth. He relied on his superior knowledge of pedigrees to feel certain when other breeders were truthful. "Those who knew him know that no man in Kentucky in his time was so well posted in pedigrees, and none was more careful and thorough in his investigations," Busbey wrote. "He made no mistakes. He was the one man that sharpers avoided."[50]

Alexander had assembled at Woodburn an excellent band of broodmares and three valuable stallions: Lexington (standing for a breeding fee of $200), Scythian (with a $75 breeding fee), and Australian (with a $50 fee). He kept careful records of the Woodburn broodmares and their progeny in a printed guide called a *catalog* that he published privately each year. He was believed to be the first of American breeders of Thoroughbreds to produce such a catalog; he certainly was the first to print a catalog of horses and livestock he offered for sale in the public auctions he held at his farm. The Woodburn catalog for 1864, for example, noted that the broodmare Nebula was the dam of Asteroid but had not produced a foal in 1864.[51]

The original owner of Nebula, Jack Pendleton Chinn, had sent the mare to Woodburn for safekeeping during the war; Alexander came into ownership of the mare during that time. Alexander's friend Richards, of Georgetown, had done the same with the stallion called Australian, selling him to Alexander soon after the start of the war. The intent of these horse owners to put their horses in safekeeping on Alexander's estate must have seemed ironic as the war progressed. Alexander's neighborhood grew quite dangerous, with outlaws stealing Asteroid and other valuable trotters and Thoroughbreds. All Kentucky was a dangerous place during these times, and Woodburn Farm was no exception, despite what all had wanted to believe. Alexander had thought he would be safe from marauders because, as a British citizen, he flew the British flag. But he was not safe, as events would show.[52]

Americans of this time had some basic knowledge of Woodburn Farm, partly because travel writers had begun visiting the estate prior to the Civil War. Visitors had written glowingly, describing a vast property situated at the heart of a region "undeniably [the] 'game bed' of the United States, in blooded horses, stock, and chivalrous sons and daughters . . . [where] horses were brought out, and led around for our inspection, and negro boys attended us everywhere."[53]

Visiting writers unfailing painted the squire of Woodburn as a kind and charming gentleman farmer of cultivated manners. They told how he resided without a wife in a home that his slaves made comfortable for

Robert Aitcheson Alexander lived in this home, which had retained its log facade along one side, evoking imagery of the late eighteenth century and the early nineteenth, when Bluegrass Kentucky stood at the edge of the Western frontier. (*Harper's New Monthly Magazine*, October 1883, 729.)

him. They described how he had enlarged his home over the years from its log-cabin beginnings to a house of ample proportions that retained the log-cabin facade on one wing. Alexander had filled the house with elegant furnishings, which customarily drew comment from his visitors. Visitors also reported on the pleasing hospitality that he dispensed with ease at his laden table. If nothing else, this picture of Woodburn Farm was helping reinforce emerging images of Kentucky horse country as a place stocked with fast horses, of "negroes" attending the horses and guests, and of a patrician gentry class that dispensed hospitality in the fashion of knightly cavaliers more often associated with the Deep "Cotton" South.[54]

Whether this vision of Kentucky horse country was to remain relevant to the new world of Thoroughbred racing was another question entirely. The new capitalists getting into the sport were bringing their own culture to the game; they brought an urbane style that disconnected their practices from the quasi-plantation traditions of Kentucky horse country. The English-type coaches in which they traveled to the races represented one expression of this break from Bluegrass tradition; the private stud farms they were building close to the city of New York represented still another. These new farms featured the latest improvements in the training and housing of horses and, thus, did not entirely resemble the older, established farms in Bluegrass horse country. In these and other ways, it was clear these new men were bringing their own ideas to the sport. The cultural practices and iconography that had linked Thoroughbred racing with rural, Deep South plantation imagery and traditions before the war now teetered between the new, urban style and antebellum obsolescence.

Alexander might not have felt a connection to these new men from the Northeast like Travers and his group. He appeared uninformed about their identities, perhaps even disdainful of the position they already had assumed in the sport. On at least one occasion, he referred to Kentucky's owners not by name but as "some New Yorkers," as though dismissing their identities and relevance to the sport as he knew it in Kentucky. A slip like this might have seemed unconscionable to racing enthusiasts in the Northeast, however, where men like Travers considered themselves the essence of New York society and sport. But Alexander continued to see the Bluegrass as central to the sport. He had the best horses. His horses had the proven bloodlines. He held the power in Bluegrass Kentucky, where other horse breeders looked to him for leadership. If "some New Yorkers" wanted to play at his level, perhaps it was understandable for him to assume that they would have to play his way.[55]

This might have been one reason why Alexander ignored, at first, the pleas of Travers and his group to bring Kentucky and Asteroid together in the Saratoga Cup. Besides trying to reestablish his racing stable after the war, he was meeting during the Cincinnati race meet in June with other leaders of the Western sport. They were attempting to bring order to horse racing in Kentucky, Ohio, and Missouri now that the war was over. Unfortunately, the intensity of the desire for the race between Asteroid and Kentucky was building in the Northeast just as Alexander was deeply engaged in his organizational efforts.

Alexander met with these men to establish an orderly racing circuit in the Western region. With Alexander representing the Woodlawn Course in Louisville, they worked out a plan so that the various meets in these states would not overlap or run simultaneously. Their concern was to put racing back on a sound and orderly basis without delay. With so much to consider in their own region, they might not have been thinking at that particular moment about the rise of the sport in New York. It must have seemed an odd paradox when a representative of the Saratoga Race Course arrived at the Cincinnati track to begin taking bets on the showdown between Kentucky and Asteroid, to take place in

New York, where the new men of the turf seemed disinterested in the Western sport.

While Alexander attended these important organizational meetings at the Cincinnati race meet, his horses also fared exceptionally well on the racecourse there. This was remarkable, considering that he was only beginning to reorganize his stable after the two raids on Woodburn Farm: one in the autumn of 1864, when thieves took Asteroid, and then the most recent raid, in February 1865. The story of Asteroid's theft was well known to racing enthusiasts across the United States, as general newspapers and *Wilkes' Spirit* had reported on the incident.

In the autumn 1864 raid, thieves disguised as guerrilla fighters had made off with Asteroid along with trotters and other Thoroughbreds from Alexander's well-stocked stables. With Alexander and others in mounted pursuit, the horse thieves rode into the Kentucky River, situated close to Woodburn, in an attempt to escape. The youth riding Asteroid apparently never knew the animal was the famous, undefeated racehorse. When friends of Alexander's led by Major Warren Viley and Zeke Clay managed a few days later to catch up with the outlaws and ransom Asteroid for $250, the boy riding Asteroid simply remarked that it was the best horse he'd ever sat on. It turned out the boy was none other than a notorious outlaw who went by a woman's name: Sue Mundy. A crowd of well-wishers in Versailles, not many miles from Woodburn, cheered Asteroid as he passed through town in the company of his rescuers on his way home to Alexander's estate.[56]

The raiders who rode into Woodburn Farm in February 1865 were smarter: they asked for Asteroid by name. In a letter Alexander wrote about the incident to his brother-in-law, Henry Deedes of Chicago, Alexander described how the clever work of his horse trainer saved Asteroid: "In the dusk of the evening the trainer gave them an inferior horse and so saved the best horse in my stable."[57]

This raid was much more serious than the first, for the thieves threatened the lives of Alexander and his close acquaintances who were with him at the time in his house. As Alexander recounted, the outlaws held the wife of his farm manager, Dan Swigert, and others at gunpoint inside the main residence while they ordered Alexander to provide them with horses. It is important to point out that these men were not guerrillas or freedom fighters, as Alexander originally thought them to be. They were deserters from their Confederate platoons who were riding with a notorious outlaw from Missouri, William Clarke Quantrill. They rode into Woodburn disguised as U.S. soldiers, but Alexander soon realized that they were the same lot who had robbed him of horses six months previously. The outlaws had also shot and killed a neighbor and fellow horseman, Adam Harper, at the adjoining Nantura Farm. When the column of men disguised as soldiers rode into Woodburn at dusk this February day, the outlaws were holding the elderly Captain Willa Viley, a neighbor of Alexander's, as prisoner to serve as their guide.

"Alexander for Gods [*sic*] sake let them have the horses," Viley pleaded with his friend. But Alexander ignored the old man. He was busy trying to stall the raiders. He went into the residence, where he had told Swigert's wife and others to barricade themselves in the dining room. He found one of the outlaws pointing a cocked pistol at Swigert's wife even as she held a child in her arms. Another guerrilla "had his arms full of guns of all sorts which he had got from the stable where Swigert's and my arms had been put by the Negroes," as Alexander wrote Deedes. One of the outlaws turned and pointed a pistol at Alexander. It is easy to imagine that, had things turned out differently in the struggle that followed, Alexander might have died and the horse industry in Kentucky would not have developed as it did.[58]

"I knocked the pistol away from the line of my body and seized the fellow," Alexander wrote. He saw that the man had been drinking just enough to make him dangerous and realized that he had to incapacitate him before he could harm anyone. Standing close by the door, which opened into a hallway, Alexander reported, "I made an effort to throw him out of the room fearing the pistol might go off and shoot someone in the room." He continued: "I was unable to throw him out at the first effort, but as I had seized him in such a way that I had my left shoulder against his right shoulder and was thus somewhat behind him, in making the effort I felt his right knee come into contact with my left and it instantly occurred to me that I should trip him."[59]

The scuffle escalated in the hallway. Alexander threw the outlaws out of the house and saved Mrs. Swigert and the children from harm. But he could not save all his horses. Nor could he save old Willa Viley.

The outlaws took their prisoner with them to another farm, where the exhausted man fell off his horse. He died soon after at Stonewall Farm, the home of his son, Warren Viley.

The raiders took fifteen Thoroughbreds and trotters from Woodburn Farm. Two of the trotters later died: one from a wound in its back and the other, called Abdallah, from exhaustion. Alexander valued the stolen horses at $32,000. Despite that huge loss, it went unsaid that he was fortunate the outlaws had not taken away his breeding stallions, including Lexington, or the undefeated Asteroid. Still, he took no more chances this might happen, sending some three hundred horses by train from Woodburn Farm. He sent many of them to Illinois and did not return them to Woodburn until August 1865, four months after the war had ended. Alexander appeared completely discouraged over the disruption to Woodburn's activities when he advertised all the Woodburn horses for sale, including Lexington, at war's end and several times throughout that summer. But, in the end, he decided not to sell. By that autumn, he had Lexington and the other stallions back at his Bluegrass estate.[60]

In September 1866, more than a year following the running of the Saratoga Cup, when their showdown originally had been expected to take place, Asteroid was preparing for a race against Kentucky at the new Jerome Park in New York when he suffered a serious inflammation known as a "bowed" tendon. His racing career ended with that injury. Alexander sent the horse home to Woodburn Farm to stand at stud.

Kentucky never returned to the state for which his breeder, John Clay, had named him. He won twice more at Jerome Park in September and October 1866 before he, too, retired to stand at stud. Travers, Hunter, and Osgood sold him to Leonard Jerome for $40,000—an astronomically high price at that time but one thought to be a sound investment. "Mr. Jerome, his present liberal owner will find him a better paying stock at $40,000 . . . than any to be found upon the Broker's Board," predicted one racing editor. More surprising than the high purchase price was the location where Kentucky would stand throughout his breeding career. His home would not be anywhere close to Bluegrass horse country, where the leading stallions had been headquartered for some decades prior to the Civil War. Jerome had built lavish quarters for Kentucky close by Jerome Park.[61]

Wilkes' Spirit of the Times, speaking as always with some measure of pride in New York, heartily approved of this decision. "Nothing about the Park, from the grand stand and club-house to the rustic arbors which surmount the wooded knolls, surpasses Kentucky's home in taste and style," the editor wrote. "It stands upon a hill, and the paddocks are on three sides of it, so the great horse can stand at the door of his hall and overlook his mares in the happy valley. We enter by sliding doors his reception hall, 40 feet by 20 and 12 feet high, wainscoted walls and ceiling, and grained in black walnut, with ash and pine panels. The groom's room is to the left; the feed room to the right. The doors in the center lead to Kentucky's box, 15 feet square, wainscoted with pitch pine, oiled." Not a single writer who had visited Woodburn Farm had described Alexander's barns in such a way as to seem so lavishly appointed. And perhaps they were not.[62]

Jerome had followed the lead of colleagues, including August Belmont and Milton Sanford, in developing his own breeding farm close to the city of New York. Belmont built the Nursery Stud near Babylon, Long Island, and Sanford, a textiles magnate, constructed what might have been the most elaborate, up-to-date Thoroughbred farm in the United States. He called his farm, which he had located near Passaic, New Jersey, the Preakness Stud. Soon, more would follow this trend. The perplexing question of why these new titans of the turf were building farms so far from racehorse country had to be of concern to Bluegrass horsemen. If the Northeastern horse owners were to retire their leading racehorses to stallion careers in New York, what was to be the future of Bluegrass breeding operations?

Certainly, Alexander's aloofness at the height of the Kentucky-Asteroid frenzy in 1865 had not helped form agreeable relationships with these Northeastern men. He had forfeited an excellent opportunity to join West with East when he ignored these new titans of the turf— or, as he called them, "some New Yorkers"—whose rapidly rising power and control of the sport he seemed to have difficulty comprehending. But the new moguls of Eastern racing also had erred in assuming that the race should be held at Saratoga. They, too, would have benefited from forging stronger relationships with the horsemen of the West in Bluegrass Kentucky, for Kentucky horsemen possessed unrivaled expertise and controlled the most prestigious equine bloodlines.

When the new moguls of racing began building their own farms in the East and—most importantly—retiring their best horses to breeding careers at those farms, Kentucky horsemen must have felt concern. They surely envisioned a future that might not include their interests, at least to the extent that they had held before the war. The Saratoga Race Course had seized an important moment in 1865, bringing to prominence men who would play the most significant roles in the sport for decades to come. Alexander had dropped the ball once. He would not make the same error twice. Now he began initiating damage control intended to join Kentucky horsemen with those of the Northeast. The hope was for Bluegrass Kentuckians to reclaim their preeminence in the Thoroughbred sport, as the center of the racehorse world. An extraordinary amount of work lay ahead.

chapter **TWO**

The Greening of the Bluegrass

Some 460 million years before horses like Kentucky and Asteroid appeared on American racetracks, central Kentucky and Middle Tennessee formed their destiny as horse country. This occurred during the Ordovician Period, a time of major plate collision of the earth's crust, along with volcanism on what would become North America. Continents moved, mountains formed, and vast seas opened into a shallow marine shelf that was to form the central portions of the east-central United States. Surging seas swept over this shallow shelf, bringing with them the millions of invertebrates that left behind a precious natural gift, their fossilized shells, which gave rise through the millennia to a particular form of limestone rock, the building block that horsemen have long believed is critical to raising a strong-boned racehorse.

The structure of this rock includes the calcium carbonate that composes most limestones. However, and more importantly to horse breeders, the composition of this particular limestone includes a heavy concentration of phosphate, an occurrence that Professor Frank Ettensohn, a geologist at the University of Kentucky, has stated is relatively uncommon and occurs in few other places outside the Bluegrass. Ettensohn has theorized that the phosphate plays a greater role in growing a strong horse than does calcium carbonate by itself. During the early nineteenth century, Bluegrass horsemen appeared unaware of the contribution the phosphate made to the rock; they believed that the limestone itself was responsible for the exquisite flavor found in beef

54

and sheep raised on this land. They believed that the limestone made the same contribution to those strong-boned horses raised in the Bluegrass, horses they described as "hickory-boned." These nineteenth-century Americans might not have realized fully the composition of the limestone, yet they still seemed aware that the soil drew its strength from it. In 1865, the *Louisville Journal* attributed the quality of Bluegrass livestock to "the stratum of blue limestone which underlies the whole country at the distance of from ten to twelve feet from the surface, and perhaps has some effect on the grass."[1]

The soil, the limestone, and the Kentucky bluegrass that grew on this gently rolling land continued to fascinate observers who wrote about this verdant section of the United States. In 1876, the Harvard professor Nathan Southgate Shaler, a geologist and paleontologist, wrote that Bluegrass land was "surpassed by no other soils in any country for fertility and endurance." Around the same time, an article in the *London Daily Telegraph* cited the mineral benefits that horses in the Bluegrass received from the soil. In 1980, the University of Kentucky professor Karl B. Raitz succinctly described the Bluegrass region as "a broad limestone plain which has been etched on a structural arch of Ordovician limestones and shales." Noting the phosphatic content in combination with calcium, he wrote: "The gently rolling terrain is underlain by phosphatic Lexington and Cynthiana limestones which decompose into exceptionally fertile silt loam soils.[2]

Early in the nineteenth century, central Kentucky and Middle Tennessee both became known as "the Bluegrass," the name taken from the Kentucky bluegrass that flourished in their fields. No one has ever produced definitive answers on whether the legume that made the reputation for these regions actually possesses a blue hue and whether it is native to these states or originated someplace else, perhaps in Europe. "Whether the grass of the Blue Grass region be indigenous, or transplanted here at an early day by artificial means we have not room to discuss," observed the *Lexington Transcript* in 1889, adding: "Anyhow, it lies at the foundation of our immense stock business. . . . It makes fine whisky, cattle, trotters and runners, and gives strength to our men and symmetry and beauty to our women." Thus, even though no one knew the origin of the grass, folktales abound about *Poa pratensis,* more commonly known as Kentucky bluegrass.[3]

Some say that, if you observe the grass in this region just at dawn, when the dew lies heavily on it, you will see a hint of blue. The folklorist R. Gerald Alvey has related still another way in which people have attempted to explain the presence of this supposedly blue-tinted grass. He told how people observed a bluish vein running through the limestone and believed that the constantly decomposing blue limestone was responsible for the blue grass. Most importantly, people believed even decades before the Civil War that livestock in this region absorbed through the grass the important minerals that the limestone rock gave up into the rich soil. Equally as important in their eyes were the natural springs that spilled water infused with the same minerals into farm ponds and streams where livestock drank.[4]

Bluegrass breeders learned early on how to exploit this natural agricultural gift of the soil and turn it into a rich resource, combining the nutrition that it provided to grazing animals with their own ever-widening knowledge of equine pedigrees. Long before the mid-nineteenth century, Americans recognized that the strongest, fastest racehorses came from the Bluegrass region. This had occurred not by accident, but thanks to the gift of the land and the breeders' continuous attempts to upgrade the quality of their stock.

After the Civil War, the unexpected rise in the number of fabulous horse farms under construction in the Northeast represented a new direction for the sport, one that challenged popular notions about the unique value of Bluegrass soil and grasslands. In fact, the owners of these new estates appeared to have ignored altogether the benefits that Bluegrass horse country offered, with its mineral-rich land and the superior equine bloodlines. The trend was becoming obvious to all: Belmont, the society leader and banker; Travers, the financier and president of the Saratoga Race Course; Milton Sanford, the textiles mogul; and the Lorillard brothers, Pierre and George, heirs of the vast tobacco fortune, were building their own horse farms to complement the growing number of racetracks in the Northeast. Just as men like these already had shifted the center of racing away from the South and the border states, now they appeared to be starting a new trend by developing their own breeding farms in New Jersey and New York. Bluegrass breeders undoubtedly would have viewed this as problematic to their interests, for it hinted at the possibility of horse country becoming obsolete or at least diminished in relevance. Either way, the problem threatened to hit directly at the pocketbooks of Kentuckians. Just as breeders were regrouping after the war, trying to replenish their stock or rebuild their farms so that they could begin earning an income again, extremely wealthy men in other states were seizing those financial opportunities out from under their grasp.

This increasingly popular trend reached a critical point when the racing career of that highly accomplished racehorse Kentucky came to a close in 1866. As we have seen, Travers and his group sold the horse for a record $40,000 to Leonard Jerome on the horse's retirement to the stud. Instead of returning to the state of his birth, however, Kentucky stayed in New York, moving to new quarters close to Jerome Park to begin his breeding career, stinted to mares whose owners had no intention of sending them to breed to stallions in the Bluegrass. Two years later, in 1868, Belmont purchased Kentucky from Jerome for the purpose of installing the horse at his Nursery Stud on Long Island. In fact, Kentucky never returned to stand at stud in the state for which John Clay had named him. No one in the Bluegrass took this lightly.

Breeders in Tennessee also made an effort to get back in the business of breeding and raising racehorses; this, too, would provide more competition for Kentuckians. In Tennessee's historic horse country near Nashville, where Andrew Jackson had founded a racecourse before becoming president of the United States in 1829, breeders took the lead in restarting their programs from the premier plantation of that state, Belle Meade. This particular horse-breeding operation had been recognized for its quality and the quality of horses it produced since long before the war. Within two years after the war, it took a significant step toward regaining some of its renown by holding its first yearling auction. Neighbors of Belle Meade, many of them breeders of Thoroughbreds, depended on this plantation for guidance and organization at a time when they were attempting to find a niche in the new marketplace.[5]

"With the probable exception of Woodburn Farm" in Kentucky, writes Ridley W. Wills II, this queen of Tennessee plantations, Belle Meade, "was considered America's greatest breeding establishment." During the 1870s and 1880s, the estate's renewed success would see it achieve nationwide recognition once again, largely through annual yearling sales held at the plantation and also, for a time, in New York.

The farm also gained renown for the valuable stallions it stood at stud, among them Bonnie Scotland, Enquirer, Vandal, John Morgan, Iroquois, and Luke Blackburn. General William Giles Harding, the master of the plantation for forty-four years, was recognized after his death at age seventy-eight in 1886 as a man who "had done as much for the breeding interests of Tennessee, and perhaps for all America, as any man in the nineteenth century," according to Wills. As Wills also points out, Harding's generalship of Belle Meade attained such renewed standing for the plantation after the war that it "was one of the few places where the Old South was brought over into the new."[6]

The great mansion, paddocks, and pastures stocked with fine horses led Northern horsemen who visited during yearling auctions to believe that this was what the Old South had looked like during the antebellum period. Six columns, each twenty-two feet in height, composed the portico of the residence. The columns, each cut in two sections of limestone taken from quarries on the plantation, represented the craftsmanship of Belle Meade slaves. The appearance of this house undoubtedly figured into notions that Americans constructed decades later, after the demise of Belle Meade, when Kentucky's Bluegrass horse country assumed the mantle as representative of the Old South. The portico of Belle Meade was well recognized throughout the United States, for writers had been describing the columns since before the Civil War. "It is true that the massive towering stone pillars that are seen in front, impress one more with the idea of extravagance than utility," wrote a newspaper correspondent for the *Nashville Union and American* in 1854, "yet they so agree in architectural beauty with the whole, that economy would even not seem to require their removal."[7]

Despite the devastation that its herds and physical structures suffered, Belle Meade was able to recover fairly quickly from the ravages of the war. Unlike other plantations in that part of Tennessee, it had not lost all its stock to armies or raiders, partly a result of the family having ingratiated itself with the Union army officers who made Belle Meade their headquarters. "The horses taken did not include any of Harding's valuable brood mares," Wills writes. "In his report, the officer said the mares were exempted from impressments until the 'will of government' was known." Breeding operations resumed rather quickly

Belle Meade plantation, near Nashville, rivaled Woodburn in the production of Thoroughbred racehorses. It resumed its horse-breeding operation soon after the Civil War. The main residence was the iconic Southern horse farm. (Photograph by the author, 2008.)

after the war. General William Jackson began to assist his father-in-law, General Harding, in operating the plantation and, most especially, the horse-breeding endeavors.[8]

In central Kentucky, the war had greatly compromised livestock breeding operations. Robert Aitcheson Alexander wrote from Woodburn to his brother, Alexander John Alexander, in 1864:

> The sale was almost a failure from the fact that the Covington [KY] Railroad was not repaired so as to allow trains to run through (a bridge having been destroyed by [John Hunt] Morgan) and the fear of the men from the more Northern States that a raid would cut them off or they might not be able to get their stock away. There were only 3 or 4 men here from across the [Ohio] river and only one purchase.
>
> The sheep brought more money than anything else. . . . I sold no trotting stock. Twelve head of thoroughbred later brought 3180 or 265 a head and 11 head of mares and fillies (Thoroughbred) brought 2270 or 206 each. I sold a Lexington mare out of Kitty Clark for $1000. . . .
>
> I am by no means satisfied with the condition of things here but cant [sic] do anything to change my stock from Ky till I go to Chicago.

In another letter to his brother, Alexander wrote in 1865: "I have got my colt brother to Norfolk back from the guerillas, but man *owning* him having been captured. I had to pay the captor $500 but as the horse seemed little the worse for the long sojourn amongst the rascals *except in condition* I am well satisfied to get him at that rate."[9]

As in Tennessee, central Kentucky breeders restarted their bloodstock operations as well as they could, under the circumstances, in an attempt to join the new market. Quite quickly, they realized that they might be able to expedite the process if they received state aid. Governor Thomas E. Bramlette readily supported the growing horse industry and chartered a cooperative association that organizers named the Kentucky Stud Farm Association. Alexander and others leading this initiative included William S. Buford, F. P. Kinkead, and Abraham Buford of Woodford County, and Benjamin Bruce, John Viley, and James

A. Grinstead of Fayette County. All were among the leading livestock breeders in central Kentucky. They intended for the association to develop its own breeding farm along the lines of the national stud in England. The English stud operated on an egalitarian principle, providing equal access to stallion service for all owners of mares.[10]

Organizers in Kentucky intended the association to provide members with the means to recommence their livestock breeding, no small matter considering that many had ended the war facing the loss of breeding stock, farms, and their labor pool, which, in most cases, had been their slaves. The group planned to purchase a farm, although there is no evidence that the plan ever got this far. The intention was to fit out the farm with paddocks and stables for horses, making it suitable for the raising of Thoroughbreds. The group also intended to purchase broodmares and at least one stallion, with the intention of auctioning the offspring when they reached the yearling stage. The Kentucky General Assembly and the Kentucky Senate chartered the new organization on January 26, 1866, and waived the customary incorporation fee of $100. Apparently, the state legislature perceived the need to support and accelerate the start of this group's work. The Kentucky Stud Farm Association must have seen the need to help all breeders by providing easy access to a stallion and mares. Unfortunately, there is no evidence that this group ever inaugurated its well-intentioned program.[11]

The association's charter clearly noted that the war had made necessary the formation of this group, stating: "The injurious effects of the late war have been most seriously felt by those who have been engaged in the breeding and raising of horse stock." Alexander's Woodburn had not been the only farm raided. General Abe Buford, Alexander's neighbor, had been another breeder hard-hit with impressments by the armies and theft by outlaws. "Most of the blood stock belonging to General Buford were [sic] lost and sacrificed in '63 and '64," reads one report.[12]

In addition to the raids on Woodburn Farm and the Buford place, the stables of Alexander Keene Richards, Willa Viley, John Clay, Major Barak Thomas, and many others suffered devastation. Likewise, so did two large stables owned by a Union sympathizer, James A. Grinstead, that were located at the Kentucky Association track. The Confederate raider John Hunt Morgan and his men set fire to those stables. Not far from the racecourse, at Ashland, the late Henry Clay's estate where his son, John Clay, had raised the horse Kentucky, Morgan and his men took Thoroughbreds valued at an estimated $25,000. Among these was the highly prized mare named Skedaddle. If Clay had not chosen to take Kentucky northeast to sell in 1863, he might have lost this colt as well. John Hervey, in his history of racing, wrote: "The idea that Kentucky did not suffer more than negligible damage to her thoroughbred interests by the war is . . . wholly erroneous. Its ravages, of which those committed by [General John Hunt] Morgan were the most terrible, affected her best blood and finest individuals."[13]

As Kentucky's horse breeders began to regroup and rebuild, they faced problems different from those experienced farther south in Tennessee. In Tennessee, the gentry class of landowners relied on its own resources to become a self-sufficient breeding business once more. Kentuckians, on the other hand, were intent on attracting outside capital investment to their business of breeding and raising horses. The Kentucky idea held considerable potential for expansion but, from the start, proved difficult to carry out. Northern capitalists viewed investment in Kentucky after the war as highly problematic. Kentucky's expanding reputation for violence and lawlessness led to the fear that bloodstock, farm property, and, most of all, people were unsafe in central Kentucky. Southern states on the whole had quickly acquired a notorious reputation for lawlessness after the war, but newspapers in the Northeast frequently singled out Kentucky. One Northerner stated that in no way could New Yorkers "live and safely conduct business in any section of the South."[14]

The other problem was the farm labor pool, which evaporated in the months following the war's end. Without a labor pool, the farms could not function. The farm labor pool before the war had consisted largely of slaves. Even before the war had ended, slaves had begun to enlist in the U.S. Army or flee to army camps, hoping to receive protection. After the war, freedmen fled in great numbers to Lexington and Louisville, seeking employment as well as safety from the violence they soon began to realize would be their likely fate in the rural areas. The Ku Klux Klan or vigilantes assuming the name of the Klan were terrorizing and killing black folk throughout the Bluegrass countryside. This environment could hardly have appealed to any capitalists from outside the state who might have considered locating a breeding farm in central Kentucky or, at the very least, boarding their bloodstock there.

Adding to the labor problem was the confusion over slavery and freedom: where did one end in Kentucky and the other start? The status of slaves as freedmen remained uncertain in this border state because Lincoln's Emancipation Proclamation of 1863 had freed only those slaves in rebel states. Slaveholding Kentucky had not gone through the war as a rebel state. Kentucky had remained loyal to the United States after a brief period of neutrality, sending 50,000 Kentuckians into the Union army. Another 25,000 Kentuckians had chosen to enlist in the Confederate army, leading to some confusion about which side Kentucky actually supported. The real story about the war from the perspective of Kentuckians, however, was the number of men who did not enlist in either army. A total of 187,000 Kentuckians chose to stay out of the war, as John Clay had. They simply stayed at home. As William W. Freehling suggests, those numbers told much about the way Kentuckians essentially regarded the war. "Those figures placed Kentucky last among southern states in percentage of whites who fought for the Confederacy and first in percentage of whites who fought for no one," Freehling writes. Small wonder, then, that many remained confused about the status of slavery during and after the fighting since government policy concerning slaves was turning out to be different in Kentucky than in the South.[15]

To complicate matters, some 23,000 black Kentuckians had joined the Union army late in the war, on a promise from the U.S. government that they would be granted freedom for themselves and their families. But slavery itself was not outlawed in Kentucky with the close of the war. That would not occur until the passage of the Thirteenth Amendment in December 1865—an amendment to the U.S. Constitution that Kentucky's legislature actually refused to ratify. Many Kentuckians who had owned slaves gave them up only reluctantly and with a great amount of resentment toward the federal government. Numbers of slave owners also refused to honor the federal law that granted freedom to black soldiers who had enlisted with the Union army. "Whatever their status, Kentucky's black population received contradictory advice," writes Marion B. Lucas. "Federal officials proclaimed their freedom; slaveholders considered them fugitives." The way slavery finally ended in Kentucky was with the Thirteenth Amendment becoming law and federal troops making sure the law was enforced. As a result, whites took out their anger on blacks, many of whom fled for the cities or the North. The turmoil resulting from this situation left the farms without much of a labor force to work the fields or tend to bloodstock and livestock.[16]

With the status of former slaves in flux, the labor pool largely vanished on the farms and at the racecourse. A new racing periodical, *Turf, Field and Farm*, published in New York, recognized this problem during its first month of publication in August 1865, noting: "We fear the unsettled condition of labor in that state will interfere to a great extent with trainers in getting the right kind of hands for stable purposes." The import of this statement, coming from a periodical published by two Kentuckians named Sanders and Benjamin Bruce, whose financial backing came from Woodburn Farm, cannot be underestimated. It appeared as though Kentuckians were sending up a white flag on the labor crisis. "Prewar production capacity was only slowly reestablished," according to Peter Smith and Karl Raitz.[17]

White landowners throughout the South exacerbated the labor crisis by harassing freedmen; border-state Kentucky also experienced this trend. "Whites were obsessed with subordinating the newly freed blacks, and looming racial turmoil would make southern labor unproductive and unreliable," Edwin Burrows and Mike Wallace write in their history of New York.[18]

Two months after its inaugural issue, in what was undoubtedly a public relations ploy, *Turf, Field and Farm* attempted to paint the labor situation in a more positive light. It reprinted an article published in the *Louisville Journal* that attempted to point out Kentucky's "many advantages to the Northerner proposing to settle in the South." The article extolled "the celebrated 'blue-grass region'" of the state and its agricultural advantages for beef cattle, sheep, and horses, noting that "the flesh of the beef cattle and the sheep of that region possess an exquisite flavor and tenderness unknown to the leathery meats of other States." As mentioned, the *Journal* agreed with the well-received belief concerning the superiority of Bluegrass soil, ascribing its advantages to the "blue limestone" underlying the region.[19]

The article also argued against the possibility of a protracted labor problem by predicting a bright future for free labor somewhere in Kentucky's future, anticipating "those 100,000 slaves who yet remain in bondage, liberated, and the trained labor and skill bestowed upon the fair fields." The author of this article did see Kentucky's future grounded in agriculture and not in industry, however, writing: "As a manufacturing State, probably Kentucky will not, for some time at least, attract much attention." But, in a direct appeal to capitalists who might be enticed to purchase farmland or horses within the state, he pointed out that two wealthy Kentuckians—Robert Aitcheson Alexander and Brutus J. Clay, the latter the owner of a vast cattle farm called Auvergne in Bourbon County—were men of cultivated manners who had spent great sums of money on their livestock. The problem was that the Northeastern capitalists were not inclined to wait for this ethereal future to take shape. Thus, they began building their own horse farms in New York and New Jersey. Meanwhile, Kentucky horse breeders "were faced with the problems of rebuilding the productivity of their land and of maintaining a genteel way of life without a reliable source of labor," as Smith and Raitz have written. Thomas Clark also noted: "The shortage of labor on the postbellum estates was so critical that at one point a widespread campaign was launched to encourage foreign laborers, including Chinese coolies, to settle in Central Kentucky."[20]

Bluegrass landowners then hit on an idea to encourage former slaves to return to agricultural work. They made small plots of rural land available, either without charge or at greatly discounted prices. They customarily sectioned off these portions of land at the rear of their estates away from public view, thus completely changing the landscape from its appearance under antebellum practices, which saw slaves occupying cabins within sight of the main residence. But much had changed with freedom, even the landscape. The point was that the landowners were offering laborers an opportunity to live on land that they could call their own. The labor problem did, in fact, sort itself out somewhat as a result of these rural hamlets. Smith and Raitz have suggested that the central Kentucky horse-farm landscape might never have evolved as it did into a collection of park-like estates had not the landowners provided laborers with access to land of their own and, thus, a place to live near the farms where they worked. Still, even after landowners initiated this practice, the farm labor problem did not immediately resolve itself. Two years later, *Turf, Field and Farm* continued to report on the labor problem, noting that hemp and tobacco production had fallen off "owing to the derangement in our labor system."[21]

By 1867, labor problems continued to plague the farmlands of central Kentucky. Offering a suggestion, *Turf, Field and Farm* reprinted an article from a Northern newspaper, the *Philadelphia Sunday Mercury,* extolling the appeal of Asian workers. This article cited physical and social characteristics of Asians, in particular Chinese immigrants, that landowners perhaps would find more appealing than those ascribed to ex-slaves: "The Coolies are interesting to a foreign observer who remembers that they have come from the land of Vishnu and Brahma, the ancient seat of wonderful civilizations, where the Ganges is a god. . . . The men are mostly very handsome and graceful, well formed and supple, with olive skins, straight features, white teeth, long, silky black hair, and lustrous dark eyes, full of passion."[22]

Turf, Field and Farm reflected the popular thinking of these times—and the labor concerns of farm owners—in citing racial characteristics and superimposing stereotypes on a hierarchy of labor. In an article titled "The Five Races of Man" published in 1867, it intoned: "Race is established by climate and mode of living . . . with differences so strongly determined that they are perpetuated hereditarily. . . . The very characteristics which form the Caucasian variety and which separate it from the varieties give it intellectual prominence . . . [and] make it the superior of all others." This argument neatly ordained that blacks belonged in the fields and the stables and not in mainstream society living as the equals of whites. It mirrored the arguments that Southerners had put forth before the Civil War when they had justified slavery with patriarchal notions. Antebellum Southerners convinced themselves, and tried to convince outsiders, that they stood as the heads of their plantations and gave orders for the good of their slaves, much as a father stood as the leader of his wife and children.[23]

The depleted labor pool continued to pose problems for Kentucky farms, despite the effort to develop rural hamlets. By 1871, some counties, including Fayette, in the heart of the Bluegrass region, attempted to interest white labor in farmwork. At the same time, some people felt that Kentucky would be better served by the voluntary emigration of blacks to Africa—a timeworn argument seen as the clear way to remove blacks from American society. Henry Clay, an antebellum patron of Thoroughbred racing and breeding in Kentucky, had patronized this movement decades before the Civil War. Six years after the war, Kentuckians continued to debate the colonization movement. A letter published in the *Frankfort Tri-Weekly Yeoman* in 1871 extolled the appeals of Liberia, describing that African country as possessing "every luxury."[24]

No one appeared to have found the solution for launching a Kentucky horse industry with the scope and scale that would make it competitive with the racing and breeding operations of the wealthy men who were embracing the Northeastern turf. The depleted labor pool, the depleted numbers of bloodstock, and the simple lack of wealth needed if Bluegrass Kentuckians were to compete with the industrial and Wall Street wealth of New Yorkers made the prospect appear grim. Those bookend regions of the Bluegrass, Kentucky and Tennessee, both bore the burden of these postwar encumbrances.

Kentucky and Tennessee consequently entered the new world of postwar racing and breeding at a disadvantage. Nonetheless, some differences in the way in which breeders in these two states sought to regain their niche as horse country became apparent almost from the start. Almost immediately, Kentuckians sought outside capital investment. Tennessee breeders seemed content to work with what they had. These different approaches would determine the individual futures for these Northern and Southern sections of the Bluegrass, for, by the early twentieth century, central Kentucky alone would become known as the Bluegrass. By that time, Kentucky had secured outside capital, had developed a professional class to manage the horse industry, and had avoided the antiracing laws that shut down the sport forever in Tennessee. The Southern portion of the Bluegrass posed a cautionary tale: the death of racing led to the end of the breeding farms in Tennessee. The result was that Americans soon forgot that Middle Tennessee at one time had shared the Bluegrass region with central Kentucky.

Kentuckians continued their struggle with the new world they faced after the war when Bluegrass horse country took another blow. This was the death of Robert Aitcheson Alexander in 1867 at the age of forty-eight. He died at Woodburn on December 1, following some years of poor health. He had long been known to be "feeble." Three weeks before his death, he fell ill, then rallied briefly before relapsing. *Turf, Field and Farm* summed up his passing as "an irreparable loss to the country." This estimation was not exaggerated, at least as far as horse racing and breeding were concerned. Bluegrass Kentucky especially would feel the loss of Alexander, for his death left a leadership void. None among Bluegrass landowners had proved the visionary that he had been in assembling the finest stallions on the most elegant, efficient farm before the war, then in spearheading the recovery of horse breeding in Kentucky after the war. Moreover, he had possessed the financial fortune to carry out his visionary ideas. His vision, combined with his fortune, had ensured Kentucky's place as central to horse breeding before the war. He was only beginning to pull the breeding business out of its postwar malaise when he died. Now the question became one of who, if any, would take his place.[25]

Alexander's death in fact ensured that Kentucky would take a different course than Tennessee. Kentucky's gentry landowners learned to rely on the organizational skills and business acumen of a middle class of professionals, enabling the state's horse business to expand, albeit slowly. More persons involved in the local industry provided the business with a wider base.

As for who would step into the leadership vacuum, the answer proved to be Alexander's handpicked associates. Alexander's great strength, in addition to his visionary qualities, had been his skill in delegating responsibility to individuals who, like the squire himself, saw the large picture. Alexander had groomed his trusted associates for leadership; even before his death, they proved themselves exceptional choices in their roles. Dan Swigert was one. He served as the manager of the Thoroughbred horse division of Woodburn Farm. He had worked alongside Alexander in steering the course of Woodburn; following the squire's death, he stayed on at the farm for two more years. Then, he began purchasing his own horse farms, eventually acquiring Preakness Stud near Lexington, renaming it Elmendorf Farm. Swigert would play a key role later in the nineteenth century in linking New York turfmen with horses.[26]

Two more key associates of Alexander's were Sanders and Benjamin Bruce, whom Alexander had partially funded when they established *Turf, Field and Farm.* In their positions as copublishers of this weekly periodical, the Bruces assumed roles as arbiters of the turf. North and South, Americans respected the two brothers for their ability to select top-choice racehorse prospects, for their auctioneering talents, and for their vast knowledge of equine pedigrees.[27]

Sanders D. Bruce, a Lexington native, published the first
volume of the *American Stud Book* in 1868, eventually
selling his work to the Jockey Club in 1896. With his
brother, Benjamin Bruce, he founded and published *Turf,
Field and Farm* in New York. (Courtesy of the Keeneland
Association.)

Class status differentiated Alexander's protégés from the plantation owners of Tennessee who single-handedly resumed their breeding operations. Swigert and the Bruce brothers belonged to the middle
class. As such, they foretold the expansion of Kentucky's horse industry
through a professional class joined in mutual interests with landowners.
An expanding number of professionals began emerging in the Kentucky

Benjamin Bruce, a native of Lexington, copublished *Turf, Field and Farm* in New York with his brother, Sanders Bruce, then returned home to Lexington to begin publishing the *Kentucky Live Stock Record* in 1875. His publication later became the *Thoroughbred Record* and, eventually, the modern-day *Thoroughbred Times*. (William Henry Perrin, *History of Fayette County, Kentucky* [Chicago: O. L. Baskin, 1882], 147, in possession of the Lexington Public Library.)

horse business. Middle-class folk would make their living as pedigree experts, as recordkeepers and statisticians, as journalists reporting on the turf, as jockeys recognized as professional athletes, as horse trainers acquiring similar professional status, as gamblers and bookmakers, and as owners and operators of racetracks. If they did not make Lexington their headquarters, they traveled to and from it with increasing frequency throughout the latter nineteenth century. The yearling auctions at Belle Meade attracted many visitors, including the Bruce brothers, but they came to buy, not to set up shop in the region. If nothing else, Lexington was closer geographically to the Northeastern capitalists whose investment breeders sought. But the demographics of Lexington's horsemen also were changing to include an aggressive professional class.

Periodically, the Bruce brothers served as auctioneers at the yearling sale at Belle Meade, giving further credence to an increasing awareness that Lexington's professional class of horsemen held wide respect among gentry horse breeders. Sanders and Benjamin Bruce dispensed advice and circulated with ease among wealthy persons, who became their clients. They did not grow up as members of an elite class, yet, as professionals, they possessed the knowledge and expertise that members of that elite class were realizing they needed to access if they were to succeed in the new postwar racing world.

The Bruce brothers had grown up in Lexington in Gratz Park, a fashionable residential area several blocks north of the city center. The Bruce family home was situated on one side of the park; on another side lived John Hunt Morgan, a friend of Sanders Bruce's and the eventual husband of the Bruce brothers' sister, Rebecca Bruce. The brothers' parents, John Bruce and Margaret Ross Hutton Bruce, belonged to the upper middle class and, consequently, could afford to live in this desirable neighborhood that lent them social connections as well as respectability.

Sanders Bruce was born August 16, 1825; Benjamin was born December 19, 1827. Both developed an early passion for horse racing and for learning the pedigrees of racehorses. Sanders and Morgan at one time owned a stakes-winning horse of some regional renown called Doty. The two friends also went into the hemp manufacturing business together as well as co-owing a crockery store. Benjamin, meantime, graduated from Transylvania University in Lexington with a degree as a doctor of medicine, although he soon turned from medical practice to mercantile pursuits. The brothers' lives took a more serious turn toward the horse racing world when Sanders acquired the Phoenix Hotel sometime before the war. Horsemen traveling through Lexington favored the Phoenix, allowing Sanders, serving as the hotel's manager and proprietor, to expand his social and business network.[28]

The most opportune acquaintance the brothers made was with Alexander. Perhaps as a result of the interest these three men shared in equine pedigrees, Sanders Bruce, in particular, began to assist Alexander at Woodburn Farm, more or less as a factotum. Before the war, visitors to Woodburn Farm had noted the presence of Sanders carving the roast of mutton served at Alexander's table on one occasion when the squire had entertained guests in his rambling, rustic home. The circle of contacts Sanders had begun making at the Phoenix Hotel enlarged at Woodburn, where he met the Northeastern textiles mogul Milton Sanford before the war. Sanford provided financial backing when the Bruce brothers, along with a Lexington horseman named W. A. Dudley, founded a commercial enterprise they called the Kentucky Importing Company. The company sent Benjamin Bruce to England in 1860 to seek out yearling fillies to purchase and send to Kentucky, where they would be auctioned as prospective broodmares.[29]

The Civil War interrupted the lives of the Bruce brothers and led to a situation that few in the North would have understood. The brothers actually represented the war in microcosm as it had played out in Kentucky, for they chose to fight on opposite sides. Sanders joined the Lexington Chasseurs, a unit of the state guard that generally attracted Union loyalists. Benjamin went into the Confederate army, making his way to New Orleans in the well-mounted company of the horse breeder Alexander Keene Richards. The Bruces's sister, Rebecca, also figured in this story of Kentucky families divided during wartime: as previously mentioned, she had married John Hunt Morgan, whose destiny was to make him a notorious Confederate raider.[30]

The swift manner in which the Bruce brothers reunited in New York at war's end underscored a peculiar curiosity characteristic of Bluegrass Kentuckians: they could and did set aside their philosophical differences over the war when it came to doing business, particularly the horse business. The financial backing that the brothers received for *Turf, Field and Farm* also revealed a combination of geographic interests that strongly reflected Kentucky's long-standing ties with Northern business. On the one side, Alexander represented Kentucky interests in helping the Bruces set up *Turf, Field and Farm.* Their other backer was Milton Holbrook Sanford, who had made his fortune manufacturing blankets for the Union army during the war and was a horse owner representative of the new direction the sport was taking. Later, Joseph Cairn Simpson of Chicago purchased an interest in *Turf, Field and Farm.* And, in 1868, when Sanders Bruce required financial backing for volume 1 of the *American Stud Book,* he received assistance not only from Alexander but also from Simpson and another Chicagoan, John J. McKinnon.[31]

Sanders and Benjamin Bruce managed to have their new periodical up and running by the first week of August 1865, just in time to defend the honor of their benefactor, Alexander, when the rival *Spirit of the Times* assailed him over the Asteroid-Kentucky controversy. Considering the timing of the publication of volume 1, it might have seemed like Alexander had installed the Bruce brothers in New York with his own public defense in mind. More likely, *Turf, Field and Farm* represented a business opportunity for the financial backers and the publishers. The stated purpose of the periodical was to represent the horse industry. It went without saying that, to the Kentuckians involved in this venture,

The headquarters of *Turf, Field and Farm* in New York occupied this building at Printing House Square facing City Hall Park, near Broadway. The *New York Tribune* building stood close by. "We are now in the very midst of the leading weeklies of the city," wrote Sanders and Benjamin Bruce, the publishers of *Turf, Field and Farm*. (*Turf, Field and Farm*, June 1, 1867, 337.)

the interests of the Bluegrass horse industry would be represented as well. Alexander gave the Bruce brothers free rein to operate their venture, and they proved the perfect pair to carry Alexander's vision forward. And so they began their work, promoting Bluegrass land, soil, and breeding at the critical juncture when racing stood poised to go national after leaving its antebellum regional traditions behind.[32]

Newly installed in New York, the Bruce brothers would have seen firsthand how the extravagantly appointed, large-scale horse-breeding operations under development in New York and New Jersey might pose competition for Bluegrass breeding interests. In this, they had an advantage most Kentucky horsemen did not, the latter being too preoccupied at home with attempting to restart their operations after the war. *Turf, Field and Farm* published descriptive articles about these Northeastern horse farms, welcoming their owners to the turf world in the deferential manner these moguls would have expected. At the same time, these articles could have served as a warning to Kentucky horsemen that others besides themselves planned to enter the postwar market for racehorses in a major way. Bluegrass horsemen reading between the lines would have recognized the urgent need to recenter the horse world on their own region. Meantime, the Bruces ingratiated themselves into this world of Northeastern wealth, advising the new men of the turf. They played both sides of the growing divide, which appears to have been Alexander's purpose. For their own part, the Bruces thus enhanced their own net worth. They were business opportunists of another breed—those who went north after the war instead of south.

The horse farms of capitalists under development in the Northeast rose as elaborate testaments to their owners' wealth, expressions of material excess far beyond the scale of the Bluegrass gentry estates. Country squires in Kentucky and Tennessee bred and raised horses on farms or plantations graced with lovely homes or even mansions. But these farms were not entirely devoted to raising horses, as were the new farms in the Northeast. Neither were they endowed with the most modern equine facilities of the like under construction in New York and New Jersey. Woodburn Farm was a marvel for its architectural practicality and park-like landscape, and it stood alone in Kentucky in this respect. But, while verdant, woodland pastures were the hallmark of Kentucky farms, material excess characterized the new farms in the Northeast.

In New York and New Jersey, men who owned racehorses stated their social standing in overt fashion. Their habit was to ensure that their elite status was "manifested in the construction of country house, rural estate, and competitive stable complexes," writes one historian. For example, William Vanderbilt's sixteen-stall stable in what is now midtown Manhattan included a carriage house, an indoor exercise ring for the horses, and a full city block of pasture between Forty-third and Forty-fourth streets.[33]

One of the first to build a farm and training center in New Jersey had been Sanford, the friend of Alexander and financial backer of Sanders and Benjamin Bruce. Of all the new moguls resurrecting the Eastern turf world, Sanford was more of a maverick than most, for he had begun a business relationship with Alexander as early as 1860. He seemed intent on buying up as many sons of the great sire Lexington as Alexander would allow. (Alexander had closed off the breeding of Lexington on the open market in 1864, limiting the stallion thereafter to the private service of Alexander's mares. Woodburn Farm continued to sell offspring of Lexington at the farm's annual yearling auctions, hence the accusation of Northerners that Alexander controlled the market prices of this stallion.) Sanford particularly desired to own racehorses sired by Lexington out of mares sired by another great horse known as Glencoe. This combination of bloodlines had worked well in the Bluegrass, and Sanford, out of all the turf moguls, founded his program on emulating Bluegrass practices. Alexander no doubt influenced him to great extent. Consequently, while other men of the Northeast raced almost exclusively in New York and New Jersey and, later, at Pimlico Race Course in Maryland, Sanford was racing a stable of Lexington's offspring in New Orleans in addition to the Eastern tracks. The track at New Orleans had risen, phoenix-like, from the wartime years.[34]

For his racing activities in the Northeast, Sanford built a private training facility and breeding farm at Preakness, New Jersey, on property situated back in the Preakness hills. He named this country retreat the Preakness Stud Farm. Typical of the new Thoroughbred farms going up in this section of the country, Preakness Stud featured the most modern touches while also retaining a timeless rural charm.

Like Sanford, the new turf titans typically expressed nostalgia for the past in the traditional, rural charm their modern horse estates evoked. They incorporated a rural motif because they relied on these estates to provide a respite from the noise and pollution of city life. Thus, the Thoroughbred and trotting-horse nurseries of New Yorkers served a dual function. They existed in order to replenish the racing stables of their owners, and they also provided their owners with country estates where they could slip away from the city, perhaps escaping into a nostalgic idea of a life people believed had existed before the onset of industrialization.

A sporting periodical of the day expressed the essential character of these rural estates: "The thoroughbred colts graze in the meadows and sport over the lawn and, when tired of the noise of the city, the proprietor can retire to this lovely spot, and realize that freshness, peace and quietness, of which poets delight to sing, and which constitutes the charm of country life." This was Preakness Stud in 1866. Sanford could not have escaped to the country quite so easily if he had built his rural retreat far away from New York, in Bluegrass horse country. Thus, he built his farm in New Jersey, apparently with the belief that he could realize success the equal of Bluegrass horsemen by importing Alexander's best bloodlines into New Jersey.[35]

Sanford had constructed two new barns, but of greatest interest in 1866 was a facility still under construction: the training barn. This polygonal building had so many sides it was nearly circular. The interior included stalls for the horses living there and an indoor training track so that they could be exercised inside during bad weather. No one in the Bluegrass had built an indoor track; Sanford, with all his money, was running ahead of the Kentuckians with this concept.[36]

Sanford had arranged that water from a nearby brook would be pumped hydraulically into reservoirs. He even arranged a measure of security for the horses, stocking the reservoirs with small fish whose purpose was to control the algae but also, more importantly, to warn the horse grooms "in case of any attempt to poison the water, a precaution . . . borrowed from England." But then, every phase of the very idea of those country places becoming popular in the United States had been borrowed from England. Protecting the water source was the least of it.[37]

Sanford's new stud farm was one of an increasing number of such facilities in New Jersey and New York. August Belmont bought an estimated eleven to thirteen hundred acres in Babylon, Long Island, calling his country place Nursery Stud. Here, he intended to retire to stud the best horses from his racing stable. At the center of this property he constructed a "handsome modern structure" of a home with twenty-four rooms. The house stood on a rise that made the building appear "so lofty that we should think the Fire Island Lighthouse and the sea might be seen from the top of it on a clear day." The perfectly smooth green lawn sloped to a lake of thirty acres in size. On the other side of the lake, away from the main house, Belmont built a trout-hatching pond, a farmhouse, five cottages, two silos, barns, pastures, pens for hogs and chickens, and fields for growing hay, wheat and rye—"a self-sufficient community," remarks Belmont's biographer David Black. Belmont also built a bowling alley behind the main house.[38]

Belmont's stables for his Thoroughbreds (as distinguished from those for his carriage horses) numbered twenty-seven stalls; the Nursery Stud design included a bunkhouse for fifty stable lads, more stabling for extra horses, a trainer's house, a gristmill for the horses' feed, a blacksmith shop, and an indoor training arena connected to the main stables by covered walkways. The indoor track actually looked more like a conservatory, for one side of the roof was completely covered with glass. This produced pleasing aesthetic effects but also aided the horses: the increased amount of light afforded by the glass roof left no dark corners around the indoor track where horses might spook from the shadows. The surface of the indoor training course was covered with tan bark. A bank of straw five feet tall and three feet wide at the top formed an inner "rail" designed to protect the horses while they exercised. A smaller circle inside this straw rail provided room for horses working at slower exercise, giving them their own space without interfering with the horses working at faster speeds.[39]

The centerpiece of the Nursery Stud was the one-mile outdoor racetrack with its own grandstand, of which Black writes: "August could sit [there] all by himself if he wished and watch his horses race. August had created a village, an ideal world where he could retreat." With country estates like Nursery Stud and Preakness Stud, Belmont and others in his class were closing themselves off from lower social classes by constructing their own spheres. Apparently, it was equally important to them that their racehorses share this private sphere.[40]

As an increasing number of these rural retreats sprang up close to New York, it was becoming clear that the new titans of the turf were, indeed, bypassing central Kentucky and Middle Tennessee as places to build their lavish new farms. The power shift became increasingly evident with the construction of more stud farms. The Lorillard family, moguls in the tobacco business since 1826, saw one brother, George, develop Westbrook Farm for Thoroughbreds on Long Island while another brother, Pierre, developed 1,244 acres into his Rancocas Stud in 1875 in Jobstown, New Jersey. Francis Morris, whose racing colors had been registered longer than those of any family in the United States, was another whose breeding farm was situated close by New York. Upstate in New York, a wealthy gambler and horseman named Charles Reed built a breeding farm for Thoroughbreds near Saratoga Springs.[41]

First came the farms; then came the breeding stallions. Kentucky had retired to the new broodmare and stallion quarters that Jerome built at his racecourse; he was followed by another horse of high quality, Jerome Edgar, whom John Morrissey, the founder of the original Saratoga Race Course in 1863, had purchased for $3,000 from John Clay. Jerome Edgar retired to a breeding career at the Valley Brook Stud on Long Island. The breeding of racehorses was expanding with each new horse retired to stud in the Northeast. One indication of this expansion was the stallion advertisements published in sporting periodicals. Stallions advertised to stand at stud for the 1866 breeding season were located in Massachusetts, New Hampshire, New York, Missouri, Tennessee, Virginia, Texas, and, of course, Kentucky. The breeders of Bluegrass Kentucky had come out of the war realizing that the South's stranglehold on the sport had been broken. Kentucky breeders now had serious competition, with the outsiders paying scant notice to the criterion everyone had formerly agreed was critical for raising a sound, fast horse: the importance of raising a racehorse in the Bluegrass.[42]

The Bruce brothers had promoted the magic of Bluegrass soil and water to a nationwide audience from the start of their business in New York. As we have seen, one article they published in 1865 "celebrated" the Bluegrass, praising the "exquisite flavor and tenderness" of the meat produced there. The article went on to predict a bright future in agriculture for Kentucky, especially so after the slaves were set free. It cited the state's renown for the production of racehorses, in particular at Woodburn.[43]

One of *Turf, Field and Farm's* most brilliant initiatives was to bring the Civil War hero General George Armstrong Custer to central Kentucky in 1871. Sanders Bruce brought the general to Lexington for the express purpose of writing glowing reports about Bluegrass horse country. Custer did not disappoint. He wrote a series of five articles in the form of lengthy letters to the editor, using the nom de plume Nomad. In his first article, he praised the beauty and functionality of the horse farms. In later articles, he doled out kind words tempered with a measure of critique concerning the quality and honesty of Bluegrass trotting matches and Thoroughbred racing. Regardless of what he wrote, Custer brought attention to horse country. For this initial visit, Sanders Bruce had arranged for a small group of horse country's power brokers to accompany Custer through his tour of selected farms. Intent on showing him the Bluegrass at its best, this group had orchestrated every phase of the horse farm tour, in the first of several visits to Lexington that Custer was to make.[44]

Bruce and his colleagues had counted on Custer's celebrity to bring attention to the Bluegrass, a tactic that the horsemen of central Kentucky would polish to perfection through a long line of invited celebrities to follow. Thus, the Bluegrass horse business must credit Sanders Bruce with inaugurating a marketing practice that has endured into the twenty-first century. Not only did most Americans recognize Custer; he also had made acquaintance with the right people in the Northeast, people who could be useful to Kentucky horsemen. He had cultivated friendships with John Jacob Astor, August Belmont, Levi Morton, Leonard Jerome, Jay Gould, and Jim Fisk, all wealthy and powerful New Yorkers whom Kentuckians would have loved to bring into their sphere within the Bluegrass. Custer would die in disgrace at the Battle of the Little Bighorn in June 1876, leading some 260 of his men to their deaths. But he did not die disgraced in the view of horsemen of central Kentucky. He had suited their purpose perfectly, marketing the Bluegrass in his articles for *Turf, Field and Farm*.

A November day greeted Custer when he stepped off the train in Lexington to meet some of horse country's movers and shakers, including Sanders Bruce. The latter's connections with Woodburn Farm remained strong and would be utilized on Custer's tour. Alexander had died four years previously, in 1867, leaving Woodburn to his brother, Alexander John Alexander, who spent most of his time traveling. The latter did not express an interest similar to his late brother's in the operation of the farm; Alexander's death truly had left a vacuum in vision and power that men like Bruce had stepped in to fill. Woodburn continued to operate as the premier racehorse-breeding farm in the United States, briefly under the direction of Swigert, and then under the inspired management of Lucas Brodhead following Swigert's resignation. Bruce had planned the tour with a visit to Woodburn as the highlight, and Custer eagerly anticipated seeing Woodburn and its breeding stock. Bruce possessed the ego and moxie to match Custer's egocentric per-

HARPER'S WEEKLY.

A JOURNAL OF CIVILIZATION

VOL. VIII.—No. 377.] NEW YORK, SATURDAY, MARCH 19, 1864. [8.00 FOR FOUR MONTHS. $3.00 PER YEAR IN ADVANCE.

Entered according to Act of Congress, in the Year 1864, by Harper & Brothers, in the Clerk's Office of the District Court for the Southern District of New York.

BRIGADIER-GENERAL GEORGE A. CUSTER.—PHOTOGRAPHED BY BRADY.—[SEE PAGE 187.]

General George Armstrong Custer, better known as an Indian fighter, also owned racehorses and hoped to purchase a farm in the Bluegrass when he retired from the military. He died in 1876 at the Battle of the Little Bighorn, riding a former racehorse he had acquired on a visit to Lexington. (*Harper's Weekly*, March 19, 1864, cover, courtesy of the U.S. Library of Congress.)

sonality. As the publisher of articles the general previously had written from Indian Territory, Bruce knew how to manipulate this cultural icon who had emerged from the Civil War with an intriguing reputation for daring bravado, his reputation matched only by his famous visage enlivened with long, golden hair that hung from his head in generous curls. He had arranged an overnight stay at Woodburn for the general, highlighted by a visit to the renowned stallion everyone longed to meet—Lexington. As a tourist in horse country, Custer could not have asked for more.

Most Americans link Custer's name to his checkered career as an Indian fighter in the West. Less well known was his great appreciation for racehorses, a passion he pursued wholeheartedly during a brief posting to Elizabethtown, Kentucky, from 1871 to 1873. The U.S. Army assigned Custer and the Seventh Cavalry to Elizabethtown, believing it was capable of accomplishing what law enforcement in Kentucky had failed to do: putting a stop to the widespread lawlessness that the Ku Klux Klan and other white supremacist groups had wrought in a reign of terror directed against Republican voters and blacks. Rather than chasing Klansmen through western Kentucky, however, Custer spent most of his time in Louisville purchasing horses for the army's use. From Louisville's most popular hotel, the Galt House, the trip was a mere five-hour train ride to Lexington, according to Custer's calculations.

"I wish I could describe what delight my husband took in his horse life," wrote the general's wife, Elizabeth "Libbie" Custer. *Turf, Field and Farm* had also brought attention to Custer's equestrian talents and admiration for horses, noting: "The General knows a good horse when he sees it and finds music in the clatter of flying feet." Libbie Custer described her husband's dream as owning a "Blue-grass farm with blooded horses." She wrote how he hoped to retire to horse country following his army career. Custer loved to associate with other horsemen and could speak knowledgeably with the best of them on equine pedigrees. He had even participated in horse racing during an army posting in Texas prior to his arrival in Kentucky. During the Civil War, he had attended trotting races in Buffalo, New York, and Thoroughbred races at Saratoga. He appeared greatly pleased to visit Lexington, where the conversation, as he quoted a friend, consisted quite agreeably of "nothing but horse,

horse, horse." He observed: "[Even] the youngest boy, white or black, can correctly trace the pedigree of every prominent horse, and give the time of every prominent race, with the place of each horse. He would not be a Kentuckian of the Blue Grass region if unable to do this."[45]

Custer's first article in his series from Bluegrass country revealed his fascination with the region right from the introduction, as he wrote: "Being desirous of taking a peep at the flyers of the Blue Grass region in their Winter quarters, I stepped aboard the early train from this city to Lexington." Two days of fine dining in Kentucky mansions in the congenial company of like-minded men awaited Custer. His hosts had arranged to meet him close by the train station at the Phoenix Hotel, where they began with a midday meal. Then the group set off in two horse-drawn carriages for Woodford County and the neighborhood surrounding Woodburn Farm.[46]

Two hours later, the men arrived at the residence of Benjamin Gratz, the owner of a farm adjoining Woodburn some fourteen miles west of Lexington. The group dined and spent the remainder of the evening talking about horses, a conversation topic that might have been Custer's favorite. "The stranger is struck with the universal importance attached to horses and their history," Custer commented. The group retired early; plans called for an early start to Woodburn Farm. Custer awoke the next morning to see a servant building a fire in the room where he had slept. Just as his article told readers much about Bluegrass horse farms, his description of this early morning domestic routine revealed how he and others of his time regarded persons of color.[47]

The servant, he wrote, "an overgrown fifteenth amendment, entered our room for the purpose of building a fire. Col. Cook, arousing from a comfortable slumber, and anxious to learn the hour, inquired of the girl, 'What time is it?' 'Oh, de cows done gone long go.' The Colonel, half awake, repeated his interrogatory, to which the ebony representative replied as before, 'De cows done gone long go.' Now as neither the Colonel or myself had ever informed ourselves at what hour Blue Grass etiquette required the cows to be 'gone,' we were left in ignorance of the hour of the morning. Our doubts on this point, however, were soon removed by Col. Bruce popping his head in at our door."[48]

The referenced Fifteenth Amendment was, of course, the constitutional amendment granting suffrage to black men, a subject hotly

The facade of the main residence at Woodburn Farm has undergone a variety of changes. The house was built originally in the Italianate style. Robert Aitcheson Alexander never lived in this house. He lived across the Old Frankfort Pike at his family's former log home. Colonel William Buford built the nucleus of the Italianate house on property he had purchased when a portion of Woodburn was sold. Following his death in 1848, his heirs sold the land back to Woodburn Farm. Alexander John Alexander, who became the owner of Woodburn on the death of his brother, Robert Aitcheson Alexander, made the former Buford house his residence. (Postcard from the collection of the University of Kentucky Libraries, Special Collections.)

debated in the North and the South as well as in the border state of Kentucky prior to ratification of the amendment in 1870. In the years to come, the debate would take on new meaning as it shifted into the sport of horse racing. At the time of Custer, however, Kentucky had refused to ratify the Thirteenth, Fourteenth, and Fifteenth amendments, which had, respectively, outlawed slavery in the United States, granted citizenship and full protection under the Constitution to blacks, and granted them the right to vote. With Custer feeling comfortable enough to write about the servant as he did—and Bruce agreeing to publish his remarks—the two men revealed a disdain for blacks that readers of Custer's articles apparently would not have found offensive in either North or South. Custer, a Northerner whose boyhood home was Ohio, appeared to feel no differently about blacks than did the Kentucky-born Sanders Bruce. The Civil War, which began as a fight to keep the United States together and wound up as a fight to end slavery, had been over for six years; however, blacks had gained freedom in name only and generally received little respect.

Sanders had intended the visit to Woodburn as the highlight of the tour; he did not disappoint Custer. When Custer wrote his article, he devoted more space to describing the Woodburn operation than he did to any other farm: "The princely estate," as he called it, "embrac[es] four thousand acres of the richest and fairest soil in the world, with its trotting stables and exercising grounds at one point, its stables and walks for runners [Thoroughbreds] at another, while midway are to be found the immense stables and pastures of the fine herds of shorthorn cattle and Southdown sheep."[49]

Custer also observed Sanders Bruce making close observations, "with pencil and note-book in hand," of the Thoroughbred weanlings intended for sale seven months later at the annual Woodburn auction of yearlings held in June. Bruce, as Custer noted, made notes on the weanlings for "his Eastern friends," who probably would commission him to bid on these horses at the auction. Two years previously, Bruce had picked out a yearling named Harry Bassett for a racehorse owner from the Northeast named Colonel David McDaniel. He acquired the yearling for $315 for McDaniel; within two years, in other words, by the time Custer visited Woodburn, Harry Bassett had developed into a champion three-year-old racehorse. His success was bringing increased attention to Bruce and his innate talent for picking out yearling racehorse prospects. The Bruce brothers served their Northeastern clients well, working as a conduit between New York and the Bluegrass. Custer realized how this worked, with the Bruces having the ability to sell their services as go-betweens because they not only knew where to find horses but also were able to link the buyers with the sellers. Later generations would call such persons *bloodstock agents*. During these postwar years, the Bruces simply represented themselves as two brothers offering their services in just about any phase of the nascent horse industry. They represented the beginnings of the professional class that was only emerging in the sport, bringing order and business practices to horse racing and breeding as the two businesses embarked on their expansion. Custer's writings helped them along their way.[50]

"Ah, Colonel, you're cum to look at de colts agin, has ye. You beats dem all a namin' de fastest ones," remarked a man Custer quoted in his article, identifying him as "the sable old functionary" of the Woodburn stables, a man who probably was a former slave and "who has been born and bred among the thoroughbreds of Woodburn." Black persons worked in great numbers at Woodburn, as previous visitors had observed in the articles they wrote about this large livestock-breeding operation. Depending on the job categories they filled, a few received more respect than others.[51]

One such man was the horse trainer Ansel Williamson, sent to Woodburn during the war as a slave on loan from Alexander's close friend in Georgetown, Alexander Keene Richards. Williamson returned to Richards a free man late in 1865 but not before he had taken the Woodburn horses through several successful racing seasons during the war. Alexander trusted Williamson to the extent that he allowed him to travel with horses to the new Northeastern tracks during the war. Asteroid's success on the track marked the high point of Williamson's horse-training career. Alexander revealed the respect he had for Williamson's ability with a horse when he named a Thoroughbred for the trainer, calling it Ansel.

A painting of Asteroid by Edward Troye shows Williamson preparing to lift a saddle onto the horse's back while the animal's jockey adjusts his riding boots, preparing to mount. The jockey is "Brown Dick," a black youth whom Alexander had purchased as a slave when the boy was age seven, taking him to Woodburn to train him to become a rider. Brown Dick left Woodburn in 1869, transitioned into the role of a horse trainer, took the name Edward D. Brown, and developed two horses— Ben Brush and Plaudit—who would win the Kentucky Derby after they left his care. Custer quite possibly might have encountered Williamson or Brown Dick on his many visits to racetracks. He probably would have spoken to either with greater respect than he showed the domestic employee who stoked the fireplace at the Gratz farm because horse racing relied on the talents of black men like Williamson and Brown Dick

Lexington's fame as a sire, acquired during the nineteenth century, remains unequaled in the history of the turf. He led the sire list in number of winners among his offspring for sixteen years. He was purchased on his retirement from the racetrack by Robert Aitcheson Alexander for a then-record $15,000 and stood at stud at Woodburn Farm. (Henry William Herbert, *Frank Forester's Horse and Horsemanship of the United States and British Provinces of North America,* vol. 1 [New York: Stringer & Townsend, 1857], facing p. 386.)

to sustain the operation of the sport in these early postwar years. They won the respect of whites.[52]

Custer described several of the trotting-horse breeding stallions he saw at Woodburn. Then he turned to the Thoroughbreds, remarking that some of the young offspring of Asteroid looked well. He also took a look at Asteroid, who was turned out in a pasture. But the horse who remained to be seen was the king of Woodburn's horses, Lexington, the sire of Asteroid, Kentucky, and Norfolk as well as so many other Thoroughbreds whose success on the racecourses had underscored the breeding prowess of their sire. Custer reacted to his audience with Lexington as though laying eyes on a king.

"As his groom drew back the bolt and opened the door which admitted us to the distinguished presence of this famous horse," Custer wrote, "we involuntarily felt like lifting our cap, and with uncovered head and respectful mien approach this great steed as if we were in the sacred presence of royalty." Lexington had long ago lost his sight. Custer noted that, instead of the horse turning to look at his visitors, as any horse with eyesight would, the blind stallion relied on his hearing to reveal the presence of Custer and the others at the door of his stall. "Lexington assumed an attitude of intent listening," Custer wrote, "pricking his ears as if to determine by the sounds of the voice who we were and the occasion of our visit." A handler led the great horse out of his stall, removed the animal's blanket, and stood the horse for further inspection. After pausing here to enjoy the moment, Custer and the group moved on to inspect two other Thoroughbred stallions, Planet and Australian.[53]

Much more awaited Custer. Bruce and the Woodburn manager, Brodhead, had arranged for the general to dine in the mansion. The new owner of Woodburn, Alexander John Alexander, happened to be traveling to California and so was not present; Brodhead served as host. "Gen. Custer" and his group "spent a day and night with me last week and seem to be well pleased with their visit," Brodhead would write to Alexander in one of the letters he routinely sent the owner of Woodburn to update him on the daily workings of the farm. Brodhead, like Bruce and Swigert, represented the emerging professional class that was taking on important functions in the world of fast horses. He had "supreme control of Woodburn Stock Farm and its valuable herds and stables," Custer remarked. His filling this role enabled Alexander to travel and live his life largely as an absentee owner—a lifestyle that remained uncommon in the Bluegrass at this time but by the turn of the century would become the norm. Brodhead, as Custer wrote, played out his role in a polished, professional manner and "received us with that marked courtesy and cordial hospitality which has ever characterized the proprietors of this justly noted establishment." He might have been alluding to the former owner, Robert Aitcheson Alexander, who remained on the farm much of the time and greeted visitors himself. But times had changed at Woodburn, as they had changed in all of horse racing.[54]

Bruce, working in tandem with Brodhead, had intended for the dinner at Woodburn to impress Custer every bit as much as his visit to the great estate. Mentioning the mansion in his article—for the new owner of Woodburn had chosen to live in a grander house than the former log cabin that Robert Aitcheson Alexander had occupied across the road—Custer went on to describe their meal. "Two items—important ones, too—I must mention," he wrote. "A piece of Southdown mutton, served in the perfectness of Southern style, and Alderney milk of such rare and exceeding richness as to cause one only accustomed to city living to wonder whether he had ever really tasted pure milk before." The milk and the mutton would have come directly off the farm, for Woodburn raised these specifically named sheep and cattle. The meal suggested more of the richness indigenous to the Bluegrass that Custer already had noted in his tour of the Woodburn stables and grounds.[55]

The remainder of Custer's tour went pretty much the same, with an impressive orchestration of showing the finest Bluegrass farms and winding up with another night spent in a Kentucky mansion: this time at the McGrathiana farm of Hal Price McGrath. The fortune that McGrath had built from running gambling houses in New York with his close friend Morrissey had enabled the Kentuckian to engage in a far more expansive way in horse racing and breeding. Kentuckians and many others knew him as a man of great hospitality; a stop here during the farm junket was a must for Custer and his party.[56]

Custer, appropriately charmed, wrote how they sat down to "a champagne supper, which Delmonico [the famed New York restaurateur] could not have excelled. In keeping with his deserved reputation for hospitality, McGrath also opened up his stores of bourbon for the enjoyment of those assembled. As Custer wrote: "There were some choice spirits there besides those which were bottled." He mentioned some who had attended, including a "turf" writer, Joe Elliott, of the *New York Herald*, who was en route to New Orleans to write about the races in that Southern city. Another he named was a Colonel Morgan, the brother of the late General John Hunt Morgan—"of Confederate fame," as Custer noted. Just as the Bruce brothers had reunited to forget their political differences after the war, so had some notable horsemen, businessmen, and landowners of the Bluegrass. Former Confederates could feel comfortable in the presence of a Union army officer. Their host, McGrath, had not fought in the war, choosing like John Clay to pursue his business interests instead. For McGrath, these interests had consisted of running his gambling rooms from New Orleans to New York. "A jolly old soul was he," Custer wrote of McGrath, but the point was this: when it came to selling horses or promoting the idea of Bluegrass horse country, ex-Confederates lined up alongside former Unionists to accomplish their purpose in Kentucky.[57]

Custer departed central Kentucky following this whirlwind tour, returned to the Galt House in Louisville, and wrote the first of his five dispatches about his impressions of horse country. Bruce, as his host, had executed a perfectly planned marketing ploy in persuading the general to write these articles for *Turf, Field and Farm,* for Custer was promoting the notion that the Bluegrass had not lost the natural qualities that had made it the source of sound, fast horses before the war. If the Bluegrass had two qualities that no other region possessed, it was the abundance of superior Thoroughbred breeding stock and the unique land these horses grazed on. The soil of this rich land had made the Bluegrass in the beginning; promoters like the Bruce brothers were working hard to fix this idea securely within the imaginations of the nation's wealthy sporting men.

The marketing plan that Robert Aitcheson Alexander had envisioned with his financial support of the Bruce brothers was moving in the direction he had hoped prior to his death in 1867. Alexander had forfeited one opportunity when he failed to send Asteroid to race Kentucky. Seizing another chance, Alexander did not fail a second time. The results he set in motion by financing the Bruce brothers in their ventures would aid the Bluegrass greatly in reinforcing the notion that this region was America's true racehorse country. Nature's work here, begun some 460 million years before Asteroid and Kentucky raced onto the stage, benefited horses in ways that the fad for Northeastern farms could not possibly match. But it would take Northeastern turfmen another thirty years to fully realize this.

chapter THREE

A Killing Spree and a Hanging Tree

The 1870s, the decade when General Custer visited the Bluegrass, brought to prominence a horse Americans came to call the King of the Turf. His owner had named him Longfellow. Bred and born in Kentucky, Longfellow was big and brown but not entirely handsome, for his head lacked the finely chiseled appearance characteristic of the classic Thoroughbred. He possessed a somewhat unfortunate profile. His face curved downward like the lower end of a whiskey jug, convex where it should have tapered in a straight line to his nose. Any horseman would have called him *Roman nosed* in the parlance of the turf. His owner and breeder John Harper called him the best thing ever on four hooves.

Robert Aitcheson Alexander had been dead three years and his protégés the Bruce Brothers were only five years into ramping up their marketing machine at *Turf, Field and Farm* when Longfellow ran his first race in 1870, at age three. Over the next three years, Longfellow and Harper would have much to do with the way outsiders perceived the Bluegrass region. People thought of Harper and saw neither a Southern cavalier nor a Southern colonel. In Harper, they saw remnants of a wild and untamed West.

Longfellow was the genuine article, a fast Kentucky racehorse, the very notion of which helped reinforce Bluegrass Kentucky's position as the cradle of the racehorse. Harper, whose twenty-five-hundred-acre Nantura Farm lay adjacent to Woodburn, sent Longfellow into New York and New Jersey to defeat horses that the turf moguls reeled out of

Americans called Longfellow the King of the Turf during the early 1870s. His owner, John Harper of Nantura Farm in Woodford County, shown here with Longfellow, saw three family members killed in two separate incidents. Harper likewise engaged in violence. He ordered a mock lynching of two African Americans on his Nantura Farm. (W. S. Vosburgh, *Racing in America, 1866–1921* [New York: Scribner Press, 1922], facing 86.)

their stables one after another to challenge him. Longfellow was "beyond question the most celebrated horse of the 1870s," wrote the historian Walter S. Vosburgh. "No horse of his day was a greater object of public notice. His entire career was sensational. . . . People seemed to regard him as a superhorse." People sought to snatch long hairs from his tail as keepsakes. He traveled east in a boxcar emblazoned with his name on the exterior.[1]

A writer for one of the Eastern sporting journals once asked Harper whether he had named Longfellow after the popular poet Henry Wadsworth Longfellow. Harper replied that he had not heard much about the man. He said he gave the brown colt that particular name because he had the longest legs "of any feller I ever seen." His folksy, backwoods manner in describing the horse and his self-acknowledged lack of formal education made Harper seem like a throwback to Kentuckians of the frontier era. The frontier had long since passed by Kentucky, yet the image remained, even after the Civil War.[2]

In the practice of the day, Harper had sent his broodmare Nantura to a stallion standing at stud not too far from the Harper home place. The stallion stood at the Bosque Bonita Stud, which belonged to an ex-Confederate cavalry officer, General Abe Buford, who had lost most of his horses during the war. Bosque Bonita was only two miles from Nantura Farm. Thus, the mating arrangement was convenient. It also proved fortuitous. The stallion Harper had chosen for his mare was Leamington, an imported horse whose destiny was to prove him a rival worthy of Woodburn Farm's renowned Lexington. Leamington's stay in the Bluegrass was brief, only one year, his owner then moving him to Pennsylvania within easy reach of New York breeders. But, in siring Longfellow, Leamington helped stamp the direction that horse breeding would take in Kentucky, for Longfellow became not only a popular and successful racehorse but also a valuable sire.

Unlike most Thoroughbreds, Longfellow did not race at age two because he was ungainly and nonathletic. His legs had grown faster and longer than his body had developed; it would take another year for the body to catch up. When he matured, he grew into an extraordinarily tall Thoroughbred of seventeen hands, the equivalent of five-foot-six at the top of his shoulders, called withers. He raced with considerable regional success at age three. When he reached four years of age, Harper took him to the Northeastern tracks, whereupon his career shot to the heights at the national level. It was in the Northeast that he earned his reputation as the King of the Turf. Unlike Woodburn Farm's Asteroid six years previously, Longfellow earned this title because he had raced not exclusively in "the West," as people of the time referred to all regions across the Appalachian Mountains, but against the best horses of the Northeast.

Longfellow was a marvel. So was his owner, Harper, in the view of Eastern racing patrons. Harper brought a touch of the exotic into their lives. He appeared quite unlike anything they were accustomed to seeing even among the many other Kentuckians who traveled northeast to the new racecourses. Like the Kentuckians, Eastern folk began calling Harper by the familiar name of "Uncle John." And, just as Longfellow had stamped himself the genuine Kentucky article, so did his owner.[3]

Harper gave the appearance of a wizened Kentuckian who had spent a lifetime in the company of horses. The finishing touch that stamped him as exotic was the frock coat he wore, a coat evocative of an earlier time in Kentucky, somewhere at the margins of the antebellum era and the frontier as it moved west. One person described Harper as "an animated ghost, with his white hair streaming in the wind. It is a queer sight to see this venerable bachelor . . . tottering along after his only love—a horse!" Harper posed a reassuring, idealized connection to older, more steadfast days that people wanted to believe had been more reliable than the present, which seemed always in flux. Harper stood as a nostalgic anchor in an ever-more-industrialized world.[4]

Horse-racing patrons clung to this comforting notion of Harper even after revelations of his darker side: information that fixed him squarely within the culture of violence raging all throughout border-state Kentucky and the South. "All hope abandon, ye who enter here," the *New York Times* wrote about Kentucky's raging violence and law-lessness. During Harper's lifetime, Kentucky ranked as especially law-less within a violent Southern culture that did not appear to place a high value on human life. As newspaper readers throughout the United States learned, Harper experienced multiple encounters with crime that represented both ends of this lawless spectrum. On the one hand, crime had victimized his family, leaving his brother and sister dead in a home invasion in 1871; this occurred not many years after he lost another brother, Adam, during a guerrilla raid on the home place during the war. On the other hand, Harper served as an accomplice to a racially motivated vigilante incident in response to the deaths of his brother and sister. He ordered a mock lynching to take place on his farm in the hope of forcing confessions from two of his African American employees. As both the victim and the perpetrator of crime, Harper stands out as an excellent case study illustrative of the violence raging at every social and economic level throughout the state.[5]

Violence and lawlessness explained much about why the new men of the turf avoided Kentucky when choosing to develop horse farms in the Northeast. The *New York Times* opined: "So long as these mid-night assassins continue to ply their trade within the shadow of the State Capitol, Kentucky has no claim to be considered a civilized State." Southerners, and also Kentuckians, were aware of this stigma adversely

Kentucky was famed for its fine women, excellent bourbon whiskey, and Thoroughbred racehorses, including the nineteenth-century champion Salvator, pictured on this circa 1910 postcard. But not to be ignored was the state's reputation for violence and lawlessness. Note the pistol and the group of masked night riders on their way through a tobacco field. (Collage of "Kentucky's Fame," ca. 1910, Kramer Art Company Postcard Proofs, 1999PH10.46, Kentucky Historical Society.)

affecting their regional economies. "We have reason to believe that a large number of our Northern friends earnestly desire to emigrate to the South ... and we fear they may be deterred from doing so by the publications [of Ku Klux stories in newspapers]," stated a letter to the editor of the *New York Daily Tribune* in 1871. Kentucky held the distinction of having one of the highest crime rates in the nation during the latter part of the nineteenth century. "The 'Ku Klux' are pretty bad," commented the manager of Woodburn.

This notorious reputation led to a widespread belief among outsiders that the commonwealth was too unstable for capital investment. Some observers blamed the widespread lawlessness on the lax system of justice prevalent in the commonwealth. Others placed the blame for this high crime rate partly with the people of Kentucky. "Frontier violence, wars, racism, nativism, alcoholism, duels—all fueled the commonwealth's aptitude for violence," James Klotter has written. "The prewar years only set the stage for the postwar actions that followed and made it easier for them to occur." The *New York Times,* which routinely reported on the lawlessness throughout the commonwealth, wrote tongue-in-cheek that Kentucky would be a delightful place to live if a person enjoyed "personal affrays and private assassinations." In the words of Robert Ireland: "While nineteenth century Kentucky produced fine horses, hemp, and whiskey, she excelled most in crime."[6]

Kentucky's upper classes shared in this public penchant for violence. The *New York Times* once commented that even the state's "best society literally streams with gore." Landowners and elected officials might engage in violent crimes or at least turn a blind eye to their existence. As Ireland writes: "The *New York Times* branded county officials as 'particeps criminis.'" This only darkened outsiders' perceptions of the state, for, if the leading citizens of the commonwealth were bound up in lawlessness, how was Kentucky to rid itself of the violence that seemed endemic to all layers of the social fabric?[7]

While the dilemma seemed unsolvable at the time, the degree of lawlessness did not appear to be in dispute. Kentucky and the former Confederate states to the South did, in fact, exhibit a higher rate of violence than the Northern states, according to popular belief as well as published literature. In one example, Klotter cites the 1880 book *Homicide, North and South,* by H. V. Redfield. The author chose Kentucky as one of three states emblematic of Southern disorder and identified it as having more murders in 1878 than eight other states combined. The *New York Times* also singled out Kentucky as especially violent. Giving a word of caution, Klotter does point out that some reportage on Kentucky violence in the *Times* stemmed from regional animosities that lingered after the Civil War. Stories of lawless incidents in Kentucky frequently originated in Cincinnati, a trade rival of Louisville's; Cincinnati wished to portray Kentucky in a negative light. But Klotter still reaches the same conclusion that Americans had reached for decades following the Civil War. "The accounts, biased though they might be," he writes, "were essentially correct: Kentucky *was* a violent place."[8]

Kentucky's ever-darkening reputation adversely affected economic development, as the pattern of horse farms developing in the Northeast had suggested. The *New York Times* took note of this in 1878 while also chastising Kentuckians for their own role in their state's worsening reputation. "[Kentucky] needs development; but she never will get it . . . until she suppresses effectually the spirit and practice of butchery with which her tarnished name is associated," the newspaper suggested in frank and certain terms. It warned that, even if the commonwealth didn't care enough about itself to guard its reputation, "material interests demand that she should use all her powers to compel respect for law and order within her bounds." In other words, Kentucky needed to own up to the harsh fact that it would continue to fall behind other states in economic development—until the state itself chose to clean up its lawlessness. But that appeared unlikely. The *New York Times* reported: "We have an admission from the highest Democratic authority in the State of Kentucky that constant outrages are committed against persons and property by bands too powerful for the officers of the law to cope with."[9]

As incidents at the Harper family's Nantura Farm demonstrated, this violence could strike within residences on famed Bluegrass farms just as it did throughout Fayette County. The *New York Times* concluded: "The peaceable people of Kentucky are today in more danger from outlaws and murderers of their own race than they were at the dawn of the century from hostile Indians." The lawlessness did not stop with the Harpers on their Nantura Farm. Nearby in Fayette County, residents petitioned authorities for police protection in 1876 "to render their houses and property . . . more secure than they have been for a number of years." The violence was still going strong in 1890 when the U.S. Census reported, as Klotter writes, "that Kentucky had more homicides than any state except populous New York." Ten years later, in 1900, Kentucky violence arrived at its zenith with the assassination of Governor William Goebel.[10]

Newspapers were rife with stories about Kentucky violence, and many Americans read newspapers daily during the latter part of the nineteenth century. Consequently, a great many people read about the killings at the Harper family's Nantura Farm, for the Harpers' great wealth in land, money, and racehorses made for a titillating tale of the type newspapers and their readers accepted as the spice of real life. Perhaps, a century later, revelations about Harper's ordering up a lynching party would have tarnished his memory in the sport's narrative and diminished by association the reverence afforded his champion racehorse

Longfellow. But this is not what occurred in Kentucky as it evolved during Gilded Age America.

The Harper tragedy began unfolding three months before Custer's tour of horse farms. John Harper's brother, Jacob, and sister, Betsy, both elderly, suffered a brutal attack by an unknown assailant or assailants who broke into the Harper residence during the night of September 11, 1871, at Nantura Farm. The farm lay near Midway, some fourteen miles west of Lexington at the heart of early racehorse country in Kentucky. This was the same rural neighborhood that had Woodburn Farm at its center. When the break-in occurred, John Harper was away from home at the races in Lexington. He was preparing Longfellow for an important race to take place that week at the Kentucky Association track. Harper was asleep in the barn where he had installed Longfellow at the track when a loud banging at the stable door awakened him. With him were his favorite nephew, Frank Harper, and the stable lads whose job was to care for the horses.

Whoever was outside the barn door had made a great commotion, having bumped into a warning mechanism that Harper had laid across the door before all inside bedded down for the night. The mechanism served as a crude burglar alarm. "The door liked to have hit him," Harper would recall two years later during his deposition for a court case. The noise also woke the young stable lads sleeping in the loft. One of them shouted down from his bed made of fluffed-up straw, demanding to know what their unknown caller wanted. The caller answered from outside the door that he would very much like to visit Longfellow. To those inside the barn, the request seemed ludicrous, a stranger wanting to see the famous horse in the middle of the night.[11]

"It was a darn pretty time of night to want to see Longfellow," Harper recalled the youths mumbling as they awoke. The stable lads, clearly annoyed at being awakened, shouted again from the loft, as Harper recalled later, "that if he wanted to see him he would have to come in the morning." Morning was a time when most racehorses received visitors, during training hours, when they had their exercise on the track and then stood for their baths and walked to cool out following their gallops. Something about this midnight visit at the barn seemed so alarming that those inside the stable understandably would not have unlocked the door under any circumstances.[12]

The stranger did return at daylight. Receiving the visitor at a more civilized hour, Harper invited him into the stable, telling him that, if he waited until the lad had cleaned off the horse, then he could take a proper look at Longfellow. Harper apologized and said that he needed to hurry away to observe his other horses training on the racecourse. He left the man at the stable with Longfellow's groom. A short time later, while close by the racecourse, Harper was priming a water pump when he received the news about his brother killed at Nantura and his sister lying near death. He forgot about the stranger at the barn and would not remember him until much later. He left right away in a horse-drawn buggy for the two-hour ride back to Nantura Farm, fourteen miles away.

Harper arrived at Nantura to find a crowd of perhaps thirty or forty persons standing around in the yard outside the family residence. The scene inside the house would be described in all its horrific detail in newspapers from the *New York Times* to the local papers in Lexington. Jacob Harper's body lay diagonally across his bed with one foot hanging over the edge. His left cheek had been crushed, as though with an ax handle. His bed had been drenched in blood that had dried by the time John Harper arrived.[13]

The local magistrate, the sheriff, the doctor attending Betsy Harper, and the Harper neighbors and relatives had already formed a hypothesis about how the assailant or team of killers might have gained entry to the house. The Harper home was a weather-beaten building in rundown condition; a window close by Jacob Harper's bed had needed repairs for some time. The catch for fastening the shutter was broken. Persons investigating the scene quickly surmised that the home invaders had gained easy entry through this window.[14]

It had not been out of character for the Harpers to ignore the need for window repairs. People widely knew the brothers and their sister as miserly, eccentric types. "The economical, almost penurious habits of the Harpers were well known," the *Frankfort Commonwealth* commented. John Harper was so reluctant to spend money that he had a habit of bringing his own wood to the racetrack in order to cook meals for his stable help and his horse trainer. He also dressed simply, in jeans, looking a lot more like a frontiersman than a Bluegrass landowner and breeder of Thoroughbred horses.

In reality, the Harpers were well-off. According to speculation, they possessed at least $500,000, hoarding great amounts of money in bonds and cash. Rumor also held that they kept huge sums of money in their house at Nantura. "The impression was general that they kept their treasure concealed about the house," the *Frankfort Commonwealth* noted. Longfellow's upcoming race might have led someone to suspect that the Harpers had more cash than usual on hand the night of the home invasion. The horse was to race that week against another turf star named Enquirer; people so greatly anticipated the race that the railroads had scheduled extra trains to bring patrons out to the track. Quite a few persons had known that Jacob Harper had planned to wager $500 on Longfellow in this race, even though he usually bet no more than $5 or $10. Someone might have broken into the house in search of this cash.[15]

Outside the house, the neighbors had found a meat ax lying on a tree stump. Here was the murder weapon, or so they reasoned. W. A. Moore, the magistrate, looked the situation over and announced that the assailant must have used the ax handle rather than the blade to kill Jacob Harper and wound his sister, for the handle showed evidence of clotted hair. Whether the hair had belonged to a human or an animal was a forensic detail no one appeared to consider. All simply seized on the idea of the ax handle as the weapon.[16]

The neighbors and local officials found more evidence: hoofprints leading from the house to a place where someone had hitched two horses in a lot at the front of the property. They also discovered a human boot print matching a size 6 shoe. The boot print revealed a peculiarity that all hoped would make it easy to find the actual boot and, thus, the killer: the top piece of the leather shoe appeared to have projected over the sole of the boot, making a clearly identifiable mark in the dust. A few people noticed at the time that this appeared to match the boot of a young relative, John W. Harper. He was the son of John Harper's other (and least favorite) nephew, Adam Harper. No one acted on this observation about the boot. All were preoccupied with turning their suspicions to easier targets: the African American domestic help.[17]

Young John Harper cried out, in the presence of Uncle John, "Let's kill the damned negroes." Witnesses described the youth as in a wild state, driven to tears. Old Uncle John Harper thought this murderous suggestion over and agreed. Not long afterward, he told some of his closest friends and relatives that, if they strung up the "negroes" and choked them for a while, perhaps they might reveal who had broken into the house and killed Jacob.[18]

The local sheriff also did his part to hurry the process along. Before the mock lynching occurred, the sheriff had rounded up five more blacks, whom he took into custody on the charge of "suspicion." Among these were a boy called Will Pryor, who tended the fireplace in Jacob Harper's bedroom; Will's father, Sam Pryor, who disappeared the morning after the killing, thus focusing suspicion on himself; Henry, a stable boy; Will Scott, a man arrested at the racetrack in Lexington; and Tom Parker, whom the Harpers had owned during slavery. Eventually, the sheriff released all five. Taking them into custody had been entirely in keeping with customary practices, for suspicion of crime in Kentucky and the South usually fell first on persons of color.

The mock lynching did not take place in the heat of passion despite the younger John Harper's urgent plea to "kill the damned negroes." John Harper commissioned a number of neighbors and relatives to carry out the mock hangings only after the sheriff failed to build a case against anyone else. The vigilantes called themselves "ku-kluxers," employing a frequently used reference to the Ku Klux Klan. Whether these men actually were a part of the Klan is not known, but they did know how to mimic the Klan's practices. They rode their horses to a place on Nantura Farm where they tied up a woman named Darkey and a boy named Henry and strung them up from two separate trees. Their intent had been to force confessions. But the two offered up nothing to their assailants, perhaps because they knew nothing at all. Deciding this was a waste of time, the vigilante party lowered Darkey and the boy to the ground—still alive. Not revealed was the extent of any injuries they might have suffered or whether the two incurred psychological damage. However, as one in the lynching party had said, they put the two "to a pretty severe test."[19]

These two had not been afforded due legal process, as had the other five African Americans that the sheriff had arrested. But, by this point, tempers had grown as short as the list of suspects. Henry was, perhaps, a son or a grandson of Darkey, whose name has also been spelled as Darky and even given as Darcus. The woman and boy lived in a little frame house some fifty or sixty feet behind the main Harper residence.

For quite some time, Darkey had engaged in a quarrel with old Betsy Harper. John Harper's sister appeared to quarrel a lot with her domestic help, but her rancor had reached its highest pitch with Darkey. The quarrel itself had fully escalated during that summer of 1871, when

John Harper was leaving on the train with Longfellow to campaign the horse at racetracks in the Northeast. The black employees in the house at Nantura had reached a state where they paid attention to no one but John Harper; with Harper away at the races, things apparently did not go well. Someone who knew the Harpers well described Darkey as "a very devilish old negro woman" who treated Betsy Harper impudently. This was the only excuse Harper needed sometime later when he ordered the mock lynching.[20]

By summer's end, Harper and Longfellow had returned home with the horse a disgraced hero: even though he had won the Monmouth Cup and defeated August Belmont's Kingfisher in the Saratoga Cup, he had lost his most recent race to Helmbold, a horse he had defeated in the Monmouth Cup. His race coming up in Lexington the week of September 11 would be critical if he was to redeem himself in the public's opinion. Hence, the great number of patrons expected at the track and the extra number of trains brought in to transport people to the races. Harper was packing Longfellow's equipment, preparing for his journey to Lexington, when his sister delivered an ultimatum: either Harper banished Darkey from Nantura, or she, Betsy, would leave the farm. Harper left the matter undecided. He planned to resolve the situation when he returned home from the races later that week. In the interim, he forbade Darkey from entering the family home while he was away.

Whether Darkey wielded the meat ax to kill Jacob and Betsy Harper is not known since the mystery of the killings never was solved. But she did draw suspicion to herself. Soon after Jacob Harper's death, people noticed that she was the only one of the servants who did not inquire about what the family had learned as the day went on. Harper relatives noticed her hiding outside the open window at Jacob Harper's bedroom, eavesdropping while they carried on discussions about the killing in the dead man's room.[21]

Other, more leading clues about who might have killed Jacob Harper went ignored in the initial confusion surrounding the crime scene. One of the most puzzling of these was why the one nephew, Adam Harper (the least favorite), seemed preoccupied with demonstrating how the assailant must have been a right-handed man. He must have been right-handed, according to Adam's explanation, to have effectively landed blows on the *left* side of Betsy Harper's face. One friend of the Harpers remarked that he actually thought this to be quite interesting when, the next morning at breakfast, he observed Adam Harper carve the meat with his *left* hand. He wondered whether Adam could have been trying to deflect suspicion away from himself. This same person also noticed that young John W. Harper's boot matched the oddly shaped print outside the house. But this friend of the Harpers said nothing at the time about the suspicions that he deduced from these clues.[22]

Sometime after the mock lynching had failed to produce confessions, the neighbors, relatives, and local authorities began to turn their suspicions away from the African American employees of Nantura Farm, focusing instead on Adam Harper. Custer wrote in *Turf, Field and Farm* after visiting John Harper three months later: "The theory of the neighbors regarding the murder of the brother and sister of Uncle John Harper is, that instead of being committed by negroes, as was at first suspected, the real perpetrator of the horrible deed is a relative." The suspicion turned in this direction when people became aware of the contents of the wills of Jacob, Betsy, and John Harper.[23]

According to these wills, any of the three siblings who survived the others was to inherit the Harper wealth. On the death of the last of these three, nephews Adam and Frank (the favored nephew who had been at the track with John Harper) were to inherit the Harper land and money. Two female relations also stood to inherit. Now, at last, the odd midnight call on Longfellow and John Harper at the racetrack barn in Lexington began to make sense. People began to consider that someone might have tried to kill not only Jacob and Betsy that night, but John and his favorite nephew, Frank, as well.

Betsy Harper had given the strongest indication of this possibility before she died. "It must have been one of our own," she had muttered feebly from her bed. Then John Harper recalled the midnight visit to the racetrack barn. It had seemed suspicious at the time; it seemed more suspicious in light of the killing of his brother and sister. Harper also revealed that he was followed from the track all the way to downtown Lexington by a stranger he thought was the same man who had stopped by to see Longfellow the morning after the mysterious nighttime visit. He grew concerned for his safety.[24]

The rural residents of the farms close by Nantura and the town of

Midway began to whisper that Adam Harper must have been the killer. The gossip reached such proportions that internecine tensions also began to build. Eventually, Adam Harper sued a cousin, J. Wallace Harper, for slander. He asked $500,000 in damages, accusing the cousin of defaming his reputation by identifying him publicly as Jacob and Betsy Harper's killer.

Adam Harper lost his lawsuit. The killer never was identified, although most continued to believe that Adam indeed had been responsible for the Harper deaths. Old John Harper's role in ordering the "ku-kluxing" of the woman and boy at Nantura was brought out during the trial, but nothing came of this revelation. The *New York Times* expressed outrage over the mock lynchings and speculated that indictments would be forthcoming. None were. Uncle John's role as advocate of the "ku-kluxing" failed to result in indictments even as it failed to blemish his character—or the reputation of his popular racehorse, Longfellow.

The trial, conducted in Georgetown, the seat of Scott County, following a change of venue from Versailles in Woodford County, brought some high-profile persons from the horse-racing world to the witness stand. One of these was Hal Price McGrath, John Morrissey's associate at the Saratoga Race Course and a partner with old John Harper in the ownership of racehorses. Adam Harper's son, John Harper (the nephew who had urged others at the Harper house to "kill the damn negroes"), concluded the day following the verdict by drawing his pistol on the defense attorney's brother when he encountered him at a hotel in Georgetown. The ending was a perfect commentary on the state of violence prevailing in Kentucky at the time. The Harper tragedy was a high-profile incident that revealed just how deep within the Bluegrass this state of violence reached, for it affected the wealthy and landowners as well as common folk.

This situation was something that not even those master drumbeaters the Bruce brothers could ignore in their efforts to promote Kentucky horse country. The Bruces treated the Harper incident as delicately as they could in the pages of *Turf, Field and Farm*. They permitted Custer to revisit the killings with a brief treatment in his article about his horse-farm tour three months later—but *brief* was the operative word. The less written, the better, for the prevailing lawlessness was overriding the brothers' work and giving credence in the Northeast to those newspaper stories about violence in the Bluegrass. The lawlessness in horse country stood as one more reason that the new titans of the turf might be better served building Thoroughbred farms in the Northeast rather than in Kentucky.[25]

From other news stories, Northeastern turfmen would have realized that the Harpers did not stand alone among Kentucky's racing fraternity in being touched by crime. Eight years following the Harper incidents, Thomas Buford shot and killed the Kentucky Court of Appeals justice John Milton Elliott. Buford was the brother of one of central Kentucky's most respected horse breeders and major landowners, General Abe Buford of Bosque Bonita Farm. Thomas Buford, according to reports on this fatal shooting, felt driven to assassinate Justice Elliott because the latter had written a ruling upholding a lower court decision that caused Buford's sister to lose her farm. Buford stopped Justice Elliot on a street in Frankfort and raised his pistol, shouting: "Die like a man." Such was life in Kentucky.[26]

Violence and danger never seemed far removed from the realm of turfmen in Kentucky. In 1879, Captain T. G. Moore of Crab Orchard, Kentucky, a well-known owner of a racing stable who patronized Eastern tracks, shot and wounded the founder and president of the Louisville Jockey Club, Colonel Meriwether Lewis Clark Jr. The latter was the grandson of the explorer William Clark of Thomas Jefferson's Lewis and Clark expedition to the Pacific in 1803. Clark had informed Moore that he could not race his horses any longer at Louisville until he paid money that he owed the track. Clark then struck Moore to make his point, threw the man out of his office, and lodged his foot against the door to keep Moore from forcing his way back inside. Moore's response was to fire a shot at Clark through the glass door with his pistol, wounding Clark in the chest. "Doubtless the thickness of the glass prevented the wound from being fatal," read a report of the incident. Clark himself often waved a pistol at others whom he wanted to threaten. Eventually, Clark pointed the pistol at himself, committing suicide in 1899.[27]

Violence also managed to stalk Richard Ten Broeck, the man who had sold the horse Lexington to Robert Aitcheson Alexander. Ten Broeck also had owned and operated the once-fashionable Metairie Race Course in New Orleans before the Civil War. Later, he became a

Kentucky horse breeder. Harper named a fast colt Ten Broeck in honor of this man who had raced horses in partnership with him. Ten Broeck was in his sixties and retired from gambling and operating racetracks when in 1874 he nearly lost his life over an incident on a train.

Ten Broeck was living in Kentucky at the time, on a farm he had purchased near Shelbyville. He had realized sufficient success that the *New York Times* referred to him as "the well-known Kentucky stock-raiser." Having one day boarded a Louisville to Shelbyville train, he found himself in the same car with one General Walter Whittaker, with whom he was, apparently, acquainted. Whittaker was notoriously unstable, having stabbed and killed a lawyer in Shelbyville, shot and killed another man in Frankfort, and spent time in an asylum after suffering a blow to the head in yet another altercation. The two men fell into conversation, Whittaker took offense at something Ten Broeck said, and Ten Broeck wisely removed himself to another car. However, when Ten Broeck disembarked at Shelbyville, so did Whittaker, who pulled a pistol and shot Ten Broeck, seriously wounding him. As with other stories about lawless incidents in Kentucky, this one received coverage in the *New York Times*.[28]

Klotter once quoted a nineteenth-century judge who exclaimed in frustration: "Human life in Kentucky is not worth the snapping of a man's fingers." Given the incidents that had affected even Kentucky's most recognizable turfmen, one would think not. The *New York Times* observed: "From no state of the South today come such frequent and continuous reports of brutal murders and whippings by Kuklux and other secret organizations. . . . This is a very singular position for a State of the American Union to find itself in during the latter half of the nineteenth century." Kentucky stood in a singular position, indeed. But this singular position was not helping the state economically.[29]

Despite his complicity in the near lynching at Nantura, Harper continued to fascinate Northeastern racing fans. Custer, when he interviewed Harper in Kentucky in 1871, asked the question that every sportsman had on his mind during that autumn: Did Harper plan to return Longfellow to the races the following year? From Harper came these words, as Custer presented them in his peculiar vernacular: "I don't say I am agoin to run again any particular horse, but I do say I am goin to git my horse ready, and when the time comes I am agoin to the races at Long Branch [New Jersey] and will run Longfellow agin any horse that wants to run agin him, and, gentlemen, thar's no livin horse can run with my horse if he is in fix to run." The vernacular, like Harper's wild appearance, depicted him not as a wealthy landowner but as a backwoodsman.[30]

In 1872, Harper did return the horse to the Northeast. Man and horse departed Kentucky in a boxcar that Harper had outfitted with a banner reading, "LONGFELLOW ON HIS WAY TO MEET HIS FRIEND HARRY BASSETT IN THE MONMOUTH CUP." Blazing across miles of railroad track on its way to New Jersey, Longfellow's boxcar must have prompted a curious mix of images among those who saw it pass by. The King of the Turf rode in that railroad car, as all would have known from the sign. People ran to the railroad sidings, hoping to get a glimpse of the famous horse when the train made a stop. Riding with Longfellow, as people also would have realized, was the man who had lost his brother and sister in a most brutal and widely reported Kentucky crime—an incident that gave many pause, for not even the Bluegrass gentry appeared safe in Kentucky.[31]

As Harper had predicted, Longfellow defeated Harry Bassett in the Monmouth Cup. When the two met again in the Saratoga Cup, however, the story took a sad turn. Longfellow twisted his left front shoe on the way to the post. It cost him everything. He ran the entire two and a quarter miles on the twisted shoe, his jockey whipping his sides furiously while the great horse struggled unsuccessfully to catch Harry Bassett. This senseless effort ruined Longfellow. The twisted iron shoe became bent over double as the horse pounded on it all the way through the race. Longfellow returned to the unsaddling area walking on no more than three feet, with the shoe embedded in the soft portion of the sole of his left front. Writers chronicling the event told how old Harper stood on the track with tears streaming down his face. The Eastern writers who had become so fond of Harper and the folksy ways he brought from Kentucky waxed as overwrought in their prose as the old man himself appeared on realizing the horse was ruined. Old Harper sadly told the writers: "I'm taking him home."[32]

And take him home he did. The two Kentuckians, man and horse, returned to Kentucky on the railroad that had brought them up to the new center of racing in the Northeast. They went back to the Bluegrass,

The Harper family memorialized its two greatest horses, Longfellow and Ten Broeck, with grave markers at their burial sites on the family's Nantura Farm. (Courtesy of the Kentuckiana Digital Library.)

where Longfellow had a career as a breeding stallion that equaled or even exceeded his racing career. By 1891, the King of the Turf had become the king of sires, reaching the pinnacle as the number one Thoroughbred stallion in the United States.

Harper did not live to see Longfellow's reaching the pinnacle of the breeding industry. Nor did he live to see another horse he bred, the one called Ten Broeck, achieve renown as a top racehorse during the middle and latter part of the decade. Uncle John died in 1874. The Nantura Farm horses became the property of the old man's favorite nephew, Frank Harper, who continued the operation of the farm and racing stable. Frank Harper campaigned Ten Broeck through a rivalry with the inaugural Kentucky Derby winner, Aristides; through an East-West showdown at Pimlico Race Course against the titan that Pierre Lorillard owned, Parole; and, finally, through the defeat of the California-based mare Mollie McCarthy in a famous race at Louisville. Ten Broeck's regular rider, Billy Walker, was the same who mentored the jockey Isaac Murphy and who would eventually become the trusted adviser of a renowned Kentucky horse-farm owner, John E. Madden. Ten Broeck and Billy Walker inspired a folk song of the era of which the opening lines went:

> Down in Kentucky where Ten Broeck was born,
> Dey swore by his runnin', he came in a storm.[33]

Mention of John Harper's complicity in the mock lynching at Nantura Farm never went beyond the initial reporting on the slander trial of his relative. But memory of the terrible killings of Harper's brother and sister remained long affixed to the story of Longfellow. No doubt the brutal deaths of two white landowners mattered more in popular ideas about the Bluegrass than did the near deaths of two African Americans. Still, the outcome was the same: proof positive that not even the landed gentry of Bluegrass horse country stood aloof, or even protected, from the lawlessness in this unstable, violent place. Small wonder that men of the turf in the Northeast shunned Kentucky for their own countryside when building their new horse farms.

chapter FOUR

"All the Best Jockeys of the West Are Colored"

Longfellow was only beginning his stud career in 1873, still keeping his name and the Bluegrass region in the news, when another Kentuckian started down a career path that would bring a similar attention to this place and to notions of who and what Kentuckians were. This was Isaac Murphy, an African American born during the Civil War and raised in Lexington. His destiny was to make him one of the most successful jockeys of all time, one of a handful of riders who helped elevate the significance of their profession from laborer to athlete. During a time when the owners and trainers of racehorses were only beginning to recognize publicly the key role that jockeys played in the success of these animals, Murphy in particular showed that a black man from former slaveholding Kentucky could win financial wealth, the respect of whites in his home state, and respect as a star athlete in New York, where white jockeys were more commonplace. Like Longfellow, like Harper, like Woodburn Farm and Asteroid, Murphy became an icon of Bluegrass horse country. Unlike the others, his place in the pantheon of Bluegrass leaders endured over no more than a limited period of time.

His career path paralleling the success of Longfellow, Murphy was by the late 1880s arguably the leading jockey in the United States, with newspapers and sporting journals lauding his success. Longfellow reached his apex as a breeding stallion in 1891 with wide acclaim as the leading sire in terms of number of winners that year on North American racetracks. All memory of John Harper's authorized mock

The Hall of Fame jockey Isaac Murphy, a resident of Lexington, won the Kentucky Derby three times. He ranks as one of the most successful jockeys of all time; his record of winning 44 percent of his races has never been matched. He is shown here, the only black man among whites, attending a clambake held in New Jersey in 1890 to celebrate Salvator's victories. (Courtesy of the Keeneland Association.)

lynching at Nantura Farm during Longfellow's racing days lay forgotten in the flush of the horse's success as a sire. Meantime, in a generous display of good feelings indicative of fluid racial relations, Americans overlooked Murphy's wild boast that he made more money in a year than U.S. president Benjamin Harrison's cabinet members. To most, it did not seem to matter that Murphy, a black man, revealed a certain arrogance in making this bold statement.[1]

Earning at least $20,000 annually, Murphy indeed ranked as the highest-paid athlete in the United States. Toward the end of his riding career, he also became a racehorse owner, not unprecedented for a black man because Dudley Allen of Lexington bred, trained, and was an ownership partner in the 1891 Kentucky Derby winner, Kingman.

But, while turfmen continued to praise the great horse Longfellow for generations following his death in 1893, they quickly forgot about Murphy soon after his death in 1896. This occurred because, during the late 1890s, a lot changed for black men who aspired to greatness in Thoroughbred racing.

Murphy's story illustrates how black jockeys and horse trainers who gained national prominence and respect in the sport eventually found themselves shuffled to the rear of the bus. Moreover, the sport quickly wiped from memory all that they had achieved in the way of personal success during the post–Civil War expansion of horse racing. Murphy was not the only black horseman denied a place in the narrative of Thoroughbred racing as it would be told for the next fifty or sixty years. Yet, as the jockey whose career record of 44 percent winners remains untouched, the erasure of his story was the most remarkable development in the sport's narrative.[2]

Murphy did not live long enough to see black horsemen denied prominent positions in the sport. He might, however, have suspected that this shift lay just over the horizon. In 1890, the Northeastern moguls who owned Monmouth Park in New Jersey temporarily banned him from that racecourse for a questionable ride on a horse that might or might not have occurred through his own fault. Northeastern newspapers that had consistently praised Murphy for his outstanding talent and his qualities as an upright citizen turned on the jockey as though they had never written a good word about the man. Stories began to surface about his consumption of large amounts of alcohol, and, in fact, his contemporaries believed that he was drinking to excess, for authorities suspended him on this account at the Latonia Race Course in northern Kentucky, near Cincinnati. But during an age when white jockeys similarly consumed a great amount of alcohol—this was part of the regimen for recovering physical strength after sweating off pounds in the sauna—Murphy emerged as the scapegoat.[3]

The turning point for black horsemen came with the rising racism in Northern cities like New York and Chicago. Black horsemen had never dominated in numbers at racetracks in the North, as they had in Kentucky and the South, but Northerners had afforded them a professional respect. However, the Northeastern moguls of the turf who had changed the sport so radically brought cultural changes that eventu-

Edward Dudley Brown, born a slave, went from winning the Belmont Stakes as a jockey to winning the Kentucky Derby as a horse trainer. He also developed two more horses that would go on to win the Derby for other racing stables. He was elected into Thoroughbred racing's Hall of Fame. He also owned racehorses. (Courtesy of the Keeneland Association.)

ally began to affect Kentucky racing as well. Northeasterners were sufficiently powerful to alter the face of the sport from one of mixed races to one of entirely white faces.

"These new people, meaning New Yorkers, Northerners, who have barged in and taken over much of the breeding, don't understand the Negro, say the veterans," reads one explanation of this cultural turn. As a consequence, the turf began to forget about its famous black horsemen: champion jockeys like Willie Simms, James "Soup" Perkins, Shelby "Pike" Barnes (the national leader in number of wins in 1888), Tony Hamilton, Monk Overton, George "Spider" Anderson, and Oliver Lewis (winner of the inaugural Kentucky Derby in 1875), and trainers like Ansel Williamson (the winner of the inaugural Kentucky Derby), Ed Brown (widely respected in both North and South as a horse trainer), and William Walker (who held an important position at Hamburg Place, advising the owner of the farm, John Madden, on which sires would be most suitable to breed to the Hamburg Place mares).[4]

White turfmen, who by the early twentieth century had assumed all the power in Thoroughbred racing, wiped from the sport's collective memory all recollection of black horsemen. They accomplished this by choosing to ignore the significant role that African Americans had played in developing a national profile for the sport. The outcome disclosed still another way in which the epicenter of power in Thoroughbred racing had shifted almost entirely to the Northeast, the influence of which was affecting cultural practices in horse racing everywhere.

Murphy's story would remain stricken from the sport's narrative until one bright Sunday morning in March 1961, when two men searching the grounds of a cemetery in Lexington discovered the jockey's grave site. Eugene Webster and Frank Borries Jr. pulled back the weeds hiding a small, crumbling concrete marker identifying the site. The moment marked the beginning of a major turn: the rediscovery of a past in Thoroughbred racing in which black horsemen had played highly significant roles in developing the sport.

Borries had learned about Murphy while reading old sporting publications. Finding the grave had become his obsession. But, after more than three years of searching, he had experienced no luck until meeting Webster, a resident of the neighborhood surrounding the African American Cemetery No. 2 on East Seventh Street. Webster told Borries he knew the location of the grave.

The story about the lost grave illustrates how effectively white patrons of racing had written highly successful black men out of history. This March day in 1961 actually was the second time Murphy's grave had been rediscovered. Thirteen years following Murphy's death, the same Eugene Webster had taken some concerned horsemen from the Kentucky Association track to the jockey's grave. According to what Webster told Borries, the horsemen, presumably black, had heard that a wooden marker at the grave had disappeared. They wanted to replace it so that the site would not become forgotten. They sought Webster's help because they did not know the location of the grave.[5]

In 1909, Webster had been able to show the way to the site because his father, Richard Webster, had taken him there many times. Once he and his companions arrived at the site, the horsemen poured a concrete marker there. But, according to Webster, they did not know how to stamp Murphy's name into the concrete. Therefore, they left the new marker in place without a name to connect it with the jockey. Until Webster took Borries to the site in 1961, the grave and marker had lain forgotten in the tangle of weeds that overtook the African American cemetery after years of neglect.

The loss of local knowledge about the location of the grave or even about Murphy seems ironic given that the jockey had been a national celebrity as well as a local hero. Newspapers had devoted a great amount of coverage to his funeral in 1896 and the large procession that accompanied the casket through the city streets. *Turf, Field and Farm* had described the procession as "the largest funeral ever seen at Lexington, Ky., over a colored person." This information might have been incorrect—thousands of persons had attended services in 1854 for a black minister named London Ferrill. The numbers must have seemed impressive, however, and among those in attendance were such white dignitaries as Colonel James E. Pepper, the owner of a horse farm in the Bluegrass, and James Rodes Jewell, a prominent local judge. Murphy's family sent out engraved invitations to the services. Jockeys, horse trainers, and horse owners sent floral arrangements. Lincoln Lodge No. 10 of the Colored Masons, a group to which Murphy had belonged, adopted a resolution declaring that "the community has lost one of its best and most successful citizens." The lodge also recognized him as a

Isaac Murphy's grave site became lost in the weeds at the African American Cemetery No. 2 in Lexington. Eugene Webster (shown here) and Frank Borries Jr. rediscovered it in 1961. Murphy's remains subsequently were moved twice: first, to the original location of the Man o' War memorial on Huffman Mill Pike, then to the newer site of the Man o' War memorial at the Kentucky Horse Park. (Courtesy of the Keeneland Association.)

model man of the Victorian Age, noting that "a faithful and loving wife has lost a discreet and devoted husband."[6]

The well-attended funeral had seemed only fitting at the time. As one of the leading athletes in the United States, Murphy had risen to a position that enabled him to dictate the terms of his riding contracts to the wealthy men like mining kings, wizards of Wall Street, and robber barons who were taking control of the turf. Admittedly, his ability to negotiate on equal terms with these tycoons represented a marked departure from the experience of the average African American, but he was a star in the emerging postwar world of sports. He wore his fame with dignity and was renowned for his honesty in a world of jockeys where the majority possibly were not the most honest of souls.

Murphy was born in 1861, a free black, on the farm of David Tanner near Lexington. Originally, he used the surname of his father, James Burns, who died at the Union army's Camp Nelson, south of Lexington, in Jessamine County, during the war. Murphy's mother, America Burns, took the boy to Lexington, where they lived with her father, Green Murphy. Soon after Isaac began riding winners at the racetrack, he took his grandfather's surname.[7]

Murphy's riding career developed within a larger world greatly conflicted about the place that African Americans were to occupy as new citizens. For a short time, perhaps a few decades, Thoroughbred racing appeared willing to give space and recognition to talented black athletes. This placed black horsemen on an exceptional plane, differentiating their lives from those of most other African Americans. For, even while black jockeys and horse trainers received praise and respect for their work, the average African American faced frightening times, both in the border states and in the South. African Americans in the North faced discrimination and segregation even if whites did not subject them to the extreme violence more peculiar to the former slave states. Northern whites welcomed freedom for blacks in principle only; the reality of seeing increasing numbers of blacks flee Southern states for the North was repugnant to great numbers of Northerners and a reality that they had not considered until the war ended. Throughout the South and border states like Kentucky, whites no more equated equality with freedom from slavery than did Northern whites. African Ameri-

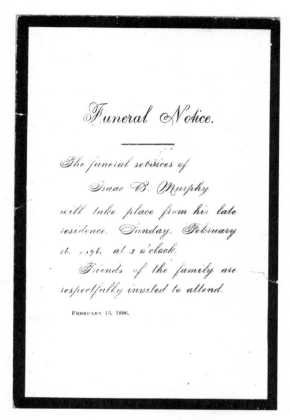

Funeral Notice.

The funeral services of Isaac B. Murphy will take place from his late residence, Sunday, February 16, 1896, at 3 o'clock. Friends of the family are respectfully invited to attend.

FEBRUARY 13, 1896.

An engraved notice of funeral services in Lexington for Isaac Murphy in 1896. A large crowd accompanied the funeral procession through the city streets. White dignitaries attended, and jockeys, owners, and horse trainers sent flower arrangements. (Courtesy of the Keeneland Association.)

can horsemen like Murphy were the exception, arguably because they served a purpose in rebuilding horse racing after the war.[8]

The reality of the newfound freedom from servitude in Kentucky, as in the Southern states, was simply a transition to another form of subservience in which whites expressed a firm determination to maintain racial and, therefore, social control. The personal brutality that had characterized the master/slave relationship transformed quickly after the war into lynchings and mob violence. George Wright has written that "white violence became so widespread that many of the northern freemen's aid societies that operated in other former slave states, helping the blacks in the transition from bondage to freedom, avoided Kentucky for fear of the lives of their workers." Whites forced numerous blacks to leave Kentucky, and many of those blacks went north or into the West. Wright saw evidence that blacks who achieved financial prosperity attracted violence as they "threatened the entire system of white supremacy." John Harper's authorizing a mock lynching at Nantura Farm in 1871 suggested how strong the desire was in the Bluegrass to retain white supremacy. The timing of his action was significant. It occurred in the wake of political and social changes that were challenging whites' position.[9]

Emancipation had wrought seismic changes in the social fabric of Kentucky, and whites were not acquiescing willingly to the new social order. They found it repugnant not only that former slaves enjoyed freedom but also that, with the ratification of the Fifteenth Amendment (February 3, 1870), these freedmen had gained the right to vote. The notion of blacks voting shook the very foundations of the ideology that whites had promulgated in order to justify slavery: that blacks were savages unfit for citizenship, most especially in a nation founded on republican ideals of self-government. White Kentuckians took up the cry of their neighbors to the south. They argued that the amendment was a fraud forced on decent American citizens in violation of the U.S. Constitution. Aaron Astor has inquired into this outrage over the Fifteenth Amendment, studying its effects specifically on the first-ever biracial elections in Harrodsburg, Kentucky, during August 1870. Astor quotes an article from the *Harrodsburg (KY) People:* "[The Fifteenth Amendment] forced to the polls a vast horde of men, utterly ignorant of the duties and responsibilities attached to the new position into which they had been thrust by the bayonet and by congressional corruption." A riot broke out in Harrodsburg, resulting in the deaths of both black and white men.[10]

Astor is among a cluster of historians who are beginning to take seriously the old saw that Kentucky seceded from the Union only after the war was over. His inquiry, uncovering a visceral opposition to the Fifteenth Amendment, gives credence to this reoccurring popular notion. Arguably, nineteenth-century white Kentuckians did find this amendment so repugnant and so threatening to white supremacy that they began to believe that the South had been right all along in seceding from the United States.

Along with Anne Elizabeth Marshall and Luke Harlow, Astor represents an emerging group of historians who have argued that this postwar epiphany for white Kentuckians evolved into a Confederate identity for the state. These three have drawn their conclusions in different ways, but the result has been a more nuanced look at how and why Kentuckians from some sections of the state, including the Bluegrass, saw themselves as Confederate and Southern to a greater degree following the war. At one time, historians thought that they saw this same metamorphosis, but they explained it as resentment over atrocities committed in Kentucky by the U.S. Army during the war. Astor, Harlow, and Marshall have found that widely dispersed resentment over the fall of slavery in Kentucky lay at the root of this change of mind.[11]

In Lexington, a great fear of "Negro rule" resulted in white supremacist tactics entering the political sphere. A simmering stew of resentment, discontent, and hate reached a boil in 1871, when a federal grand jury in Louisville indicted Lexington's mayor and other city officials for their actions during a riot in Lexington over black voting. A similar stew boiled over in the 1873 municipal elections in Lexington. By this time, Democrats were waging an all-out campaign to keep Republicans out of office in the city, fearing that, if they won control of the local government, they would place black persons in authoritative positions, including those of police officers. They also feared that, if Republicans held office, they would permit black children to attend public schools.[12]

Democrats played on these phobias by instilling a fear of "Negro rule" in the white population. The *Kentucky Gazette*, the newspaper that supported the Democratic Party in Lexington, warned readers that it behooved every Democrat to vote as if his life and property depended on it. It warned that a "black canaille" was out to overtake municipal government. "The white men of Lexington are not going to permit the niggers to rule this town," the *Gazette* trumpeted, as though issuing a call to arms. The election process saw white officials denying blacks the vote in 1873. As in 1871, federal authorities arrested city officials and took them to Louisville for yet another grand jury hearing. Predictably, the *Kentucky Gazette* expressed its outrage. "The interference of Federal authorities in the local affairs in Lexington is a gross outrage," it declared.[13]

The *Gazette* kept hammering home the alarming implications of the black vote, pointing out what it interpreted as the increasingly threatening presence of blacks throughout the city. Not mentioned was the fact that, during the slavery era, blacks had been equally visible on city streets while performing tasks and errands for their owners. In the meantime, concern over the new biracial society became increasingly evident at the state level. Bourbon Democrats, a conservative wing of the party that represented aristocrats and landed gentry, spoke out at the Democratic convention about their grave fear of the "revolutionary Republicans" attaining their goal of black social equality and, thus, in the Democrats' eyes, despotism in the commonwealth.[14]

The sociologist Gunner Myrdal would reach the obvious conclusion in the 1940s: that an American dilemma had existed since the Civil War over "what to do with the Negro in American society." However, the white turfmen of Kentucky and the South began to agonize over this dilemma only some thirty years later. Until that time, they were not the least bit concerned about black Americans occupying important positions at racetracks; they viewed blacks as simply continuing to occupy the same jobs they had held as enslaved persons, jobs as jockeys, horse trainers, and caretakers of horses. Eventually, Northern turfmen persuaded their colleagues in Kentucky and the South to change their minds. By the early twentieth century, black jockeys found themselves unwelcome in the starting gate everywhere from New Orleans to Kentucky and on to New York and Chicago. It was as though horse owners, horse trainers, white jockeys, and the public had reached an unspoken agreement that no longer would it do to have black men sitting on flashy racehorses in the spotlight.[15]

In Lexington and Louisville, in New Orleans, Memphis, and Nashville, in fact, at racecourses throughout the South and the upper border states, black jockeys and horse trainers had predominated in numbers throughout the slavery era and for perhaps thirty years following the Civil War. Some former slaves, including Ansel Williamson and

Edward Brown, discovered widespread fame within the sport following the war. Others, like Murphy, were born during or after the war and never knew slavery. Collectively, they formed the greatest repository of knowledge about racehorses, for the care, training, and riding of these animals had been the province of slaves in the South. Older black men mentored the young boys who apprenticed to racing stables, seeking to learn the jockey craft. Southerners and Kentuckians had been so accustomed to seeing black youths riding races and black men handling the training chores, working alongside white trainers and jockeys, that they considered this mixing of races in the horse stables to be the natural order of the racetrack.

The South's white racing patrons also mixed freely with black spectators, for example, in New Orleans, where both races intermingled in the grandstands at the premier track, known as the Metairie Jockey Club. At least, they mingled freely up until 1871, when the Metairie course erected a separate stand for blacks. The jockeys had not been separated, however, and, two years later, the *New Orleans Times* was writing how "the darkies and whites [among jockeys] mingle fraternally together, charmed into mutual happy sympathies by the inspiriting influence of horse talk." The patrons, however, initiated segregation in the grandstand, perhaps in reaction to the Reconstruction work of Radical Republicans in New Orleans. Reconstruction, wholeheartedly resented throughout the South, had been intended in part to support African Americans by upholding the civil rights granted them. The editor of the *New Orleans Louisianian*, a newspaper with a black readership, urged blacks to boycott the horse races at Metairie in response to the segregation of the grandstand. He argued that this separate grandstand "pandered to the ignoble passions and prejudices of those who possess no other claim to superiority, than the external shading of a skin."[16]

Economic pressure forced a partial reversal of this segregation effort. When a new group called the Louisiana Jockey Club took control of the track from the Metairie Jockey Club, the operators partially reversed the earlier segregation order and allowed blacks to mingle anywhere in the grandstands except within an exclusive section located in the "quarter stretch" near the finish line. Still not satisfied, two African American patrons sued the track ownership, accusing the club of violating the Civil Rights Act of 1869 by refusing equal access to public accommodations. The suit evidently went nowhere. However, after Reconstruction ended in 1876, an amazing reversal occurred: black patrons regained the equal accommodations they previously had been accorded. For the remainder of the nineteenth century, blacks mingled freely with whites at the New Orleans track.[17]

In Kentucky, the sport benefited from the great numbers of African American horsemen who remained in the state after the war. These horsemen aided in the recovery of the turf in the Bluegrass since they possessed the body of knowledge about horse care and also constituted the much-needed labor pool. Jockeys and horse trainers drew attention to the sport in Kentucky with the success they achieved there and in the Northeast. But the time had not come when the sport everywhere would view jockeys as an elite class of athletes. In the view of whites, jockeys and horse trainers were no more than laborers filling jobs that whites did not want. David Wiggins, who has written on black athletes participating in the white world of sports, identified the job of racehorse jockey as one of those occupations considered fit only for blacks since it had been closely associated with slave labor. Consequently, blacks dominated this division of labor in the South after the war, just as the overwhelming number of bathhouse keepers, tailors, butchers, coachmen, barbers, delivery boys, and laundresses were black.[18]

The paddock scenes of black horsemen mingling with whites that patrons of the turf would have seen in the South were not the scenes that the revised narrative of racing depicted later. Still, blacks did, in fact, dominate the landscape at Kentucky racetracks. Black jockeys rode the winners of twelve of the first twenty-two Kentucky derbies from 1875 through 1896. Thirteen of the fifteen riders in the inaugural derby were black. No one in Kentucky considered this exceptional during that era, for the situation represented the norm. Northern patrons of the sport did, however, notice how numbers of blacks predominated in Kentucky racing, prompting the *Spirit of the Times* to remark in an 1890 headline: "All the Best Jockeys in the West Are Colored." By the West, the *Spirit* as usual meant Kentucky, for it was speaking from its authoritative location in the East. The particular article in question concerned the number of black jockeys riding at the Latonia course.[19]

Northeastern racing did not have this longtime exposure to great numbers of black jockeys and trainers. Northern racing patrons certainly saw the occasional black rider or horse trainer during the Civil War, when Kentucky stables began going north to race. Following those years, the numbers of black riders increased somewhat in the Northeast, but blacks never dominated in numbers as they had in the Southern states or in Kentucky. Northern stables tended to pluck their jockey prospects from the labor pool most readily accessible in their part of the United States: the urban streets and orphanages, where small white boys abounded, many of them Irish. The Live Stock Record told in 1894 how this process worked. A great number of boys were taken from asylums and homes of different kinds. These "little mites . . . started with horses at the age of eight or nine years old." The practice of exploiting youth and poverty was no different North or South; only skin color differed.[20]

As in the South and in Kentucky, race relations among jockeys and horse trainers existed in a fluid state that lacked hard-and-fast color lines, rules, or even legal practices that would have segregated the races. Black jockeys rode against white in the top-level races in the Northeast during the decades following the war: Murphy's greatest rival was the white "Snapper" Garrison, who was of Irish descent. Murphy did not live long enough to witness the racial clash that would occur following his death, when white riders would form a cabal hostile to black jockeys. During Murphy's era, black and white jockeys rode races alongside one another, generally without problems. These fluid relations ended shortly after his death.[21]

White jockeys did not stand alone in harboring increasingly hostile feelings toward blacks. In his biography of the black jockey Jimmy Winkfield, a native of the Bluegrass whose career succeeded Murphy's, Joe Drape tells how elite New Yorkers who patronized racing and owned horses expressed repugnance over jockeys of both races—but mostly over blacks. "Immigrants already overran the sport," Drape writes, "and for that matter, the city, encroaching on what the Jockey Club members had believed was a gentleman's game. The migration north of Southern blacks, along with the resentment it stirred in the city's new white arrivals, threatened the Jockey Club's image of what the sport of kings should look like on this side of the Atlantic." It was felt that urchins from the streets and orphanages "were preferable to the country darkies who followed idols like Murphy, Hamilton, and Simms east to grab a piece of horse racing's richest purses."[22]

Murphy's era—from the 1870s through the early 1890s—thus marked the high point for black horsemen in the racing world. The racetrack life held the promise of a way out of poverty for white and black youths; down in Kentucky, African American youths like Murphy had numerous examples of achievement to emulate. Murphy's own mentors included the renowned horse trainer Eli Jordan, a former slave who later took in Murphy and his widowed mother at his residence in Lexington, presumably after they had left Murphy's grandfather's home. The young Murphy also took advice from William Walker, a slightly more experienced jockey who expressed pride for all he taught the aspiring rider. Murphy's other mentors were white: Mrs. Hunt Reynolds, who appeared to have had a great hand in managing the operations of her husband's racing stable, and James T. Williams, who developed the careers of a number of young jockeys in Kentucky and owned a racing stable in partnership with a man named Richard Owings. Young Murphy, fourteen years old when he first climbed aboard a Thoroughbred, was fortunate to learn his craft in Kentucky, where large numbers of horsemen lived and always were on the lookout for small black boys to bring into the trade.[23]

Murphy's mother, America Burns, was a laundress in Lexington whose customers included the racing stable owner Owings. In 1873, she allowed Owings to take her son, said to be very small for his age, into an apprenticeship to teach the boy how to ride. Murphy, still using the surname of Burns at that time, did not start down his career path in a blaze of instant glory. He fell off the first horse he climbed aboard and was reluctant to try again. Williams drew on his own great finesse to persuade him to get back on the young horse that had thrown him. Murphy succeeded. He remained on the farm through 1874, although at that point he failed to attract much notice for his riding. He had not yet polished his skills.[24]

Murphy's life changed dramatically in January 1875 when his mother took him to Jordan, who was working as the horse trainer at the tracks for Williams and Owings. Jordan took the youth to Louisville to the racetrack still under construction—the Louisville Jockey Club Course, to become known later as Churchill Downs. Murphy's athletic talent blossomed while exercising horses for Jordan on the track. The two developed a father-son relationship that would endure until Jordan's death in 1884. Murphy called Jordan "the old man" out of fondness. Others, calling him "Uncle Eli," uncle being a popular way of addressing black men, recognized Jordan as a horse trainer of superior knowledge and skill. Clearly, Jordan had a powerful influence on young Murphy while instilling in him the work ethic and honesty that would take him far in his career. This was not to say that Murphy did not come to Jordan with an extraordinary focus that was unusual for a youth. "Isaac was always in his place and I could put my hand on him any time day or night," Jordan said. "He was always one of the first up in the morning, ready to do anything he was told to do or to help others. He was ever in good humor and liked to play, but he never neglected his work but worked hard summer and winter. He never got the big head."[25]

Murphy was fortunate to work in Jordan's care at the racetrack for reasons that went beyond the mentoring the older man could provide. By living and working at the racecourse as a young man, he managed to sidestep the violence of the type that John Harper had ordered carried out on two domestic servants at Nantura Farm. Domestic labor was easily replaced; skilled jockeys and trainers were not. The campaign of violence against blacks in Kentucky did not, with rare exceptions, touch those blacks holding down high-profile positions in Thoroughbred racing. Two exceptions were incidents involving the jockeys Billy Walker and Jimmy Winkfield. Walker said that the operator of Churchill Downs, M. Lewis Clark, threatened him with violence if he failed to ride an honest race in the famous matchup of the Kentucky-based Ten Broeck with the California mare Mollie McCarthy in Louisville in 1878. "You will be watched the whole way, and if you do not ride to win, a rope will be put about your neck and you will be hung to that tree yonder and I will help to do it," Clark informed the jockey. During the early twentieth century, Winkfield claimed that he received threats "from the Ku Klux Klan," according to his daughter, Mrs. Liliane Casey. But these claims of threats were exceptions within the safe haven of horse racing during decades of violence that made Kentucky a dangerous place for all, but especially for persons of color.[26]

Crimes against blacks reached such serious proportions that the Freedmen's Bureau set up an office in Lexington with the intention of protecting the civil rights of newly minted black citizens. The presence of the Freedmen's Bureau, mandated only for those states that had seceded, spoke volumes about the volatile situation in Kentucky. And events in Kentucky kept the bureau busy. Marion Lucas has cited a bureau report from 1866 detailing 58 incidents against African Americans in Kentucky, "including more than two dozen whippings and beatings of men and women, three rapes, eight attempted murders, nine murders, and one case of burning a freedman alive." The 1866–1867 report of the Freedman's Bureau in Kentucky cited 319 cases of mistreatment of African Americans. And so went the reports in succeeding years. "Much of the violence that gripped Kentucky in the years immediately following the Civil War," Lucas writes, "stemmed from the prevalent belief of whites in the inferiority of blacks. . . . The desire of the majority of white Kentuckians to keep freedmen 'in their place' allowed a minority to . . . [create] a 'system of terrorism.'"[27]

The terrorism occurred as much in central Kentucky, where Murphy grew up, as it did throughout the state. Most telling concerning terrorist activities has been George Wright's research revealing how the lynching trend in Kentucky followed a course counter to that in the rest of the United States. While lynchings did not reach their greatest numbers nationwide until 1890, their numbers had been high in Kentucky from the outset. In other words, racial hate in Kentucky had been aggressive from the end of the war on. The evidence could be found throughout horse country: less than a month before the Harper killings and the subsequent mock lynchings, whites hanged an African American at Frankfort, the state capital. On election night two weeks following the Harper killings, whites took two blacks from the jail in Versailles, the seat of Woodford County, the same county where Nantura Farm was situated, and hung them.[28]

Angered, and greatly concerned, African Americans in Frankfort and the surrounding regions sent a petition to the U.S. Congress documenting more than one hundred cases of violence from November 1867 to May 1870. These incidents included twenty-four mob lynchings, the killing of twenty-one men and three women in mob violence, and numerous incidents of beatings and whippings. Blacks found little justice. As Lucas writes: "The system of intimidation and terror, the prohibition of black testimony against whites in state courts until 1872, and the hostility of most whites toward federal involvement, made it difficult to arrest, and virtually impossible to convict, those charged with crimes against blacks." Moreover, not only did those persons of the highest social ranking in the Bluegrass—the landowners who bred racehorses— seem disinclined to come to the aid of blacks under siege; they were part of the violence. The *New York Daily Tribune* identified Kentucky's "gentry" class—its horse breeders—as one and the same as the Ku Klux Klan.[29]

In Frankfort, the state legislature surprised many Kentuckians when it began considering a bill to repeal the lash. This possibility so greatly alarmed the *Kentucky Gazette* that the editor felt compelled to warn: "Theft and violence will become much more prevalent. While the negroes were slaves they were kept in perfect subjugation by the lash, and it is its disuse that has made them such pests of society."[30]

In contrast, people simply did not read about violence inflicted on either black jockeys or black horse trainers in Kentucky. Threats of violence surely occurred, assuming that Walker and Winkfield were not exaggerating. But outright violence, or at least publicized violence, appears not to have taken place within the sport of horse racing—not until the 1890s, when racism grew exponentially in the larger world. After that time, and mirroring events in the larger society, white jockeys ganged up on black jockeys at a number of racetracks. By the end of the decade, and following the U.S. Supreme Court decision in *Plessy v. Ferguson* (1896) upholding racial segregation, black horsemen and trainers simply disappeared from their high-profile positions in the sport. But, before that time, the jockey and horse-trainer labor pool existed as integrally important to the smooth function of the sport in Kentucky. Murphy and his fellow black riders, along with black horse trainers, appeared to live their lives free of the fear of racial harassment. They were too important to the economic order of the sport, which could not operate without them.

Murphy's jockey career had risen like mercury on a hot day. He went from riding at a country course southeast of Lexington, Crab Orchard, to riding at the new track in Louisville in 1875 and at Lexington in 1876. By 1877, he was riding summers at Saratoga, where the former slave jockeys Abe Hawkins and "Sewell" had preceded him during the track's early years. He achieved great success while riding largely against white jockeys. By the early 1880s, he had moved to the sport's top echelon and was dictating the terms of his riding contracts to the wealthy men whose horses he rode. The public recognized him for the star athlete that he was, his behavior unimpeachable both on the track and at leisure in the city of New York. Walter Vosburgh, a distinguished racing official and writer on turf matters in New York, described Murphy in 1884 as "an elegant specimen of manhood . . . strong, muscular, and as graceful as an Apollo." That same year, the *Louisville Courier-Journal* commented on Murphy's renown throughout the United States, observing that the jockey looked "like a Sphinx carved out of ivory . . . familiar on every racetrack in America."[31]

In a fortunate coincidence, Murphy's best years coincided with the increasing presence of still another set of "new men" who brought big money and their own brand of ostentatious living to the rapidly expanding sport. These were the mining kings of California and other Far Western states, who began sending their stables east. Their Eastern competition consisted in great part of the Lorillard brothers, Pierre and George, who were beginning to win so many races with their vast numbers of horses that owners of the majority of racing stables would come to regard them as crushing the sport in New Jersey and New York. The Lorillards weren't really crushing all the competition, only most of it. Two more brothers who had recently joined the game would cause the Lorillards frequent anguish by crushing them in turn. These were the Dwyers, Phil and Mike, former butchers who had parlayed their business into wholesale meat distribution in New York. The Dwyers weren't the least bit interested in "improving the breed," as the sportsmen of Belmont's social set claimed to have been. Quite in contrast, the racing stable of Mike and Phil Dwyer existed solely for the purpose of setting up betting opportunities for the two brothers. They excelled at betting even as their stable of horses excelled at winning races because they bought the best horses available. They even built their own racetrack in Brooklyn, competing directly with tracks patronized by Belmont's social set.[32]

Murphy rode this expansion of racing with the mastery of an athlete playing all his best options. By the mid-1880s, he was riding for George Lorillard, Elias "Lucky" Baldwin, and the fiery Ed Corrigan from Chicago. Phil Dwyer made some huge errors in judgment by betting against some of the horses Murphy rode when he thought him to be riding the inferior horse. He lost those bets. One example was with the Freeland–Miss Woodford rivalry. In three different races at the Jersey Shore's Monmouth Park, Murphy rode Ed Corrigan's Freeland against Phil Dwyer's Miss Woodford and defeated the mare twice. As the first American racehorse to win more than $100,000, Miss Woodford was not your average mare; consequently, defeating her was no small achievement. Refusing to believe the obvious, Phil Dwyer bet Corrigan $20,000 that Freeland could not defeat Miss Woodford again in a fourth race. The Dwyer brothers put the best jockey of the times on Miss Woodford—an Irishman, Jim McLaughlin—but to no avail. Free-land defeated the mare. The race inspired lines of poetry in the press, as events of that era often did, with this particular piece telling how,

> Freeland came with a sudden dart
> At the finish, and Isaac proved too smart
> For the Dwyers' jock; how at last
> He nailed him just as the post was passed.

Murphy was raising the bar for jockeys, elevating this form of labor to a profession, an art, a niche in athletics that inspired admiration and lines of poetry. The results were paying off handsomely. The jockey was riding "first call" (first option) for the gambler/horse owner Lucky Baldwin, and they both were profiting from the arrangement.[33]

This is not to say that Murphy was participating in gambling scenarios with Baldwin. He was renowned as much for his honesty as for his riding skills. When mentoring young black jockeys, he advised them to be honest above all else—wise words in a world where jockeys of color would have been well advised to be honest or else risk personal violence. "Stoval, you just ride to win," he once advised the young African American rider John "Kid" Stoval. "Just be honest, and you'll have no trouble and plenty of money." Murphy's arrangement with Baldwin and other gambler/horse owners consisted only of his riding fees, but the fees he commanded during the height of his career made him rise to a comfortable, upper-middle-class status, financially well-off.[34]

With his rising income, Murphy surrounded himself with accoutrements appropriate to the lifestyle at this level: a move into a home that his contemporaries described as a "mansion" on Third Street in Lexington, the acquisition of his own horse-drawn carriage, a valet (who, ironically, was a white man), a respectable wife, Lucy, and so-cial standing in Lexington's upper-class black community. Lexington's white community afforded him no small measure of respect. One indi-cation of this was the habit of one local newspaper, the *Kentucky Leader*, of reporting periodically on social occasions held at Murphy's home. It described these events almost as though they had taken place at a white person's residence, although it consistently made it clear that this was colored society. Judging by these accounts, when Lucy and Ike Murphy entertained, they spared no expense and invited the highest social strata among Lexington's black residents.[35]

One time, the Murphys held a reception for the black riding star Tony Hamilton and his new wife. The *Leader* reported: "Before 2 o'clock there was a long line of carriages in front of the Murphy mansion, and one hour later the lower rooms were packed with the colored crème de la crème of Lexington." The reception was on a scale that had "sel-dom been equaled even in white circles." The newspaper described the bride, Annie Messley, as a woman "very light in complexion and quite pretty." Degree of blackness mattered and was equated by both blacks and whites with class stratification. The newspaper also carefully noted the social standing of Murphy's guests: "Isaac Murphy, Tony Hamilton and Isaac Lewis have each won deserved turf honors, and are all upright, honest men, and are well to do people." Other guests included such local African American professionals as Dr. Mary Britton, an educator who later became a physician and ranked as one of Lexington's most respect-ed citizens. On another occasion, this one marking the tenth wedding anniversary of the Murphys, the *Leader* was on the social scene once more, reporting on the event, and including the menu in the report: quails with champignons and claret, oyster patties, turkey with chest-nut dressing, croquettes with French peas, and other epicurean delights. Murphy and his guests dined well.[36]

A rich diversity existed in Lexington's African American com-munity, with Murphy and his wife clearly representing an upper mid-dle class. Ike and Lucy's widening circle of acquaintances would have brought them into contact with an impressive group of black profes-sionals: besides Dr. Britton, this would have included other physicians, pharmacists, elected politicians, lawyers, journalists, landowners, cler-gymen, building contractors, and architects. The black community was

Isaac Murphy's mansion has been erroneously identified by some historians as this house, the Richard T. Anderson house on Third Street. Murphy's mansion was of the same size and of similar design and located within two blocks of the Anderson house. No photograph of the Murphy mansion is known to exist. Like this house, Murphy's mansion contained ten rooms and had an observatory on the roof where Murphy could watch horses training or racing nearby at the Kentucky Association track. (Courtesy of Transylvania University, J. Winston Coleman Kentuckiana Collection.)

conscious of class stratification just as the white community was in its own sphere; Ike and Lucy Murphy moved to their mansion on Third Street presumably to escape their older neighborhood of Megowan Street, which was fast becoming Lexington's red-light district. It is interesting that the Murphys did not sell their house and property on Megowan Street. They became landlords, renting the house to a black man.

The move the Murphys made to the large house on Third Street suggested that they were intent on elevating their social position to a level much above the laboring class since Murphy had acquired nation-

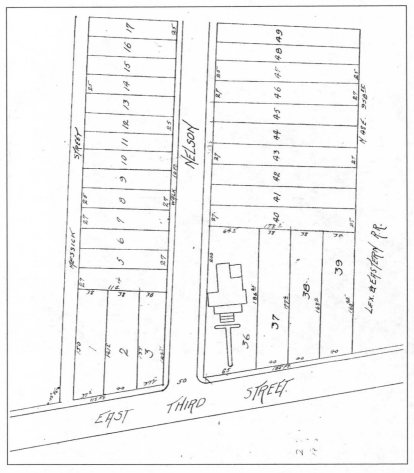

This is a plat drawing of the Isaac Murphy mansion, the only known image of the house that was situated on the roughly seven-acre plot that Murphy owned on East Third Street. The lots shown in this drawing were created after the jockey's death in 1896 and on subdivision of the property in 1903. The developer proposed that a street be run through the property, to be known as Nelson Avenue. An advertisement ("Big Sale of Lots Tuesday, April 14," *Lexington Herald,* April 14, 1903, 10) for the sale of these lots described the residence as two-story brick with bath, water, and lights. It noted that the property was situated close by the Lexington and Eastern Railroad tracks. (Netherland Subdivision, Plat Cabinet E, Slide 96, Fayette County Land Records, County Clerk's Office, Lexington.)

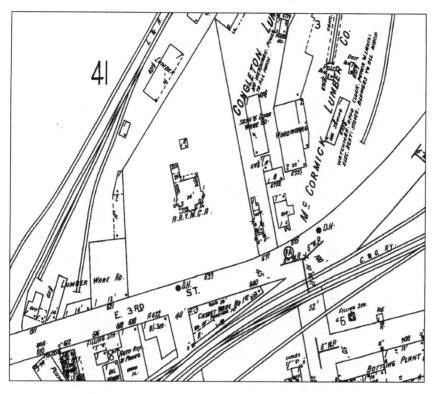

Compare the Murphy house (facing page) with this drawing for the Anderson house, a nearby mansion that has been mistakenly identified as Murphy's house. The Anderson house was situated farther east on Third Street, across the railroad tracks and near Clay Avenue. A newspaper advertisement ("Public Sale of the Most Elegant Residence in Central Kentucky," *Lexington Leader*, July 7, 1888, 4) announced a public sale of the Anderson house. Many years later, the house became known as the Railroad YMCA. (Sanborn Fire Insurance Map, 1907, University of Kentucky Special Collections, Lexington.)

wide recognition as a star athlete. This was a further indication that he was elevating the jockey profession above that of its former niche in the laboring class. Despite his rise to fame, however, Murphy might have realized that the jockey profession continued to suggest connotations connecting it with a class of labor. He revealed his awareness of this when he once said: "I am as proud of my calling as I am of my record, and I believe my life will be recorded as a success, though the reputation I enjoyed was earned in the stable and saddle."[37]

His talent in the saddle appeared to erase the color line for Murphy during these fluid times when white society remained undecided over "what to do with the Negro in American society," as Myrdal put it. The times were, indeed, in flux: lynching was on the rise nationwide as the close of the nineteenth century approached; racial segregation was on the horizon even as the lives of African Americans evolved along a track similar to those of whites in matters of status and class separation. At times, these parallel tracks crossed, as Murphy's did in the sport of horse racing. But not all blacks prominent in the sport of racing received recognition equating them with whites even if they did receive respect. Respect, like everything else, was stratified.

An example involved the house servant named Peter, long employed as the major domo of McGrathiana, the horse farm of Hal Price McGrath, the winner of the inaugural Kentucky Derby in 1875. Whites who were outsiders to the Bluegrass did not recognize Peter as their equal, yet they afforded him wide respect. Peter's reputation as an efficient, loyal house servant extended far beyond the Bluegrass and resulted in a biographical sketch written in 1874 in *Turf, Field and Farm*. Peter amused the house guests at McGrathiana, for he appeared to exercise a great amount of power. All knew that any power he appeared to possess came only at the discretion of McGrath; yet, when Peter ruled the hallway and dining room at McGrathiana, no one would have suggested this imbalance in power anywhere within his hearing. While Murphy epitomized the independent, high-achieving black man from Kentucky, Peter represented an entirely different sort of Kentuckian: the well-loved family servant, the holdover from slavery days who also, perhaps because of family loyalty, appeared to be protected from lynching and other forms of violence. The writer for *Turf, Field and Farm* got it right when he wrote of Peter: "He is one of those servants so highly prized by the rich and cultivated planter in ante-bellum times." He was, indeed, a picture of antebellum times, a throwback to an era that, ironically, was to become the future for Kentucky's troubled horse industry by the twentieth century.[38]

Picture Peter presiding over a battalion of waiters in the dining room, issuing orders "with Napoleonic decision," as *Turf, Field and*

The winning team for the first Kentucky Derby in 1875 was the horse Aristides; his owner, Hal Price McGrath; and the jockey Oliver Lewis. (Courtesy of the Keeneland Association.)

Farm described him at work. "When on duty Peter permits no subaltern to trifle with his dignity. . . . He bears himself like an aristocrat, and by the set of his hat and the cut of his coat you are impressed with the fact that he is a colored individual of no ordinary pretentions. In the eyes of Peter there is no place like Kentucky. . . . He will whisk out his broom five hundred times a day, and if no objections are made, will brush such a man's coat threadbare, and carelessly ram into his vest pocket every fifty-cent stamp or dollar bill that you thrust into his hand. . . . Peter is a type of the polite, dignified old family servant of the chivalric days before the war. He does not care a snap of his finger for Mr. Sumner's pet measure, the Civil Rights bill, for he has enjoyed more privileges by voluntary concession than could have been conferred upon him by the working of a law which appeals to or stirs up the prejudices of race."[39]

When McGrath would take his racing stable to the June race meet at Jerome Park, he would take Peter along as well. This pair of "worldly men"—the Kentucky gambler-horseman and his loyal servant, who had a penchant for betting on horses and for making conversation with the ladies—must have presented quite a contrast to other Kentuckians like the sphinx-like Murphy or even the wild and frontiersman-looking John Harper. Peter would be "in high feather" when McGrath took him northeast to the races. The black man was always on the lookout for a financial backer, persuading any likely prospect "with many bows and scrapes" to bet money for him on a horse of which Peter whispered he had inside knowledge because he worked for McGrath. Judging by the story in *Turf, Field and Farm,* Northeastern racing patrons regarded this act with paternal affection. They acquired some of their impressions of Kentuckians from this duo of Bluegrass representatives. Interestingly, the impressions gave no indication of the violence raging in Kentucky.[40]

While Northeastern whites patronized Peter's bowing and scraping for betting money at the racecourse, they appeared to think nothing odd about Murphy, higher up the social scale, dining next to them at the major social event of the summer of 1890 at Monmouth Park, a celebration given by the horse trainer Matt Byrnes at his home near Eatontown, New Jersey, in honor of the great horse that Murphy rode named Salvator. On this occasion more than any other, the respect that whites professed for Murphy intersected so neatly with the rider's achievements and fame that differences of skin color seemed wiped away from the slate of cultural and racial beliefs.

James Ben Ali Haggin's stable owned Salvator, whose rivalry with a horse named Tenny grabbed the attention of racing fans, as had previous rivalries between Kentucky and Asteroid, Longfellow and Harry Bassett, and, later, Ten Broeck, Tom Ochiltree, and Parole. Salvator and a filly named Firenze were arguably the two best horses to emerge from Haggin's vast equine empire, which comprised his forty-four-thousand-acre Rancho del Paso in California and, later, upward of eleven thousand acres at Elmendorf Farm, which he would establish in Lexington. Murphy rode both these racing stars from Haggin's stable. He was at the height of his career.[41]

Haggin actually was returning to his roots when he purchased the initial portion of Elmendorf in 1897, for he was born in Harrodsburg, Kentucky, in 1821. He had practiced law in Kentucky, Mississippi, and New Orleans before following the gold miners to California during the rush of 1849. He had not gone to California searching for gold, instead opening a law office with Lloyd Tevis in Sacramento. He did find gold, however, in the form of a silver mine in Utah in which he, Tevis, and George Hearst invested. They also invested with Marcus Daly in the Anaconda copper mines in Montana, the Homestake mines in South Dakota, and other operations, including one in Peru. Haggin had begun buying Bluegrass horses from Tennessee and Kentucky in the 1880s and won the Kentucky Derby with Ben Ali, purchased in Kentucky. He was also winning races that impressed the Northeastern establishment, races like the Belmont Stakes and the Withers Stakes. He came out on the side of those breeders who stood by the bloodlines of the great stallion, Lexington, since the dam of Salvator, Salina, was one of the best daughters of the old horse.[42]

Murphy might have heard the story of the naming of Salvator, how the colt whose sire was an English import named Prince Charlie had originally received the name Effendi. Writing *The Great Ones,* Kent Hollingsworth told how Haggin's valet, an African American, was shining his employer's shoes one day when Haggin noticed that the man's bald head was the same color as Effendi's coat. That might have been the reason, according to Hollingsworth, why Haggin renamed Effendi as Salvator, after the valet. By any name, Salvator was a top-level racehorse, winning stakes races at ages two and three. At age four in 1890, he and his rival, Tenny, gave Murphy, Haggin, and all racing fans memories of the type that sometimes come only once in a lifetime.[43]

The excitement over these two horses began building after Salvator won the Suburban in New York, defeating Tenny, among others. Murphy sat enthroned in a floral horseshoe after winning the Suburban, a custom for jockeys on winning some of the most significant horse races of that era. His adoring fans would not permit him to climb down from the floral shoe on his own but carried the arrangement, with him still enthroned, to a place where he and other jockeys gave interviews to the newspaper reporters. All the while, Tenny's owner was chafing. He believed that his horse should have won the race and so challenged Hag-

One of the most celebrated sports events of the latter nineteenth century was Salvator's defeat of Tenny at Sheepshead Bay in New York, June 25, 1890. Isaac Murphy rode Salvator to victory by the length of half a horse's head. A white jockey, "Snapper" Garrison, rode Tenny. The race inspired Ella Wheeler Wilcox to write the poem "How Salvator Won." (Courtesy of the Keeneland Association.)

gin to a rematch. The showdown was set for the Coney Island track late in June. When Salvator and Murphy stepped out on the track, the pair looked like "the idealization of horse and jockey," read a report of the race. "The crowd seemed to recognize the fact, and round after round of applause came from the masses of people in the stand, on the lawn, and, in fact, every place where a sight of the race could be obtained."[44]

Sports aficionados credited Murphy and his unflappable calm on horseback with holding off Tenny's challenge in the late homestretch to win by the length of a horse's head. The contemporary poet Ella Wheeler Wilcox immortalized the race in a poem published in the *Spirit of the Times,* a section of which reads:

138

One more mighty plunge, and with knee, limb and hand
I lift my horse first by a nose past the stand.
We are under the string now—the great race is done—
And Salvator, Salvator, Salvator won![45]

Murphy was clearly the hero on this June day in 1890, receiving the crowd's applause with the stoic visage he always showed before the grandstands. The Salvator-Tenny rivalry moved to New Jersey in July to the newly rebuilt Monmouth Park, which the New York sportsman David Withers had reconstructed on a scale previously unknown in sports. Salvator won his race at Monmouth by four lengths. The *Spirit of the Times* declared: "About the immense superiority Isaac Murphy shows over the majority of the jockeys at the present day . . . there can be no room for doubt." Two weeks following that race, Byrnes staged the famous party to celebrate Salvator's victories. Murphy sat down at the table among the white guests, among whom were "half the judicial and political 'somebodies' of New York." According to photographic records, Murphy appeared to take his place among whites with ease. He was elegantly attired in a velvet-collared coat and derby. The clambake in honor of a horse and jockey who had made a success of the season was itself a huge success. The champagne flowed heavily that day.[46]

Two days later, the bottom fell out from under Murphy's career. He reappeared on the track to ride Haggin's fast filly Firenze at Monmouth Park—and lost the race, finishing seventh. It seemed that the entire world noticed he had trouble riding the filly. The *New York Sun*, in a report reprinted in the *Kentucky Leader*, told how Murphy "was listing to the left and clinging to the saddle" during the race. Perhaps one hundred yards beyond the finish line, the filly slowed to a trot on her own, and Murphy rolled out of the saddle and was "picked up by bystanders, while others hurried forward and caught the mare." The bystanders helped him back into the saddle so that he could return Firenze to the unsaddling area. Then he forgot to ask the permission of the judges to dismount, in accordance with racing rules. His friends had to put him back on Firenze once more in order to follow through with this requirement. After weighing in on the scales, Murphy had to be almost carried to the jockeys' locker room. Rumors ran wild throughout the racetrack grandstand that he was drunk. His friends "hurried him into his clothes, secured a carriage, and drove him home."[47]

The aftermath for Murphy was suspension from the track and an immense scolding in the newspapers, for it appeared that he might have ridden while drunk. The *New York Times* exclaimed that it was "past belief" that Murphy would make such an embarrassment of himself. The *Times* pointed to the clambake two days previously as perhaps the start of a drinking binge. The *New York Sun* certainly was convinced that Murphy had been drunk, for its reporter had "heard" that the jockey was not a novice to a state of inebriation. The honest man's jockey, Murphy, denied these accusations. He told how prior to riding Firenze he had visited with his wife, Lucy, in the grandstand, where they asked the waiter to bring them a glass of mineral water. Murphy's white valet, the waiter, and the cashier at the grandstand all insisted that Murphy drank nothing but the mineral water during this short visit. Witnesses next to the jockey scales reported that they saw nothing amiss with the rider when he weighed out to ride the race. Matt Byrnes, who was Firenze's trainer and Murphy's host from the clambake, said he saw nothing wrong with Murphy when he met him in the paddock prior to the race.[48]

No one ever learned what really had happened to Murphy that day. Well known was the fact that, like many jockeys, Murphy went to extreme measures to keep his weight low so that he could ride races. Jockeys of that era believed that drinking champagne would renew their energy and, thus, offset the debilitating side effects of the dramatic weight-loss programs they endured. Murphy followed this practice and began taking "intoxicant drinks" in the years prior to his death "to aid his strength against the exertions of [weight] 'reducing' necessary to this profession," according to his friend and attorney L. P. Tarlton. Vosburgh, the respected turf correspondent in New York, revealed that Murphy had reduced from his "winter weight" of 140 pounds to 110 pounds in order to ride Salvator during the 1890 season.[49]

The possibility exists that something else happened to Murphy. The *New York Sun* reported: "There was a rumor, and a very strong one at that, that the jockey had been drugged by somebody who had bet heavily on other horses in the race." Murphy returned to his mansion in Lexington, where, according to the *Louisville Commercial*, he was "confined to his house by sickness": "Murphy has never recovered since his sickness at Monmouth. . . . He was undoubtedly sick at the time, and not drunk, as at first reported." The Louisville newspaper revealed that it had received "private information . . . that Murphy, on his physician's statement, is suffering from effects of poison probably administered to him that day at Monmouth Park. . . . The physicians [sic] declares that Murphy will never fully recover from the poisoning." When the *Kentucky Leader* interviewed Murphy, he said he could not say for sure whether he had been poisoned. "But," he continued, "something suddenly got the matter with me and I have never been well since." Whatever had happened, Murphy's career wound down rapidly from that point, with many believing that he became an alcoholic in his later years.[50]

Murphy won the third of his trio of Kentucky derbies the following spring. But his nationwide popularity had suffered immensely from the Firenze defeat and the suspicions that surrounded the incident. Despite a long and respected career, he passed within a mere few weeks from a jockey carried about on the shoulders of whites in a winner's floral horse shoe to a rider suspended by racing authorities at a Northeastern track and harshly criticized in the Northern press. With the Murphy controversy, it appeared that the public and all the racing sport were beginning to be less forgiving of black jockey stars.

In fact, news reports were beginning to appear about white jockeys forming hostile cabals against black riders. In 1900, the *New York Times* published its previously mentioned article about white riders forcing black jockeys off the turf. "[The] negro jockey is down and out," read the report, as a result of the work of "a quietly formed combination to shut him out. This edict is said to have gone out at the first race meeting of the year . . . that horse owners who expected to win races would find it to their advantage to put up the white riders. . . . Gossip around the racing headquarters said that the white riders had organized to draw the color line." A race war was looming at the nation's racetracks, and the white jockeys did not consistently lead the charge. At the Latonia Race Course, a white jockey complained in 1891 that black riders were conspiring to injure him during the races he rode. The *Spirit of the Times* considered this complaint while observing an irregular amount of accidents during the races at that track and concluded: "Whether or not there is something like race feeling and prejudice in the ranks of the riders, it is certain there has been altogether too much jostling and crowding."[51]

News reports like these might not have shocked anyone of that era, considering how sports were mirroring daily life. Racism was on a parallel course in the larger world: the number of lynchings was increasing throughout the United States and would reach its highest point during the 1890s. In a few short years, the sport of Thoroughbred racing no longer would provide the safe haven for the black stars of the turf that it had for some twenty-five years. Racing would follow in the footsteps of the larger world.[52]

Like old John Harper before him, however, Murphy had reaffirmed to Northeastern horsemen that the Bluegrass was home to some of the foremost horsemen, as well as to fast horses like Lexington, Asteroid, Longfellow, and an ever-expanding number of turf stars. Horsemen like Murphy helped make it easy for outsiders to equate the Bluegrass region with the racehorse. Sadly for those African Americans who trained racehorses and rode them as jockeys, these contributions at the sport's highest levels would soon be ignored and then forgotten as the sport's front lines, most visible to horse owners and the public, became completely white.

Blacks remained heavily involved in racing, but their duties were confined to the stables, where they were not quite so visible to the public. With American society becoming segregated, and with blacks relegated to invisibility in all aspects of life, it would hardly have seemed right for black jockeys to continue receiving the public accolades that Murphy and other black horsemen had received so freely during a time of more fluid race relations. But that time had occurred before whites finally figured out, as Myrdal would put it, "what to do with the Negro in American society."

chapter **FIVE**

Old Money Meets the Arrivistes

Isaac Murphy's 1890 Kentucky Derby winner, Riley, raced for the stable of Ed Corrigan. "Big" Ed Corrigan was an ill-tempered sort who was known to crack his cane over a man's head rather than consider the other's point of view. This did not seem to trouble folks involved in the sport of horse racing, for Corrigan had plenty of money and spent it freely in the game. He was among the vast variety of new men entering the sport in the 1880s and 1890s: in his case, a fiery maverick who cared not what others thought of him or whether he fit with August Belmont's social set, which he did not. Corrigan was his own man, and his horses competed successfully with the best. Men like him were bringing great changes to the sport that Belmont had revived in New York.[1]

Corrigan came into the game during an expansion of racing that saw the sport spread far beyond the geographic vision for New York and the elite social class division that Belmont, Travers, and Jerome had crafted for racing within their sphere during the mid-1860s. Corrigan, an industrialist from Kansas City, Missouri, situated his base of operations in Chicago. Here, an important event called the American Derby materialized. Raced in front of large crowds at Washington Park, and with purse money that grew to be quite large, this event approached the prestige and monetary value of a race in New York that Belmont and his group held so dear: the Futurity. The American Derby actually became the richest race in the nation in 1893, with a purse of $60,000, sending a subliminal alert to New York that the latter would need to add more

Ed Corrigan (shown here in profile) founded Hawthorne Race Course on the west side of Chicago in 1890 and raced his stable of Thoroughbreds throughout the eastern United States, winning the 1890 Kentucky Derby with Riley. Corrigan made his money in railroad expansion in the West and was notorious for his hot temper. (Courtesy of Keeneland-Cook Collection, Keeneland Library, Lexington.)

money to the Futurity—or else forfeit prestige. Chicago racing had been a small-time affair from 1864 on, but, with the opening of Washington Park in 1884 and General Phil Sheridan of Indian-fighting fame and Civil War notoriety as the track's president, Chicago positioned itself squarely on the sporting map. The good news for fans of the sport was the addition of much more racing. In this milieu, Corrigan was king.

Like Belmont, Corrigan was self-made. Unlike Belmont, he did not cultivate social acceptance or connections with the elite. He was born in St. Johns Crysostom, outside Montreal, and raised in Kansas City, where his family immigrated in 1860. He began his working years as a teenager, laying down railroad track in the West. Eventually, he built up his own company to contract for railroad expansion into the Far West. He and his brothers also were pioneers in building the Kansas

City Street Railway system. His association with railroads spanned an era of labor unrest, beginning with a nationwide railroad strike in 1877 that saw more than one hundred workers die in the accompanying violence. The strike occurred in the wake of the Panic of 1873 but also during a time when labor unions had begun to emerge and challenge the practices of employers and captains of industry. The wealthy in America and even the middle class viewed labor unrest "with an uneasiness that assumed almost hysterical proportions," Paul Boyer has written in his study of cities and moral order. However, the reality was that employers generally did not concern themselves with the welfare of their workers. Boyer suggests that civil disorder during the 1870s "took on a more menacing aura as a direct expression of labor unrest." The strikes and violence that broke out at railroad and industrial centers hardened business owners like Corrigan. He had seen more of the violent side of life than many when, as a self-made industrialist, he became a racehorse owner in the late 1870s. At one time, he owned or leased possibly one hundred Thoroughbreds in training.[2]

Corrigan founded the Hawthorne Race Course in Chicago in 1890, four years after the famous Haymarket Square incident, when someone threw a dynamite bomb at police who were attempting to break up a strike rally at the McCormick harvesting-machine factory. The bomb killed seven policemen; as police fired into the crowd, they killed four persons. The Haymarket incident convinced many that radicalism lay simmering in labor; this belief put industrialists on edge as they contemplated the increasing volatility of the laboring class. Industrialists, captains of industry and finance, and the socially elite distanced themselves from the rabble with the racing stables they acquired and the country estates they developed for themselves.[3]

Corrigan, unlike many other wealthy men, did not evade encounters with the working class. He simply met labor's threats head-on, the way he had learned how to handle these problems while running railroads in the West. A story about the way he handled a threatened strike at his Hawthorne track was indicative of the roughshod way he did business. He invited four strike negotiators to his office, where he dealt a knockout blow to each, laying them out unconscious on the floor. Then he went outside and announced that the pending strike was off.[4]

Corrigan did not get away clean from every instance of aggression.

In 1905, authorities arrested him at the Latonia Race Course in northern Kentucky for an assault on an apprentice jockey. According to witnesses, he had been highly upset after the rider galloped a mare too fast during a warm-up for a race. He seized the youth by the ears, pulling and twisting them, with the jockey subsequently forced to seek hospital treatment for damaged eardrums.[5]

Corrigan loved racing, and he loved gambling. He also knew how to seek out the right jockey to win the major races when his money was down. With Murphy riding the bulk of his horses during the 1880s, his stable amassed more than $1 million in winnings. Considering the arrogant and insensitive, sometimes violent manner that Corrigan displayed in his dealings with others, it is significant that he did not appear to have used bullying tactics on his jockey. In fact, Murphy seemed to hold the upper hand, negotiating riding contracts on his own terms. The horse owner needed Murphy; the jockey consequently appeared not only free to name his price but also immune from Corrigan's wild, abusive outbursts. Moreover, Murphy's reputation for honesty worked in the gambler's favor because Corrigan could trust Murphy to ride to orders. When Corrigan sent horses from his stable into New Jersey or New York, Murphy rode them impeccably. Murphy was up on Freeland when Corrigan sent that horse east in 1885 for those widely publicized races against the filly Miss Woodford.

All did not go well in the Northeast for Corrigan, however, and the tangential effect on Murphy is worth consideration. In 1891, Corrigan ran afoul of the scions of New York racing when they told him that they no longer would permit him to race in the Futurity. He sued and won his case but with the result that the society pillars of the New York turf barred him from any future participation at their tracks. Corrigan believed the real reason he was barred was that he insisted on bringing his black jockey east to ride. Or so he said. But the racial climate was, indeed, changing in the East, as Murphy had learned from his own experience and his ban from Monmouth Park after his troubling ride on Firenze.[6]

The upshot of racing's expansion, as demonstrated with Corrigan's arrival in the game, was that Belmont and his small group faced competition beyond anything they had imagined when they resurrected the sport in the North. This increasing rate of competition was compelling everyone in Thoroughbred racing to search wider for the competitive edge they believed would give them an advantage over their rivals. While Corrigan and the mining kings like James Ben Ali Haggin and Marcus Daly led a successful foray into New York from the Midwest and the Far West, competition also heated up with new men in New York getting into the sport.

The Lorillard brothers, George and Pierre IV, were two such New York men. Heirs to the industrial tobacco fortune of their father, Peter Lorillard, George and Pierre dominated Thoroughbred racing for nearly fifteen years, beginning in 1873. The brothers were plutocrats, similar to Belmont, Travers, and Jerome. They spent freely on the sporting life and sundry activities available to the idle rich. Their interests ran to yachting and trap shooting as well as horse racing. In 1885, Pierre founded Tuxedo Park—he initially called it Deer Park—in the Ramapo Mountains of the state of New York, designing this hideaway as a hunting preserve. Social events and table gambling at Deer Park grew so infamous that Emily Post found the inspiration for her *Blue Book of Etiquette* at this social enclave. Every man arriving at Deer Park drove a four-in-hand coach of the type Belmont and his friends drove to Jerome Park. Dinner guests wore evening attire that came to be known as the tuxedo, hence Tuxedo Park. Pierre Lorillard's taste in all he did ran to the extreme. His Rancocas Stud near Jobstown, New Jersey, evolved as second in size only to Alexander's Woodburn Farm in Kentucky.[7]

The founding of Rancocas Stud signaled yet another disregard of the once-popular belief in the superior qualities of Kentucky's Bluegrass soil. "I can see no reason why as good a racehorse cannot be raised in Kentucky as in England or elsewhere," wrote a correspondent from New York in the *Spirit of the Times*—but the matter was in doubt, at least as far as Lorillard and his set saw it. This is not to say that Pierre Lorillard was unfamiliar with Kentucky: he sent one of his best horses, Parole, to Louisville to run in the second renewal of the Kentucky Derby in 1876. William Astor of New York also had a horse entered in the race, one named Vagrant, who won while Parole finished fourth. But, while Astor's horse had been bred in Kentucky (his trainer was the Bluegrass horseman Jim Williams, who was the first to put the young boy named Isaac Murphy into jockey training), Parole made the long train trip to Louisville from New York. This was a rare venture into Kentucky for a horse from New York. Pierre did not run another horse in the Kentucky Derby, and, for the next four years, the race reverted generally to the province of Kentuckians. Meantime, Lorillard focused on building up Rancocas Stud and on winning the races that counted in front of his friends in the Northeast.[8]

Pierre named his stud farm for a stream that ran through the sixteen-hundred-acre estate. He put two hundred men to work building ditches for a water system to run throughout the farm. He had them build barns and paddocks and a training track. He had them remodel the manor house, adding at least a dozen rooms, and had his workers install an elaborate iron gate that he had brought for his carriage driveway from the Bowery Bank in New York. Winged Mercury stood guard atop the gate.[9]

Reportedly, Lorillard spent more than $1 million building the farm and remodeling the mansion. Inside the manor house, he dedicated one room to gaming and installed a roulette wheel. Excessive on all fronts, he had Tiffany and Company design special aluminum plates for the horses of Rancocas Stud and his racing stable—simply because he did not care for the customary heavy iron shoes. On the aluminum shoes, Pierre actually anticipated a modern trend that would see nearly all racehorses shod in aluminum, although that trend would not develop for many more decades. A reporter from Kentucky was overwhelmed when he viewed Rancocas Stud. He commented: "In extent and perfection of detail Rancocas stands alone in this country, and there is probably nothing as complete on the globe."[10]

George Lorillard installed his racehorses at Islip on Long Island, and his stable, separate from Pierre's, distinguished itself with winning the Preakness Stakes over five consecutive years. By 1878, the two Lorillard brothers dominated the sport nationwide in number of wins: a remarkable feat considering that they essentially confined their racing to New York, New Jersey, and Maryland. The brothers Lorillard so dominated the turf by the latter 1870s that they could hardly avoid racing against each other. Memorable was a well-attended East-West showdown at Pimlico Race Course near Baltimore in 1877, when Frank Harper (recall him as old John Harper's favorite nephew) brought his Ten Broeck, the dominant horse in the Midwest, to challenge Tom Ochiltree (George Lorillard's horse) and Parole (Pierre Lorillard's stable star). Parole won the race, to the great dismay of the "westerners," as the newspapers referred to the Kentuckians. The gelding's popular victory led to an Eastern phenomenon: Parole pool rooms, Parole saloons, and Parole baseball clubs, all named for the animal. Nobody was talking about the Kentucky Bluegrass when they mused on Parole's success. The focus rested entirely on the Northeast.[11]

Parole became the talk of the tracks during the latter 1870s, replacing the now-retired Longfellow as the equine star at the center of the sport. Interestingly, the two horses, though some years apart in age, shared the same sire: a horse named Leamington, who had departed Kentucky after a one-year stay, during which he had sired Longfellow. After leaving Kentucky, Leamington had been installed near Philadelphia at Erdenheim Stud. This clearly could be viewed as still another expression of cavalier disregard for the Bluegrass in its former role as the undisputed epicenter of race-horse breeding. But that was the way the turf was developing.

The Lorillards returned to the well from which Parole sprang, purchasing the entire crop of Leamington yearlings from Erdenheim Stud in 1879. One of those was Iroquois, who, shipped to England, won the Epsom Derby for Pierre, the first American horse to win this historic event (and a feat not to be repeated until 1954). This was no small achievement. New Yorkers seized on this victory as validation of the American Thoroughbred, a matter of esteem and equality that Englishmen had long disputed, believing their horses superior to those of the Americans. Pandemonium hit New York with the news of Iroquois's win. While the excitement spread throughout the city, the New York Stock Exchange suspended all trading. The *Spirit of the Times* reported: "The reporters, hosts of them, have attempted to storm Mr. Pierre Lorillard's Fifth Avenue residence."[12]

The victory was a triumph of American Thoroughbred breeding but not one for Kentucky breeding since, like Parole, Iroquois was a product of Pennsylvania. The breeder of Iroquois was a man named Aristides Welch, and he, along with his breeding program at Erdenheim Stud, was receiving a great amount of attention in the sporting periodicals for Iroquois's achievement in England. With the Bluegrass not even figuring into this transatlantic story, Kentucky as the cradle of the racehorse was a notion sinking farther over the western horizon. The Eastern rac-

Pierre Lorillard's Iroquois became the first American horse to win the Epsom Derby in England in 1881. Americans were so excited over his victory that the New York Stock Exchange suspended trading the day the news arrived in the city. (Courtesy of the New York Public Library.)

ing and breeding establishments appeared to have the business locked up in their region; the combination of Rancocas and Erdenheim studs stood at the pinnacle of this modern-day phase of the sport.

A debate over bloodlines likewise threatened to leave Kentucky at a disadvantage. Sons of the great stallion Lexington were proving unremarkable in the stud, an unfortunate development that might have attributed to the popularity of Leamington (imported from England) in his Pennsylvania home. At Jerome Park, turfmen had debated the relative merits of Lexington and Leamington as breeding stallions during casual conversation. The question was one of mere sporting competition at that point. However, with the sons of Lexington, the discussion took a different turn, down a path of disappointment. Asteroid's "waning popularity" was well known, with one commentator remarking that the horse simply was not going to duplicate his extraordinary talents in his offspring. "Breeders thought that he was such a remarkable race horse himself that all they had to do was to breed and get one like himself," was the lament. Kentucky, standing in New York, had not fared better than his rival.[13]

A noted pedigree authority observed in 1879: "The sons of Lexington had, taken as a whole, proved a failure at the stud when compared with the English importations." The writer was Walter S. Vosburgh, a New York resident who wrote bloodstock articles under the pen name Vigilant. Vosburgh's point was worth considering since the sons of Lexington were all that remained for breeders if they desired to try to replicate his bloodline; Lexington had died in 1875, and breeders expected his sons to carry his bloodline forward. Vosburgh concluded: "The sons of Lexington, though first-class performers themselves, have failed in transmitting it to their progeny. . . . The grandsons of Lexington have had the misfortune to meet a better strain in the progeny of the English horses and . . . proved inferior to them."[14]

An even greater debate questioned whether imported English stallions contributed more to the breed than stallions bred and raised in the United States. Those elite patrons of Jerome Park who arrived at the races in English coaches fell on the side of the English horses—a trend that did not at all favor the bloodlines popular in Bluegrass Kentucky. "Some of the Englishmen who belong to the Jerome Park Club will hold up their hands in horror at the idea that any one should be so bold as to assert that an American be as good as, or better than an English race horse," wrote an observer quite familiar with the beliefs of these New York elites.[15]

Belmont, who could well afford to buy whatever suited his fancy, was a major importer of English horses to his Nursery Stud. "His stallion, The Ill-Used, combines more of the blood royal of the English Stud-book than any horse in the world," the *Spirit of the Times* commented. Belmont stood two sons of Lexington at the Nursery: Kentucky (purchased after Jerome put him up for auction) and Kingfisher, a horse Longfellow had defeated. Yet he relied heavily on his English imports. He had representatives scour the auctions in England for him. "His mares . . . are the pick of the English paddocks," the *Spirit* reported. Once again, as far as this discussion was concerned, Bluegrass Kentucky did not exist. The *Spirit* concluded that Belmont's importations pointed strongly to a successful breeding program at the Nursery Stud.[16]

Down in Kentucky, Benjamin Bruce had begun publishing his own periodical in 1875, calling it the *Kentucky Live Stock Record*, in which he chided those New York breeders and their preference for English bloodstock. "It is with no little displeasure that we have noticed of late an increasing tendency on the part of some . . . breeders to deprecate the stock of their neighbors and fellowmen engaged in the same business," he wrote. He denounced the practice as "reprehensible" and suggested that this war of opinions over English versus American bloodstock be put to rest. "Some thoroughbred horsemen advocate native blood as represented in Lexington and his descendants; while others want nothing but imported English blood," he wrote. But he advocated that each side become more accepting of the other's difference of opinion. "What we condemn is the practice on the part of some who are ever ready to pass judgment upon the stock of their neighbors, without a corresponding advantage to themselves, but a marked injury to their neighbor. . . . You cannot build up a herd or stock farm by the abuse of your neighbors." Despite his advice, the controversy never did settle.[17]

In addition to this debate over bloodlines, Kentuckians sensed a growing problem with the Northeast on another front. A controversy had arisen over the weights jockeys would be assigned for a variety of races. Known as the *scale of weights,* these assignments made according to a graduated scale required older horses to carry more weight than two-year-olds, for example. The assignments were clearly specified—and differed between the tracks in New York and those in the West, including Kentucky. This difference evolved after 1876 when the American Jockey Club, Monmouth Park, and Saratoga adopted a higher scale of weights. Kentucky horsemen and those in the South spoke out against this—and suffered repercussions.

Benjamin Bruce accused Belmont's American Jockey Club of adopting the higher weight scale without consulting horse owners in other regions. Moreover, according to Bruce, the Jockey Club was attempting to intimidate those Westerners and Southerners who spoke out against the new mandate. Belmont vigorously denied this. But Bruce countered that Jerome Park was punishing him by refusing to advertise in *Turf, Field and Farm.* He regarded this as an attempt at bullying him into obeisance. The scale-of-weights controversy between Eastern and Kentucky horsemen continued for several years, but New York did not reverse its decision to adopt a higher scale. It was New York's way or no way.[18]

Even as Belmont pursued his breeding program, two racing stables of a different sort emerged on the New York scene. These were the stables of James R. Keene and the Dwyer brothers of Brooklyn, Mike and Phil. Keene enjoyed two different phases in horse racing, each situated at the opposite end of a period of personal financial ruin. Keene's first phase was entirely unlike his second, for, during his initial involvement, he did not breed racehorses. Years later, he would breed some of the most outstanding racehorses of all time. This occurred during his second phase, after he reentered the sport in 1892 and purchased Castleton Farm in Bluegrass Kentucky. But, during the first phase, initiated in 1877, he purchased racehorses that others had bred and raised, frequently paying huge sums of money. In purchasing rather than breeding horses, his operation was similar to that of the Dwyer brothers, who never bred their own racing stock.[19]

Keene and the Dwyers both were taking a vastly different approach to horse racing than was, for example, Belmont, whose passion was to breed a brilliant racehorse at his Nursery Stud. But every one of these men was similar in that each had money. Keene was already a wealthy man when he left his home in California to move to New York in 1876. He had held various jobs in California, from teacher and editor while studying law to selling equipment to gold miners. He traded on the San Francisco Stock Exchange, and, as he grew wealthy, he mingled with persons who figured prominently in California racing. Among these were Elias "Lucky" Baldwin, the founder of the Santa Anita racetrack, and Governor Leland Stanford, whose interests lay more with the trotting-horse breed than with Thoroughbreds. Keene rode a private railroad car to New York to embark on a sea voyage intended to help his health. However, he neglected to board the ship. He never made it past Wall Street.[20]

Keene has been called one of the most feared stock-market manipulators of all time. Wall Street fascinated him, and he realized quick success purchasing railway stocks. He even saved the market during 1877 when the railroad strikes threatened the entire U.S. transportation system. The market for railroad stocks crashed with this labor unrest and threatened to bring down the entire stock market. But Keene bought up all the railroad stock and, consequently, won the appellation as the man who saved the industry. He was a prideful man. In one moment of reckless arrogance, he suggested that he could teach Jay Gould a thing or two about Wall Street. Gould responded by saying that, while

James R. Keene (on the right) has been called one of the most feared stock manipulators of all time. He even saved the stock market in 1877 when railroad strikes threatened the entire U.S. transportation system. Keene purchased Spendthrift for $15,000 and won the Belmont Stakes in 1879 with this horse. Later in the century, he purchased Castleton Farm in Lexington. (Courtesy of Keeneland-Cook Collection, Keeneland Library, Lexington.)

Keene had arrived in New York in the luxury of a private railroad car, he, Gould, would send him home to California in a boxcar. The two men thus became lifelong enemies.[21]

Keene's moment as savior during the Panic of 1877 coincided with those momentous years when the Lorillard brothers dominated racing in the Northeast. The Lorillard success apparently did not sit well with Belmont's social set, who had resurrected this sport presumably for their own use. Charles William Bathgate, prominent in Belmont's set and coming from the family that had sold farmland to Jerome for the construction of Jerome Park, went to Keene and urged him to open a racing stable in an attempt to break up the Lorillards' seeming stranglehold on the sport. Bathgate suggested that Keene purchase Spendthrift, an undefeated horse they had all heard about that was racing exclusively in Kentucky and Tennessee. Keene decided to take Bathgate up on his suggestion. Accordingly, Keene's agent, who appears to have been Sanders Bruce, took $15,000 down to Lexington and purchased Spendthrift from Dan Swigert, the man who so ably had assisted Robert Aitcheson Alexander during Woodburn Farm's formative years. Spendthrift was a son of Australian, the top sire at Woodburn Farm following the death of Lexington in 1875. Spendthrift swiftly rewarded Keene for his $15,000 gamble on this steep purchase price by winning the Belmont Stakes the following year, 1879.

Keene's purchase of Spendthrift represented a financial windfall for Swigert and, undoubtedly, for Sanders Bruce, who, acting as sales agent, would have received financial compensation. The sale of Spendthrift to Keene also helped boost the profile of Bluegrass Kentucky within the realm of the Lorillards, Belmont, and other titans of the Northeastern turf. The horse's success did not bring these titans to transfer their breeding operations to Kentucky, nor did it send them to Kentucky to buy up all the available horses. But it did bring Keene back to the well that had produced Spendthrift. Bruce and Bathgate, acting as agents, purchased nine colts for Keene at the Woodburn Farm yearling sale of 1879. The least expensive of these, costing a mere $650, Keene would name Foxhall. This horse would show up the French the same way Pierre Lorillard's Iroquois had shocked the English, for he won the Grand Prix de Paris in 1881.[22]

Meantime, the Dwyers, Mike and Phil, were busy building their own racing empires from their New York base, making shrewd purchases of any horse they believed would fit brother Mike's gambling scenarios. The brothers were not interested in breeding to improve the breed, as Belmont was attempting at the Nursery Stud. They wanted immediate action rather than success that might be possible only after waiting two or three years for a foal to mature into a racehorse. Thus, they purchased ready-made racing stock, colts and fillies of at least two years of age.[23]

The Dwyer brothers came into the sport with more than enough money to play this game with rich men, for they had turned the butcher shop in Brooklyn that they had inherited from their father into a large meatpacking business. One of their customers was August Belmont. According to stories, he sold them their first good horse, one Rhada-manthus. One has to wonder whether Belmont lived to regret bringing the Dwyers into the sporting fold because they began to beat him at his own game.

Mike Dwyer was a heavy gambler whose interest lay in the money he could make on his horses in the betting ring; he did not care quite so much for the purse money they could make by winning races. People said that his brother, Phil, never bet more than $50. Mike's lifetime gambling losses, on the other hand, were huge, estimated at his death to be somewhere in excess of $1.5 million. But, though Mike lived to gam-ble, the Dwyer brothers turned their racing ventures into a formidable force. They developed one champion after another: Hindoo, Hanover, Miss Woodford, Tremont, Kingston, and Dew Drop, the first three re-membered as among the greatest racehorses of the nineteenth century.

Phil, while he did not wager much in the betting ring, gambled his money on the building of new racetracks. He founded two jockey clubs in New York and built the Gravesend racetrack, which became a thorn in the side of Belmont's sensitivities, along with those of Jerome, Travers, and their prestigious American Jockey Club. With the Dw-yer brothers' new track gaining a reputation as a haven for blue-collar horsemen and racing fans, the sport was turning in a direction that the American Jockey Club had not anticipated when it announced, on its inception, that it would make sure that the sport evolved at only the highest levels. The Dwyers were bringing blue-collar diversity to Thor-oughbred racing.

Like Keene, the Dwyers began reaching into Kentucky to find a competitive edge for their stables. And, like Keene, they found their way to Swigert, possibly by way of an introduction from Sanders Bruce. Swigert bred Hindoo, raced him as a two-year-old in the Midwest, then sent him to Saratoga, where the Dwyers purchased him for $15,000. The following year, 1881, when Hindoo was a three-year-old, the Dwyers sent him back down to Kentucky, where he won the Derby. On returning to the Northeast, Hindoo won all the major races, including the Travers Stakes.[24]

When the Dwyer brothers brought Hindoo to the Louisville Jockey Club track (Churchill Downs) for the Kentucky Derby, they were shocked to learn that bookmakers did not offer betting there. The only forms of betting at Louisville turned out to be the selling of auction pools and the French pools, an early form of pari-mutuel betting. Bookmakers had been operating at the New York tracks since 1873, and most people considered them a giant leap forward in the modernization of betting.[25]

The Dwyers thought the pools "hick stuff," as the Derby impresario Matt Winn once told the story. Consequently, when the brothers considered returning to the derby the following year, they informed the track that they would bring their colt, Runnymede, only if the track would round up some bookmakers for derby day. When the track said that it could not provide bookmakers—that none were known to operate in Kentucky—the Dwyers imported their own among the large party of guests that accompanied them to Louisville. They bet large with their bookmakers, taking a huge loss when Runnymede ran second to Apollo. But the importation of the Dwyer brothers' bookmakers made such an impression on Kentuckians that some of them, who had been auction pool sellers, became bookmakers. The effect was to change the form of betting at the track in Louisville until legislation outlawed bookmaking in 1908.[26]

During these years, the Dwyers were making good use of the secret formula for winning that they had discovered in Kentucky. This was Runnymede Farm in Bourbon County, some miles outside the county seat of Paris. Here presided two Kentuckians, Catesby Woodford and Ezekial Clay, the latter easily recognized by the dark patch he wore over one eye. The purpose of the patch was to cover injuries he had suffered in the war. Clay also was known to Northeasterners who read their newspapers as the man who had led the posse to rescue Asteroid for Alexander after thieves had taken the horse from Woodburn Farm.

When Hindoo retired from racing, the Dwyers traded the horse as a stallion prospect to Runnymede Farm in return for $9,000 cash and a two-year-old filly named Miss Woodford. She developed into the first American Thoroughbred to win $100,000. In 1895, Mike Dwyer purchased fourteen yearlings from yet another Kentucky farm owner, Milton Young, who had acquired McGrathiana Farm following the death of Hal Price McGrath. Ben Brush was in this group; he won the 1896 Kentucky Derby.[27]

This penchant for reaching into Kentucky to purchase racehorses might have seemed a profitable new turn of events for the Bluegrass, and it was—for the few persons involved. Swigert and Bruce both were acquiring comfortable financial status from the money they realized either by acting as agents for the elite racing stables of New York or by selling horses they owned for a profit. But, for the majority of Bluegrass horse breeders, the whims of these Northeastern racing stables did not trickle down. Few were the horses like Spendthrift, which had sold for $15,000. The average price seemed more mundane. For example, during auctions held at Lexington in 1877, John Clay's best yearling brought $770. Warren Viley saw bidding reach $710 for his yearling colt by Longfellow. Viley also auctioned two broodmares for $30 apiece. Woodburn Farm, as usual, got the big money for its yearlings: $3,100 and $1,050 for two colts purchased for Pierre Lorillard's account and $1,000 for one purchased for George Lorillard's account, all three sons of Lexington. But none of these prices could match the $15,000 Swigert received for Spendthrift and again for Hindoo. Other than a few horses purchased out of Kentucky sales, the major racing stables of the Northeast continued to pursue a model of breeding their own horses. Moreover, these powerful stables bred their mares almost exclusively to their own stallions. Consequently, very little traffic took place in the form of mares sent from New York down to Kentucky for breeding to stallions in the Bluegrass.[28]

Like Swigert, Bruce, and Woodburn, Runnymede Farm fared well financially. Its greatest wealth materialized later, however, during the 1920s, when the Kentucky senator Johnson N. Camden Jr. married into the family. He brought with him majority ownership in the Kentucky River Coal Company. Mineral wealth consequently expanded the horse-breeding operations at Runnymede in the same way Alexander had expanded operations at Woodburn Farm, using money from his ironworks in Scotland and another ironworks in Kentucky's Muhlenberg County. The point was this: big money did not originate in horse breeding. Rather, great fortunes made outside the sport supported horse breeding, whether on Northeastern farms or on those in Kentucky. This model would become the norm in the Bluegrass during the twentieth century, when the big money eventually came to Kentucky's horse business from outside the state.

All this is to say that Kentucky's native horsemen were not getting wealthy off their horses. Agricultural wealth simply could not compete with industrial wealth. With the exception of Woodburn Farm and Runnymede, both of which were able to expand owing to fortunes made in mining and minerals, the native gentry among Kentucky's horse breeders could not match the wealth of businessmen who came to the sport from Northern cities or mining ventures, the latter either in eastern Kentucky or in states farther west. Industrial wealth and Wall Street wealth were the engines driving the Northeastern turf and its ancillary breeding operations. Kentuckians bragged on their horses, but the fact remained that Belmont and others bred their mares almost exclusively to their own stallions. The only hope Kentuckians could hold out for enhancing their own breeding industry was to renew interest in the natural qualities of the Bluegrass soil, water, and grass. The *Kentucky Live Stock Record* pointed out the disadvantages found in horses bred on low, wet, and marshy lands: "Succulent herbage tends to the production of fat, with loose, flaccid muscle, and sinews of a similar texture, the very reverse of that which is requisite for the thoroughbred horse, or, indeed for any animal that is to be qualified for speedy or continued exertions." On the other hand, the periodical advised: "In Kentucky and Tennessee the land is dry and sound, somewhat elevated and rolling, conducing to a clean, wiry, and muscular animal. . . . Kentucky and Tennessee have bred and are breeding more first-class racers than all the rest of the States combined." Numbers alone, however, could not grow the business in the Bluegrass. The business could not return to its dominant status without an injection of outside wealth.[29]

The expansion of racing continued in the Northeast. The founders of yet another jockey club opened a new track called Coney Island in 1880 at Sheepshead Bay, New York. This group of twenty-four included some of the same powerful surnames that had attended the founding of Jerome Park and the American Jockey Club: Vanderbilt, Travers, Jerome, and, of course, Belmont. It also included two new names of significance: Keene and Lorillard.[30]

The breeding of racehorses nonetheless presented an opportunity to make or supplement a living in Bluegrass Kentucky, however. Looking to secure a greater piece of this economic pie, central Kentuckians doggedly pursued their efforts to recapture the region's former glory as the undisputed capital of the racehorse. Sanders Bruce followed his model of Bluegrass boosterism in the pages of *Turf, Field and Farm,* publishing stories about Kentucky horse farms. His brother, Benjamin, had left New York in 1875 to inaugurate his own publication, the *Kentucky Live Stock Record,* later the *Live Stock Record.* Like Sanders, Benjamin followed the practice of publicizing the Kentucky farms. The vision of Robert Aitcheson Alexander to promote Bluegrass horse-breeding activities in New York had, thus, doubled back on itself with the Bruce brothers operating on both fronts.

The Bruce brothers were fond of citing statistics that showed the Bluegrass to be the number one producer of Thoroughbreds by numbers, an example of their boosterism, but a misleading use of numbers. For example, Benjamin Bruce wrote in 1879 about the surging demand for racehorses, with Kentucky producing the most foals: 243, or nearly 50 percent of the 541 foals reported nationwide for 1878. Yet the origin of this statistic lay in the fact that nearly every farmer in the Bluegrass was breeding at least one Thoroughbred each year in an attempt to supplement his income. And this failed to tell the complete story. The business was scattered, consisting of small farmers, and lacking large capital. Twenty-five to thirty breeding establishments existed in Bluegrass Kentucky. At only one Kentucky farm did the volume of foals produced compare in numbers with the volume produced at the breeding farms of the Eastern racing establishment. This farm was Woodburn, where the number of foals produced in 1870 was seventy-two. The farm of James A. Grinstead, a leader among Kentucky breeding and racing men, was more typical: in 1870, he had some twenty broodmares. Like

Alexander, he had spirited his horses out of Kentucky during the war and essentially started over after the war ended.[31]

Going by the numbers, production at Rancocas in New Jersey as well as at the Nursery nearby on Long Island, Erdenheim Stud in Pennsylvania, and Haggin's Rancho del Paso in California exceeded the average breeding operation in Kentucky. Rancocas listed seventy-one mares on the grounds for 1879. "The intelligent horseman . . . will be struck by the strength of this stud, in the number, quality and fashion of its mares," commented the *Spirit of the Times*. The publication did not believe that these mares were always bred to the best stallions, but the point remained the same: a large operation like Rancocas held power in the vast amount of its breeding stock—and Rancocas was only one farm within the large concentration of power that lay centered on the East Coast.[32]

Benjamin Bruce dwelt on the rising trend in Thoroughbred racing: the number of dates was increasing across the country, particularly in New York. But the racing programs remained weak in talent owing to a paucity of good horses to fill the races. If Bluegrass horsemen wanted to reap the financial rewards from this growing sport, "our farmers can not do better than to buy a few head of high class thoroughbred mares to breed and meet this increased demand," he wrote.[33]

But the problem was how to acquire the best-bred mares. Once again, Kentucky horsemen could not compete with the moguls up East. "Mr. P. Lorillard is absorbing to his Rancocus [*sic*] Farm all the best mares in the country which money can purchase," reported the *Spirit of the Times*. Frank Harper, the nephew of John Harper, who had taken over the Nantura Farm horses on his uncle's death, bid $4,100 at an auction in Lexington on a mare that Pierre Lorillard also wanted. The mare's sire was the popular stallion Leamington, who had given Longfellow to the Harper family. Harper failed to get the mare, whose name was Kate Pearce. Lorillard's representative raised his bid to $4,150, and the mare went straight into the Rancocas empire in New Jersey. "Harper was anxious to get her but learned that Lorillard was prepared to go to $10,000," according to a newspaper report. All Bluegrass horsemen could share Harper's frustration. "We may add that well-bred young mares . . . are in demand in this country. . . . Those most fashionably bred are scarcely to be had at any price," the *Spirit of the Times* spoke out, joining the conversation. But who but the titans of the turf could afford to purchase these mares?[34]

The big money remained within the sphere of the Eastern jockey clubs or in the close connections that flowed from the Sanders Bruce pipeline, originating in New York and running down to Swigert in Kentucky. Until the new titans of the turf could be persuaded to relocate their breeding operations to Kentucky, no horse industry of significance or power possibly could emerge in the Bluegrass. Most horse-breeding operations on the farmland of central Kentucky were disparate and small in comparison to the operations of the Lorillards, Belmont, Welch, and others in the Northeast. They could not enjoy the ripple-down financial windfall that the relocation of the major studs inevitably would produce in Kentucky.

Nor had central Kentucky ever separated itself as the only geographic section renowned as horse country within the Bluegrass region. Belle Meade plantation, along with neighboring farms near Nashville, continued to produce top-quality Thoroughbreds for the market. Belle Meade listed ownership of sixty-seven Thoroughbred mares in 1880, a number representing a sizable operation. In 1880, Belle Meade lost a popular stallion, Bonnie Scotland, to death (the same year Bonnie Scotland posthumously earned distinction as the leading sire in North America; his twentieth-century descendants included the 1973 Triple Crown winner Secretariat and the 1989 Kentucky Derby and Preakness Stakes winner Sunday Silence). Soon afterward, Belle Meade paid $20,000 in gold for Iroquois, the winner of the Epsom Derby in 1881 for Pierre Lorillard. Enquirer, named for the *Cincinnati Enquirer* newspaper, arrived at Belle Meade in 1885 to stand at stud. Luke Blackburn, a son of Bonnie Scotland, went into the stud there in the mid-1880s and sired the Kentucky Derby runner-up of 1889, Proctor Knott. The latter two horses bore the names of Kentucky governors, Luke Pryor Blackburn (1879–1883) and J. Proctor Knott (1883–1887). Middle Tennessee as a horse-breeding region had fully recovered from the Civil War to compete successfully with central Kentucky. "Tennessee not only has the advantage of climate over Kentucky, but equally productive lands with unsurpassed grasses, while her fields are abundantly watered with never-failing springs, and these valuable lands can be purchased at a low price," a correspondent for the *Spirit of the Times* reported in 1880.[35]

One wealthy New Yorker, Charles Reed, heeded the siren call of Tennessee's Southern ambience and found himself in company with an archetypal Southern colonel, General William Jackson, whose Belle Meade plantation with its splendid residence looked every bit the part of a plantation manor home. Reed apparently thought that, by moving to Tennessee, he could find the competitive edge that others had tried to corner in the Northeast. But he stood alone in this maneuver. His powerful partners in the turf remained in the Northeast, where they thought that, by cornering the most popular bloodlines of the era, they would find their competitive edge.

This was one reason John Clay routinely took his horses to Maryland, New Jersey, and New York to race and, he hoped, to find buyers there willing to pay a greater price than he could have found in the Bluegrass. Clay had made this his practice since selling Kentucky at the Paterson track in New Jersey in 1863 and, later, another good horse called Jerome Edgar. He was still traveling the rails northeast in 1872 when he wrote to his wife, Josephine, back home on his stock farm, Ashland, about the difficulties of this lifestyle: "I am sleeping and eating in a stable 900 miles from my own dear wife, living so rough that I am sorely tried to persevere in it." Josephine managed Ashland in her husband's absence and proved as expert at breeding and raising Thoroughbreds as he was known to be.[36]

The fact that Clay made his living quarters in the stable with his horses might have represented the fashion of Bluegrass horsemen (remember that John Harper had done the same when he took his stable to the races). But this practice also might have demonstrated how Kentucky horsemen could ill afford to squander money when they took to the road. Clay estimated his monthly expenses on the road at $700, including money needed for racing his horses at Saratoga, Jerome Park, and Baltimore. This was almost as much money spent in one month as his best yearling brought at auction several years later in 1877. Back home at Ashland, a note for $7,000 was coming due in 1872. Clay informed Josephine that he had had to borrow money from Harper at the races in order to meet his expenses. He swore his intention to quit this livelihood and stay home. "Of one thing I am certain," he wrote, "and that is that whatever happens I train no more horses after this year and I wish next year was come."[37]

The fact that a son of the revered Henry Clay, five times a presidential candidate, the statesman known as the Great Compromiser, tried to meet his expenses by living in a stable said something about the reality of horse farming for those natives of Kentucky who pursued this line of work. John Clay was an odd sort who fought the inner demons of a troubled personality and was known to tip the bottle a bit more than perhaps he should have. All recognized him as a superb horseman, however. "I deem [him] among the best breeders and trainers in the Union," a writer informed the *Spirit of the Times* before the war in 1859. Clay spent more than forty years on the turf, known all the time for his unblemished honorable ways. Northern folk would have seen him as yet one more in the diverse lot of Bluegrass horsemen who frequented the racetracks, men as varied as the black jockey Isaac Murphy and old John Harper, who evoked a frontier past with his odd attire and his gray hair flying in the wind. The archetypal Kentucky colonel had not yet emerged.[38]

Like Zeke Clay, who led the posse to rescue Asteroid from horse thieves, John Clay had negotiated with the raiders of the Confederate general John Hunt Morgan for the return of a valuable broodmare and six other Thoroughbreds he owned. Clay had pursued Morgan's men after they stormed the barns at Ashland. He overtook the rebels at Georgetown, where he ransomed the seven horses for $900. Among them was a valuable broodmare prospect, Skedaddle. Clay wrote in his diary: "Stayed all night at Pratts Tavern in Georgetown after great anxiety and trouble about getting the horses from the Rebel robbers."[39]

Josephine Clay took over the operations at Ashland after John Clay's death in 1887. She was not the first woman to run a stock farm in the Bluegrass—Mary Warfield had operated Whitehall and rented pastures to the U.S. Army for the grazing of mules during the war in the absence of her husband, Cassius Clay. A small number of women in Kentucky, such as Mrs. Hart Gibson at Ingleside Stud, bred or owned racehorses during the latter part of the nineteenth century. A Mrs. Patterson, the widow of Rody Patterson, kept "high-bred" trotters at her place on Nicholasville Pike. Josephine Clay, however, stood out as a woman in the business because she operated the largest farm, owned the greatest number of broodmares, and was the most successful in the Thoroughbred business. Horses to which she had close connections in-

Josephine Clay managed the horse-breeding operation at the Ashland-on-Tates-Creek estate for her husband, John Clay, during his absences at the races. She became an expert at breeding and raising Thoroughbreds—in an era when women did not generally engage in this business. She took over the horse operation at Ashland entirely following her husband's death in 1887. (*Turf, Field and Farm*, March 18, 1898, 357.)

cluded two Kentucky Derby winners: Day Star (1878) and Riley, Ed Corrigan's 1890 winner.

Josephine Clay went outside conventional social boundaries that restricted her gender in order to promote and sell her Thoroughbred yearlings. A family story holds that occasionally she visited the Phoenix Hotel, known as the horsemen's headquarters, in downtown Lexington, where she mingled with the turfmen. She also occasionally joined the men in a poker game in the lobby of the hotel. Perhaps she was able to join horsemen in their card games because they all spoke the same language and everyone would have known her as the widow of a horseman they respected. In fact, Josephine became widely respected for her own knowledge of horses and pedigrees. She had overseen the care of their horses during her husband's frequent absences at the races. "I made a study of turf registers and became well acquainted with horse ancestry," she told the *Kansas City Star*. When William Collins Whitney of New York bought a Kentucky horse farm in 1901, people told him that the best initiative would be to buy all Josephine Clay's mares at any price. Josephine and her bloodstock held the respect of the industry.[40]

Kentucky folk knew Josephine Clay for her habit of donning a broad-brimmed straw hat and riding a horse through fields to visit each and every broodmare and its offspring. She said that she paid no more than twenty-five cents for her hats, so it troubled her not a bit when a horse would reach over and take a bite from one of them when she stopped to pat or speak to it. Some residents of the Bluegrass remarked that she preferred speaking to horses than people. They thought her a bit strange.

Her success was well known, however, for Josephine gained fame as an author as well as the owner of a horse farm. She was a woman ahead of her time, one whose achievements did not go unnoticed. The organizers of an international conference of women to be held in 1903 in Toronto sought her out to deliver an address. She was unable to attend, but she wrote remarks to be read at the conference. In her address—"Women and the Professions"—she stated that her experience in the production of Thoroughbred horses, "which is pre-eminently not a feminine occupation," stood as proof "that all pursuits are open to woman, and her only limitations lie within herself." She was a leading example of how a woman could succeed on her own in a man's world.[41]

With all her eccentricities, however, Josephine Clay presented quite a different notion of a Bluegrass woman than did the coquettish belle, a Kentucky type beginning to emerge in fiction and the imagination. Typical of this new woman was the female character in a stage play titled *In Old Kentucky*, which premiered in 1893. The script equated notions of the Southern colonel and the Southern belle with Kentucky, transposing these notions away from the Deep South and into the border state.

This popular melodrama played in New York, Boston, and Chicago in 1893–1894 and featured popular Kentucky themes: family feuding, violence, and horse racing. The cast included six Thoroughbreds. The Thoroughbreds dashed across the stage in the third act at the finish of a race held in Lexington and called the "Ashland Oaks Derby." The story line had the heroine, Madge Brierly, wishing to escape the longtime feuding of Kentucky mountain folk. She fell in love with a wealthy colo-

In Old Kentucky, a stage play that premiered in 1893, equated notions of the Southern colonel and the Southern belle with Kentucky, transplanting this imagery from the Deep South to the border state. The stage play ran for many years in various cities and became a movie. The cover for a piece of sheet music pertaining to the movie is shown here. (From the author's collection.)

nel from the Bluegrass and, as an expert horsewoman, rode his mare, Queen Bess, in the Ashland Oaks Derby. Madge Brierly overcame the treachery and snobbishness of the colonel's friends. She won the race on Queen Bess—and the colonel's hand in marriage. *In Old Kentucky* became a staple of stage shows and played for twenty-seven consecutive seasons in New York or on the road. In 1935, the stage play was remade into a silent movie. Arguably, the stage play of the 1890s played a role in influencing Americans to begin thinking of Bluegrass Kentucky in terms of the antebellum South. One account suggested that the production introduced the fictional Southern colonel. In reality, the story line was far removed from the lives of Josephine or John Clay, the Harpers, or most other native Bluegrass horsemen.[42]

The fact that the story line of this melodrama featured violence and mountain family feuding said as much about beliefs of people outside Kentucky as it did about the residents of the state. As always with notions of Kentucky violence, the result had to work against the full development of a Kentucky horse industry. Kentuckians could not deny that lawlessness continued to plague their state: the postwar violence publicized in the Bluegrass had, by the 1880s, expanded its reach on newspaper pages to include numerous internecine feuds in the mountains of eastern Kentucky.

Then, one horsemen of the powerful Northeast changed his mind about this region and its rich soil, minerals, grass, and bloodlines. Against all odds, and defying the negative publicity about violence in Kentucky, Belmont moved the breeding division of his Nursery Stud to Lexington in 1885. This decision created no small amount of editorial comment in the sporting periodicals and seemed highly surprising for a man who during the 1870s had seen Kentucky and the South as so overrun with violence that he pleaded with the U.S. Congress to investigate the activities of the Ku Klux Klan throughout the South and border-state Kentucky.[43]

But Belmont had finally come to the realization that his breeding program on Long Island was not producing the results he'd hoped for. Despite the expensive English imports, his racing stable had for a number of years not been as effective as he'd hoped. The Lorillards, the Dwyers, Keene, and others were beating him at his game. He needed a new competitive edge. And so he turned his attention to the Bluegrass and its mineral-rich soil. He decided to turn the Nursery of Long Island into a training center; he moved the bloodstock to central Kentucky to a farm he leased on Georgetown Road outside Lexington.[44]

Belmont's farm manager arrived in Lexington in 1885, fully armed because he feared bodily harm. He stepped off the train "covered all over with pistols and knives and other warlike weapons," read one report. He told Bluegrass horsemen, much to their amusement, "that all this was for his own protection only, and with no intention of attacking others, and that, finding things not quite as bad as he expected, he has quietly put most of his armory aside and out of sight." The fact that he arrived armed spoke volumes about the concern Northeastern horsemen had for traveling to the Bluegrass.[45]

Belmont had reached such a point of desperation, however, that he was willing to enter into denial over the danger and economic instability he and his farm manager had long believed existed south and southwest of the East Coast. This belief harkened to 1870, when Belmont had offered to finance an investigation of the Ku Klux Klan. But, by 1885, when Belmont made his momentous decision to transfer his breeding program to the Bluegrass, horse racing had expanded so far beyond its scope in 1865 or even 1870 that he chose to overlook his prior concerns. The violence had not ceased in Kentucky. It escalated with mountain feuds, with racial violence throughout the state, and, ultimately, with the assassination of Governor William Goebel in 1900. The renewed desire to find a competitive edge in this sport that had expanded to bring in so many new men saw Belmont revise his thinking about Kentucky. The desire to win could cloud a man's perceptions that way. The irony was that his son, August, would further entrench his economic interests in Kentucky when eventually he assumed a key role on the board of the Louisville and Nashville Railroad.[46]

For Kentucky horsemen, Belmont's moving Nursery Stud to Lexington was the greatest boost their industry had received thus far. The boosterism of the Bruce brothers and the reputation for fast horses and knowledgeable horsemen that persons like Isaac Murphy, John Harper, John and Josephine Clay, and many other Kentuckians had helped promote would begin to turn the attention of other Northeastern turfmen to Kentucky after Belmont moved Nursery Stud.

Belmont's friend Milton Sanford had preceded him and purchased

Bluegrass farm property in 1872, but Sanford had been traveling to central Kentucky for such a long time—since before the war—that Kentucky horsemen looked on him as one of their own. Belmont was the first among outside capitalists lacking long-standing ties to the Bluegrass to transfer his breeding operations there. Nursery Stud would add an entirely new dimension to the map of existing horse farms, which were predominantly owned by locals. This marked a turning point for the horse region of Kentucky. "The very fact that Mr. Belmont realized the inability of himself or any other man to breed the best horses outside of Kentucky should be born in mind today by some who claim that the East affords just as good opportunity, and who are establishing or removing their studs to the East," the *Lexington Herald* stated, tooting the horn of regional boosterism.[47]

Belmont did, indeed, cause the scales to slough off the eyes of his fellow New York sportsmen. Though he would not live to see the greatest personal consequence of embracing the Bluegrass, one could say he set in motion events that would bring his son, also called August, but a man who did not want a *II* or a *Jr.* attached to his name, to breed the greatest racehorse of all time: Man o' War, foaled in 1917 at Nursery Stud in Lexington. But Belmont did begin a trend, one that started off slowly at first but eventually brought the turf moguls of the twentieth century to the Bluegrass to establish their breeding studs.

The elder Belmont died in 1890, a time when the entire United States was beginning to undergo societal changes that would affect horse racing significantly. He did not live long enough to see his vision for racing go awry with the descent of the sport from an arena for the improvement of the horse to a sphere controlled by gamblers and dishonest men. He did not live to see Progressive Era reformers shut down racing in many states, most remarkably in New York, where Belmont's social set once had held so much power. He did not live to see the passing of the horse from a utilitarian animal to an animal with a questionable future when replaced in the early twentieth century with the automobile. And he did not see the changes that placed Kentucky at the center of a newly shaped vision of the racehorse and horse country, a vision charged with powerful meanings that saw winners and losers among whites and blacks.

This new way in which Americans came to perceive Kentucky and its racehorses brought outside capitalists to completely change the way they viewed horse country and its lawlessness, its backwardness, and all they had previously considered detrimental to investment in the region. And so Bluegrass Kentucky slowly began to regain its antebellum position of power, a position that saw it as the cradle of the nation's racehorses. However, this newly constructed image of horse country would turn the Bluegrass into something entirely different than it was before the Civil War.

chapter SIX

Winners and Losers in the Age of Reform

Each time the sport of horse racing attempted to participate in the good feelings and free-flowing money that marked the lives of at least the elite class during the supposedly carefree Gay Nineties, it took a series of unsettling blows. Racing continued to expand beyond all expectations, with more than three hundred racetracks operating throughout the United States, six in the region of New York. This vast expansion brought a proliferation of problems, not the least of these the spread of racetrack gambling into the urban poolrooms that the working and the lowest economic classes patronized.

Poolrooms (i.e., betting shops) made offtrack wagering possible, offering direct competition with the racetracks. One way in which racetracks attempted to fight the poolrooms was by forbidding the use of the telegraph on track grounds. The intention was to block the transmission of race results to the betting shops, with the hope of putting them out of business. Track owners and operators were painfully cognizant that the poolrooms "enabled people to bet without attending the races, and, hence, drew largely from the attendance at the track," as the *Spirit of the Times* noted. Monmouth Park in New Jersey did not stop at banning the telegraph. This track formulated a plan to maintain secrecy on the names of entered horses until twenty minutes prior to each race, when the track would distribute printed slips of paper with this information. As the *Spirit* reported in 1890: "The effect was that no one . . . at noon had any idea of what was going to start. Added to this, the police made a raid on the pool rooms in town, and the city business was at a standstill. The effect of this was the enormous attendance present. People could not back the horses in town and were compelled to go to the track."[1]

More worrisome to the sport than the competition these poolrooms presented was the magnet they became in drawing the attention of social reformers. One thing led to another. In a short time, reformers began to expand their critical look beyond the poolrooms to the entire sport of horse racing. In their minds, they appeared unable to separate the racetracks from the offtrack shops that functioned like parasites feeding off the sport. A groundswell of antiracing reform began building momentum in a number of states; although the movement did not evolve as a cohesive effort under a national organization, it did affect racing on a nationwide scale.

The social concern over poolrooms simmered at low decibels during the 1890s, but the concern was, indeed, increasing. Poolrooms represented only a portion of gambling options; nonetheless, the manner in which all gambling operated openly on city streets alarmed a great many middle-class citizens. According to one account about Chicago: "Clark Street was the scene of every form of gambling from galloping dominoes to whizzing roulette wheels. Leather-lunged barkers were posted along the sidewalks at strategic points urging passers-by to enter and try their luck in the glittering palaces of chance that lined the hectic thoroughfare. Poolrooms, conducted by a well-known syndicate, . . . were prominent units in this gambling layout. In these rooms, bets could be made on races run at other points in addition to Chicago."[2]

Lexington and Louisville also were home to a number of poolrooms. A Fayette County grand jury began an investigation of local poolrooms in 1892, with the judge instructing the jury that he did not intend to ignore "the great vice." The intensity of such concern escalated into the early twentieth century in Lexington and included allegations of the city police looking the other way, allowing the poolrooms to operate outside the law. The telegraph enabled the poolrooms in Lexington to offer betting on races in such places as New York and Chicago. "Young Men Ruined by Pool Rooms," proclaimed a headline in a Lexington newspaper in 1905, but not until 1909 did the Kentucky Court of Appeals put the betting shops out of business by ruling that operators of poolrooms could be held liable for breaking the law.[3]

Social concern over poolrooms merely constituted the warm-up to antiracing legislation, however. Early in the twentieth century, when Progressive Era reforms came into vogue, state legislative wallop would pack authoritative power into the escalating outcry to ban all Thoroughbred racing—everywhere. In the spirit leading up to those reforms, middle-class concern about the state of society was blaming a good number of the nation's moral ills on gambling as well as on alcohol, prostitution, and the stranglehold big business had on American progress.

America's middle class saw a multitude of reasons to feel threatened and feel inspired to initiate or at least plead for social and economic reform. As an increasing number of small businesses failed during the financial panic that prevailed from 1893 until 1897, the middle class began to look like an endangered stratum of American society. Small, family-owned businesses no longer could compete with the large corporations and conglomerates of the industrialists. Demographic changes had brought increasing numbers of Americans to the cities, but what they found there was crime, violent labor strikes, and waves of immigrants arriving from Eastern European countries to fill the expanding needs of the labor force. Middle-class Americans could turn in one direction and observe the upper classes living hedonistic lifestyles of great excess, lifestyles out of reach of most Americans. Or they could turn in the other direction and watch with horror the swelling urban slums wrought with crime, gambling, prostitution, and alcoholism. Reform-minded persons of the middle class sought to clean up these moral ills affecting society's lowest classes—and, in doing so, threatened the interests of society's wealthiest class, at least when it came to its favorite sport, horse racing.[4]

This was not to say that Lexington wholeheartedly embraced the Progressive Era reform movement, at least not in the beginning. City authorities sparred with the poolroom operators, certainly. However, the poolroom crusade turned out to be little more than window dressing. Lexington remained in 1901 where it had lingered for some time: a city "cursed with disease, high mortality rates, air pollution, poor drinking water, a wasteful taxation system, and an overall disregard for the city charter," as James Duane Bolin has written.[5]

Considering these ills, Lexington might have seemed a prime candidate for Progressive reform. Still, even at the turn of the century, the city remained under the lingering spell of a former political machine boss, Dennis Mulligan. The legacy of his iron rule of graft and spoils was a political system that operated much the same as before he had lost his control of municipal politics twenty years earlier. Lexington had too much catching up to accomplish by the dawn of the new century.[6]

A new political boss moved in to fill the vacuum—and, in a new wrinkle, Bluegrass landowners controlled this man's politics. This was William Frederick "Billy" Klair, whose political acuity Bolin compares to "an assertive and oppressive paternalism that secured power for the elite" class of the old planter oligarchy. Bolin cites Malcolm Jewell and Everett Cunningham, who argued that the early Progressive reform movement had little effect on Kentucky owing to the conservative political alignments of railroad, coal-mining, liquor, and racetrack interests with "Bluegrass farmers and political leaders of both parties[, which] retarded progressive reforms." One could suggest that, in the eyes of this group, reform was a good thing as long as it eliminated the competition the poolrooms presented to their well-loved Kentucky Association racetrack, but a bad thing if it affected the ruling power of this elite class in any way. When the Progressive movement gathered momentum and took aim at the sport of horse racing nationwide, Bluegrass horse breeders no longer stood on the side of social reform. Under a headline that read "Heavy Blow to Kentucky," the *Lexington Leader* published a major story in 1908 that stated: "The passing of the [New York] anti–race track betting bills has caused gloom. . . . The situation is indeed dark in Kentucky, where the breeding of thoroughbreds is perhaps the greatest industry in the State."[7]

Some years before this story appeared in Lexington, racing's leaders in New York had sensed the increasing desire of reformers to wipe out the sport. The *Spirit of the Times* attempted to mediate, reminding everyone of the huge fortunes invested in the breeding of racehorses. It intoned: "These valuable sports should not be subjected to injury by the resurrection of some old Puritanical blue law." However, the final word on this would not be the province of the *Spirit*. It would rest with the rising reform sentiment and proreform legislators.

New York's racing patrons were only too familiar with the cycles of repression and expansion as they had long occurred in the constant tug-of-war between reformers and sportsmen in that state. The founders of

Jerome Park must have felt the threat of reform at their flanks when they opened their swank new racecourse in 1866, for they had made efforts from the start to placate those who opposed horse racing. Men like Jerome, Belmont, and Travers thought they would accomplish this by lending their social approval and cachet to the sport, thereby giving it the appearance of wholesomeness.

Turf, Field and Farm made the argument in 1868 that the elite status of turf sports lent a wholesome character to racing, framing its argument by likening the sport in America to the sport of kings in England and Europe. "In the Old World it is smiled upon by kings, queens and emperors," it stated, "and in the New World it is patronized by wealth and intelligence, as well as keenly enjoyed by the masses. In view of these facts it is about time that the fanatics ceased to denounce the race course as an arena for the growth of rowdyism and obscenity." As periodicals of that era were fond of pointing out, the display of fashionable attire at Jerome Park might even have the beneficial effect of influencing the lower classes, thereby inspiring the masses to self-improvement. As *Turf, Field and Farm* wrote: "The imperial goddess of fashion sends forth her edicts from the Club Stand and Club House of Jerome Park; and fashion, in our country, graduates from the highest social circles to the lowest."[8]

By 1890, racing had slipped beyond the exclusive control of society leaders and any semblance of order that their social cachet could lend. The sport's expansion even led to angst among large numbers of its most elite participants. They lamented the passing of previous decades, when, at least as they recalled it, horse racing was dedicated to pure sport and not to crass commercialism. As events had evolved, the sport's rapid expansion had given rise to a three-headed monster: the number of racetracks proliferated; the tracks felt the pressure of competition and so raised purses to attract the numbers of horses needed to fill their programs; and, consequently, the tracks increasingly depended on public admission fees and on bookmakers to produce the money for these purses and other operating expenses. Previously, horse owners had provided these funds through their private club memberships and fees paid for nominating their horses to run in races. By 1890, the sport's commercial turn had become apparent to everyone. This trend would only increase in subsequent years.

The first bookmaker was said to have begun business in Philadelphia in 1866, taking bets on cricket, rowing, and racing. Throughout the next thirty years, the importance of bookmakers to racetracks had become obvious to everyone. Racetrack expenses had grown to the point that operators could not manage financially without the operating fees they charged bookmakers. Each bookmaker paid a daily licensing fee to the track, generally $100. With a racecourse in a major city having perhaps sixty to one hundred bookmakers operating during a single day's racing, the money to be gleaned from licensing fees spoke powerfully to the owners of racetracks. Need and greed became the twin devils manipulating this synergy between bookmakers and racecourses. People had long debated the pros and cons of seeing the bookmakers (and, before them, the ontrack auction pool sellers) ascend to a position of necessity in racing. "The racing code encourages speculation by legalized betting," noted *Harper's New Monthly Magazine*. "And for what? It is safe to say, to gratify the depraved appetites of about one hundred and fifty men of questionable character. Watch at Saratoga, or Jerome Park, where you please, the crowd that gathers around the pool stand. Meeting after meeting the faces are the same. Those who bid in the pools are professional gamblers. A gentleman of respectable business connections does not like to be seen in that wrangling crowd."[9]

Accompanying the proliferation of bookmakers and professional gamblers was the chicanery that goes hand in hand with the siren call of the big money to be won gambling, including horse drugging, race fixing, and the bribing of jockeys. "Legalized betting encourages promiscuous gambling; and promiscuous gambling excites passion, and points the way to fraud," opined *Harper's*. Fraudulent practices became known through articles published in newspapers and the sporting press. Because of this reportage, racing's audience certainly was aware of what was transpiring. Suspicion about the honesty of jockeys and horsemen became widespread. The sport was acquiring a poor reputation as a result of dishonest practices. Northeastern racing no longer had the aura of sport for sport's sake that Belmont and Jerome originally had brought to the game.[10]

As far south as New Orleans, fraud and commercialism had changed the sport. Writing about New Orleans, Dale Somers cites bookmaking as bearing only part of the responsibility for this change.

"Racing's integrity declined in large part because control of the sport shifted from the planter aristocracy to professional sportsmen," he argues. One could have said the same about the Northeast, by substituting "Belmont et al." for "planter aristocracy."[11]

An internecine gambling war also loomed. Bookmakers and the major gamblers resisted the primitive pari-mutuel machines that Pierre Lorillard had brought over to the United States from France in 1871, when the machines were known as *Paris Mutuel Pools* (hence the Americanization of the term into *pari-mutuel betting*). Pari-mutuel machines allowed for a minimum $5 wager when a small number of them first appeared in North America; they held the potential to appeal to patrons who could not afford the large wagers that bookmakers took. The bookmakers, in turn, had displaced the auction pools that had been the earlier form of racetrack betting. And now the bookmakers saw the machines as cutting in on their action. Heavy gamblers like Mike Dwyer detested the machines because gamblers using them could not manipulate the odds, as they could when attempting to outwit the bookmakers. No one could agree on what was best for the sport. Truthfully, few cared.[12]

Racetracks also fought among themselves. Different groups of tracks banded together into various "turf associations" with one association sometimes prohibiting the entry of horses that had raced at another. Moreover, some tracks failed to honor the rulings of other tracks, ignoring or overlooking official decisions that would have denied participation anywhere to an owner, trainer, or jockey for an infraction of the rules at the track where the ruling originated. Consequently, these rulings lacked the official backing that would have made them universally effective. The banned offenders simply moved their action to whatever racetrack would take them in.

Here, again, Kentucky racing found itself at odds with the sport in New York. On one occasion, when the New York tracks failed to reciprocally honor a ruling that barred two jockeys, this action struck the president of the Louisville Jockey Club, Colonel Clark, as a slap in the face. Benjamin Bruce used the pages of his *Kentucky Livestock Record* to lambaste the New York decision as a contemptible insult to Kentucky: "The West [i.e., Kentucky] has done everything in her power to conciliate the East, has tried to have a uniform set of rules and even gone so far as to meet the East on their ground, but with no good result." The regional tension that had been so apparent in the controversy over Asteroid and Kentucky never had completely dissipated. Periodically, the tension bubbled to the surface of the slowly stewing pot, and the sporting press occasionally took notice.[13]

The real headlinemakers were the high-rolling gamblers whose mercurial adventures at the racetracks went on full public display for newspaper readers. The great number of column inches devoted to their stories sometimes implied a suspicion of race fixing, which, in turn, drew the attention of social reformers. John Wayne "Bet a Million" Gates was one of the sport's new arrivals during the Gilded Age. He started out selling barbed wire in the West and visiting gambling palaces in the cattle towns where he sold his product. Eventually, he made his way east to Wall Street. One biographer wrote: "In an age of unprecedented industrial expansion, fantastic risk taking, ruthless exploitation, Gates was the most daring builder, the biggest gambler, the sharpest promoter of them all. He challenged the kings of the wheat pits, the lords of steel, the barons of mining and railroading, the oil and financial rules in his heedless, slashing career." According to another biographer: "For sheer daring and raw nerve none of them [i.e., the high rollers on the turf] could hold a candle to Gates." One story held that, on one occasion, he won at least $2 million on a single race. Most Americans knew that he died broke.[14]

Gates and Belmont stood in complete opposition when it came to their purposes for pursuing the sport of racing. Belmont believed that Gates and the excessive amounts of money he wagered tainted the reputation of the turf. Interestingly, Corrigan, of Chicago's Hawthorne Park, liked Gates and forwarded tips on his horses to him. Men like Gates received their inside information in various ways, among them, pressing jockeys for information on their mounts. "Many times scandals brewed from these paddock conferences between the rider and some big operator," noted the *Thoroughbred Record*. "For many years heavy bettors, like John W. Gates, Jesse Lewisohn, Dave Gideon, Dr. J. Grant Lyman, Mattie Corbett and the late George E. Smith ("Pittsburg Phil") could be seen buttonholing jockeys five minutes before the boys had mounted. . . . Hereafter the only persons who will be permitted to talk with the jockeys are the owner of the horse to be ridden, the trainers and the jockeys' guardians."[15]

By 1890, Pierre Lorillard had decided that he had seen more than he cared to of warring racetracks, dishonesty in the sport, and the increasingly critical look that social reformers were casting toward horse racing. He organized a dinner in New York, inviting twenty-four prominent patrons of the turf to hear his plea for organizing the sport. The outcome was their agreement to form a national board, beginning in 1891, for the purpose of reforming the sport. Generally, their club has been known as the Board of Control. Originally, Lorillard did not invite the Dwyer brothers despite the fact that they controlled the Brooklyn Jockey Club and two tracks in New Jersey. This appeared as a social slight and, perhaps, also an acknowledgment that the Dwyers were business competitors, operating their tracks in direct opposition to Jerome Park, the Coney Island Jockey Club at Sheepshead Bay, and Morris Park, tracks all owned and operated by New York's elite class of turfmen. Later, Lorillard changed his mind. He invited Phil Dwyer to serve on the board of directors of this "national" club. The name of the group actually was misleading, for it was not at all national; its seven members represented only the four major racing associations of the East—Sheepshead Bay, Gravesend, Monmouth Park, and Westchester—plus three racing stables, including that of John Hunter. Bluegrass Kentucky had not been included in this exclusive group.[16]

Kentuckians undoubtedly resented this latest insult to the state's standing in the sport, but they already were dealing with a more devastating problem. A mysterious and deadly disease had crept into the emerald fields of the Bluegrass during the winter of 1890. Mares had begun aborting their unborn foals at an alarming rate, and no horseman, no matter how deep his equine knowledge, knew the origin of this malady. Many wondered whether a phenomenally warm and wet January might be the cause.[17]

The foals were intended to be the cash crop either that season, when they were weanlings, or the next, when they were yearlings. The situation began to look dire: the "slipping disease," as people began calling these mysterious stillbirths, was threatening to rob the Bluegrass of its young racehorse prospects. One estimate put the loss as high as 75 percent of unborn foals. Mares of all breeds, but most importantly Thoroughbreds and Standardbreds, were losing their embryos. The telltale sign of miscarriage was generally the same everywhere: a small, bloody mass left on the ground or in the stall of a broodmare. The *Spirit of the Times* reported to its nationwide audience that Kentucky weanlings were in short supply from the 1890 crop, owing to the slipping malady. The news coming out of Kentucky was not good. The Bluegrass region had long been haunted by the notorious violence and lawlessness and now appeared tainted with unidentified germs.[18]

The disease returned the following winter and spring foaling season of 1891. Once again, horsemen wondered whether the weather might have had something to do with it, for 1891 had begun with a phenomenally warm January, accompanied by rapidly thawing ground. But no one really knew what the source of the problem was. Bluegrass breeders knew only that their pocketbooks would be affected. They feared that the news reports of this mysterious disease killing off the second foal crop in as many years could prove nearly as devastating as the actual loss of foals. They mounted a quick attempt at damage control, informing the *Spirit of the Times* that "rumors" of another year of the slipping disease were highly exaggerated. Whatever was killing the horses in Kentucky was not helping sell the Bluegrass as a desirable location for breeding farms. The impact of the foal disease threatened to steer potential investors away. Bluegrass breeders struggled with the devastating loss to their foal crops.

At precisely this time when the Bluegrass needed a boost either from public relations or development, help appeared on the horizon. The Silver Fox of Wall Street, James R. Keene, returned to horse racing in 1891. The man who had won the 1879 Belmont Stakes with Spendthrift and then sent Foxhall on a successful mission to France in 1881 was back in the sport. Americans had not forgotten his success a decade earlier when Foxhall become the first American horse to win France's greatest race, the Grand Prix de Paris, followed a year later with a victory in the Ascot Gold Cup, the renowned English race.

Keene epitomized the sort of wealthy man whose spectacular rise and mercurial fall on Wall Street fascinated America's financially strapped middle class. His story represented an amazing rags-to-riches tale. He had recovered from financial ruin and was spending heavily on horses with a newly made fortune. The ramifications for Bluegrass Kentucky were huge and came just in time to offset the devastation that the slipping disease had inflicted on the region.

The main residence at Castleton Farm in Lexington. James R. Keene purchased Castleton but visited the farm only twice. He typified the absentee owner, representing a class of wealthy men who began buying up horse-farm property in the Bluegrass late in the nineteenth century. (Ford Photo Album Collection, 1890–1904, KLGSC-FORD-77.01.007, Special Collections, University of Louisville.)

Keene had reentered the turf world by purchasing Brookdale Farm in Red Bank, New Jersey, on the death of the farm's founder, David Dunham Withers. But, before long, he, like Belmont, turned his attention to Lexington. In 1892, seven years following Belmont's move to Kentucky, he bought 600 acres of farmland that had once belonged to the Breckinridge family estate, Cabell's Dale. Keene called his new place Castleton Farm. He would enlarge the farm to 1,070 acres before selling it to another New Yorker, David M. Look, in 1911.[19]

Keene's development of Castleton Farm into the premier power-house of racing was a milestone along the path toward the Bluegrass regaining its singular renown. Americans were well aware of his financial ruin in 1884, which led to his hiatus from racing. He had attempted to corner the wheat market, pouring his entire fortune into that effort. Jay Gould, his bitter rival, had countered that action by ordering his agents to glut the market. This ruined Keene, sending him out of New York via that literal boxcar that Gould had wished on him. Edward L. Bowen quotes an account of Keene's radically altered lifestyle following his financial ruin: "I used to see him going to and from his little cottage in the country because he was, like myself, too poor to live in the city. I was poor, too, but I could still afford to have my wife's phaeton meet me at the station. Not so with Keene. He walked from the station to his house. I have seen him in the dead of winter struggling through the snow drifts, with his head lowered and his body bent, walking against the wind, a dismal figure on the chill landscape."[20]

Keene bent his body into the wind until he climbed back to the top. He engineered some major business coups for the banker J. P. Morgan and grew rich again himself. The latter had hired him in 1890 to wrest control of the Northern Pacific Railroad from Edward Henry Harriman. Keene accomplished the job by means of stock manipulation. He had always demonstrated extraordinary perception and cunning on Wall Street, and he was at his best in this instance. "Keene was a master at buying cheap, then manipulating share prices upward" until the public caught on and charged in afterward, following his lead, according to Bowen, who quotes the English writer on turf matters Edward Moorhouse: "He did not bet on fluctuations. He made them." Returning to racing, Keene imported forty-four English mares and with his son, Foxhall Keene, paid $3,000 for a son of the Kentucky stallion Himyar. The colt's name was Domino. That name would become synonymous with speed on the racetrack—and with Bluegrass Kentucky. Domino's influence on the breed as a stallion would be immeasurable.[21]

Keene could not have returned to Thoroughbred racing in a more spectacular way than with Domino. The horse was a wonder on the track, for he remained undefeated at age two, setting an earnings record that stood intact for thirty-eight years. Domino's life story could have served as illustrative of the struggles of Bluegrass horse farming and its increasing dependence on New York racing after the Civil War. Domino's breeder, Major Barak G. Thomas, a former Confederate, had returned from the war financially ruined, discovering that, while he was away, his assets had been sold to cover his debts. Practically all he had

Domino's name became synonymous with speed on the racetrack. People called this horse, owned by James R. Keene, the Black Whirlwind. He was a champion and the best sprinter of his time (1893–1895). Retired to Castleton Farm, he had a great influence on the Thoroughbred breed. (W. S. Vosburgh, *Racing in America, 1866–1921* [New York: Scribner Press, 1922], facing 162.)

left was a yearling Thoroughbred filly, a daughter of Lexington named Hira. She raced with moderate success in Kentucky. Major Thomas also traded some land he owned in Alabama for a mare named Dixie, who developed into a significant broodmare, thereby supplementing the major's income. In the beginning, Thomas did not rely on breeding horses for his sole financial support; among other endeavors, he was the general manager of the *Lexington Observer and Reporter*. But, by 1877, when he had regained sufficient financial strength to purchase 250 acres on Russell Cave Pike, he did turn the majority of his attention to horse breeding. He named his farm Dixiana, in honor of the mare Dixie, and, in an unabashed display of his personal eccentricities, he placed a sign on the iron gates at the entrance to Dixiana:

NOTHING EXCEPT
A GOOD
RACE HORSE
WANTED

***

AGENTS
FOR THE SALE OF
BOOKS, PATENT MEDICINES,
SEWING MACHINES,
AGRICULTURAL IMPLEMENTS,
HORTICULTURE &
NURSERY PRODUCTS AND
ESPECIALLY
OF LIGHTNING RODS
AND WIRE FENCES
NOT ADMITTED

***

VISITORS
OF EVERY NATIONALITY
WHO WILL COME UN TO MY HOUSE
ALWAYS WELCOME

***

B. G. Thomas[22]

Thomas raced Hira in New York because that was where you had to send a promising racehorse whether you wanted to sell it or to build its reputation so that its offspring would sell well. Eventually, the major brought Hira back to Kentucky to serve as a broodmare. Her third foal, a colt sired by Alarm and born in 1875, was named Himyar, an outstanding racehorse whose destiny was to sire Domino, the fastest horse the major bred, and the horse that would mark the return to the sport by Keene.

The major sent Domino among his consignment of yearlings to be sold in New York at the annual Tattersall's sale in 1892. Foxhall Keene purchased the colt for $3,000, and Domino went into the father-son racing stable. Thomas no longer owned the Dixiana Farm—his finan-

On Domino's death in 1897 at Castleton Farm, his owner, James R. Keene, had the horse returned to his birthplace, Major Barak Thomas's Hira Villa Farm. The horse's body was delivered to the grave site in a horse-drawn wagon. The grave stone was inscribed: "Here lies the fleetest runner the American turf has ever known, and the gamest and most generous of horses." (C. Frank Dunn Photographs Collection, KNU1987PH2-3484, Kentucky Historical Society.)

cial situation had forced him to sell out in 1890 to Jacob S. Coxey, a populist from Ohio who, in 1894, during the financial depression, was to lead bands of unemployed men—called Coxey's Army—in a march from Ohio to Washington, DC. Coxey's Army demanded that the federal government create jobs for the unemployed. Coxey, his wife, and his son, Legal Tender Coxey, accompanied the marchers. By that time, Thomas was well established at his new, smaller farm, Hira Villa Stud, where Domino was born in 1891. By 1893, the year of the nationwide financial panic and the year preceding the march of Coxey's Army on Washington, Domino had moved to the head of Keene's racing stable and acquired a popular nickname synonymous with his extraordinary talent: the Black Whirlwind.[23]

Like Coxey, Keene had set up his breeding farm in Kentucky; unlike Coxey, who would own Dixiana Farm for only three years, he would exert an enormous influence on horse breeding. Castleton Farm developed into the dominant Thoroughbred nursery in the nation in terms of champion horses produced. From 1893 through 1912, the father-son team bred 113 stakes winners, among them four of the greatest to compete on American racetracks: Colin, Commando, Peter Pan, and Sysonby. Kent Hollingsworth writes in a history of Thoroughbred champions that Keene "more or less wrote the *American Stud Book* around the turn of the century." True, Sanders Bruce had written the first six volumes of the actual stud book, yet "it was Keene's horses which provided the significant copy: Spendthrift, Kingston, Domino, Voter, Commando, Cap and Bells, Delhi, Sysonby, Peter Pan, Ballot, Colin, Celt, Ultimus, Maskette, Sweep, Black Toney, Pennant, and such. The foregoing list of champions and leading sires owned or bred by Keene suggests that racing and breeding Thoroughbreds at the turn of the century was his private preserve." In other words, Keene dominated the game.[24]

Keene visited Castleton only twice during the nearly twenty years he owned the farm. He remained in New York and on the racecourses near that city as well in Europe, where his stable also was successful. Once more seated at the pinnacle of Wall Street, he relished life as the owner of a racing stable stocked with the finest equine athletes. The recognition afforded him as the owner of the dominant racing operation in America was enhanced by the fact that he had not purchased these horses at a public sale but bred and raised most of them. This matter of pride in his home-bred horses drove his energies in the sport, much as the same pride had driven Belmont.

Keene did not personally oversee the breeding and raising of these horses. He entrusted that job, as well as the management of the farm, to his brother-in-law, Major Foxhall Daingerfield. In this practice, Keene followed a similar absentee-ownership pattern that Alexander John Alexander had initiated at Woodburn Farm on inheriting that estate in 1867 from his brother. Belmont similarly had structured Nursery Farm around this absentee-owner model when he moved the operation to Kentucky in 1885. Keene and Belmont stood in the vanguard of a new type of horse-farm owner that would begin coming to the Bluegrass in greater numbers. Major Thomas, John and Josephine Clay, and, before them, old John Harper had been farm owners of a different type, making their primary residences on these properties, and generally managing the farms themselves. Keene and Belmont represented the new type of absentee horse-farm owner soon to replace the smaller, owner-operated horse farms in the Bluegrass.

Keene's success on the racecourse brought so much attention to Castleton Farm that racing historians generally have overlooked his prior ownership of a famous stud farm in New Jersey. His purchase of Brookdale Farm had followed a model that owners of racing stables had accepted since the return of the sport to New York following the Civil War. The question, then, was why Keene changed his mind about New Jersey and turned to Kentucky.

He might have seen merit in August Belmont's decision to transfer Nursery Stud to Lexington in 1885, for Belmont had turned his track fortunes around in 1890 to become the nation's leading breeder. The success that Belmont realized off his Kentucky farm had not brought Eastern turf moguls in great droves to Kentucky, however. Something else must have changed Keene's mind.

What cannot be overlooked was the timing of Keene's purchase of Castleton Farm. This occurred in a time frame that coincided with the rise of antiracing sentiment in the Northeast. Perhaps Keene had begun to consider Kentucky as a more stable environment for race-horse breeding because thus far the state had essentially ignored the antiracing momentum building everywhere else throughout the United States.

Whatever his reasons for transferring his operation to Bluegrass Kentucky, Keene, like Belmont, overlooked the rampant lawlessness that had rendered the Bluegrass unsuitable in the eyes of a previous generation of Northeastern horsemen. In modern terms, these men assumed a sense of denial. In 1900, Kentucky violence reached its zenith with the assassination of Governor William Goebel. Some have viewed the assassination as a consequence of a fight Goebel had engaged in with the Louisville and Nashville Railroad, a powerful entity that had enjoyed considerable state government influence. Its president was August Belmont II.

The killing of a state governor aside, violence still raged in every direction in Kentucky. To the east in the mountains, feuds brought negative attention to the state. Altina Waller has argued that social change sparked these famous feuds. In her view, mountaineers feuded out of negative reaction to upheavals brought by the arrival of outsiders and industry focused on timbering and coal mining. No doubt, the mountaineers experienced displacement and disempowerment in the process of eastern Kentucky becoming colonized by emigrants from the industrial states, as Ron Eller has argued. But these are modern historical arguments. Nineteenth-century Americans read about these widely publicized mountain feuds and received further reinforcement for the notions they harbored that Kentuckians were violent and backward.[25]

The odd twist was that eastern Kentucky was beginning to be seen as the locus of violence in the state. The reality was that violence and lawlessness did not diminish in any part of Kentucky, including the horse country of the Bluegrass. From 1896 to 1896, Kentuckians engaged in a Tollgate War, tearing down or burning the ubiquitous tollgates that blocked most roads, including those approaching Lexington. People had become weary of paying tolls to pass through the gates; as things generally went in Kentucky, some took up their guns to prove their point.[26]

On the heels of the Tollgate War came the Black Patch War, a phase of vigilante violence that began in the tobacco fields of western Kentucky and spread to the Bluegrass. Night riders wreaked havoc on tobacco-growing farms, setting fire to barns. In central Kentucky, where most farms raised tobacco in addition to horses, the violence was believed to have touched Haggin's Elmendorf Farm. Newspapers initially placed blame for a barn burning on night riders. However, Elmendorf Farm claimed that this was not the case. Nonetheless, several more incidents of barn burnings in central Kentucky did point to the night riders of the tobacco wars. This reign of terror seemed like the Ku Klux Klan reprised, with a twist: during the tobacco wars, farmers felt threatened, regardless of their race. The wars were intended to unite all farms in ceasing to grow tobacco until the giant trusts met the growers' price demands.[27]

Thus, it seemed ironic when men like Belmont and, later, Keene looked to central Kentucky with capital investments in mind, considering Northeastern titans of the turf had long considered the Bluegrass too unstable for development. But, when compared to the increasingly dubious outlook for the future of New York racing, Kentucky might not have looked so unstable regardless of its lawlessness. A racing official at the Latonia Race Course in northern Kentucky remarked in 1891 that the Thoroughbred interest was so paramount and all pervading in the Bluegrass that Kentucky would be the last state in the Union to enact antiracing legislation. Keene arguably agreed with this idea. Despite two years of slipping disease in Kentucky, despite the lawlessness that continued to give the state a bad name, Keene took the plunge and purchased Kentucky land, just as interest in social reform rose higher in New York.[28]

Two years following his purchase of Castleton Farm, Keene took a bold step to protect New York racing and, as well, his huge investment in his Kentucky breeding farm. He spearheaded the organization of a new jockey club in the hope of bringing the type of reform and order to the sport that the Board of Control had been unable to accomplish. This amounted to a preemptive strike intended to negate the power and legislative influence that the social reformers were amassing. But, though they tried to clean up their own house, racing's reformers like Keene would see their own power minimized when the juggernaut that was Progressive social reform reached full flower early in the twentieth century.

The founding members of the new Jockey Club included twenty-seven elite patrons of Eastern racing. Their intention was to control racing and see it conducted to their own standards. Unlike its predecessor, the Board of Control, this group did possess the power needed to control the sport; this happened because the new Jockey Club represented racing's interests more fully than had the Board of Control. Keene wanted to see the Jockey Club organized along the pattern of the prestigious English Jockey Club, in which titled landowners ruled their sport with imperious power. Like-minded colleagues carried out his wish. In the style of his late father, who had reigned as the "dictator of the turf," August Belmont II assumed the chairmanship of the Jockey Club in 1895, taking over the reins of the sport in the Northeast, a sport that had changed radically from that which his father had ruled. He thus became the "ruling spirit" in Jockey Club affairs.[29]

One of Belmont's first initiatives was to use his influence in seeing the Percy-Gray law on a safe passage through the New York State Assembly in 1895. This law was intended to outlaw gambling on horse racing. However, as a result of Belmont's influence in the assembly, the new legislation really did not outlaw horse racing. It simply authorized a specified amount of racing by limiting the sport to the "better" tracks. This brought racing in New York entirely under the control of the Jockey Club and, thus, Belmont. Belmont and his associates saw this law as an appeasement to social reformers. The carrot held out with this law was the thousands of dollars the tracks would agree to pay annually to the state treasury, the money to be used for the benefit of agricultural societies. By the early years of the twentieth century, this money amounted to some $200,000 annually. Here was another turn in the affairs of the sport, for, from this point forward, racing would make a practice of reminding state legislators of the economic value of the sport to the state. As the amount of money increased, so, proportionately, did the appreciation of the legislature for what became known as this *sin tax*. Horse racing would be on its way to becoming big business—if social reformers remained content with the Percy-Gray law. But they did not.[30]

Pierre Lorillard, perhaps believing that New York racing could return to the hobby sport it had been decades earlier, viewed the outlawing of gambling and bookmaking as a return to a sport controlled exclusively by elites, the commercialism having been removed. Consequently, "the right class of men to own race horses will come to the front," Lorillard predicted, because wealthy men would then race their horses "for each other's money," as they once had, rather than depending on purses bolstered in large part by the bookmakers' daily licensing fees. In other words, the Percy-Gray law was intended to exclude undesirable horse owners every bit as much as it was intended to prohibit gambling offtrack. With this law, the Jockey Club began to amass formidable power in New York.[31]

In reality, the sport was not going to return to its roots no matter how dearly Lorillard and his friends might have wished it would. Expansion had taken Thoroughbred racing too far beyond the sphere of Lorillard, Belmont II, and Keene. The Jockey Club made a grave mistake in believing that the Percy-Gray law would bring order where there was none, for gambling continued despite it. Even with the law in effect, bookmakers working the New York tracks continued their business as usual—with one slight alteration. Instead of writing receipts for bets taken, they found a way around the law by acknowledging bets verbally without writing out receipts. Bookmakers paid off the winners at a predetermined place outside the racetrack gates at the end of each day. The Jockey Club remained aloof and oblivious, leaving the controlling of betting to the Pinkerton detectives. The Jockey Club erred in looking the other way.[32]

The Jockey Club amassed a concentration of power unlike anything seen previously in the sport as conducted in North America. It licensed jockeys and trainers, appointed racing officials to the tracks, allotted racing dates, and, in 1896, took over the *American Stud Book,* buying out the original six volumes from Sanders Bruce. This landed exclusive control of the Thoroughbred registry with the Jockey Club. No horse could be registered as a Thoroughbred unless it traced back eight consecutive generations as recorded in this stud book. It did not trouble racing's elite powers that Bruce's work was replete with errors and that horses might not be from the families purported to have produced them. All that mattered to the Jockey Club was that the stud book brought order and control to the sport, in an era when businessmen sought these qualities. The stud book placed a vast amount of power in the Jockey Club for the club to use at its discretion; the consequence was that all breeders of Thoroughbreds now came under its control.

The Jockey Club wrote the rules of racing, interpreted these rules, and enforced the same. It also declared that any track refusing to accept its authority would be classified as an outlaw track; horses that raced at outlaw tracks could not race at Jockey Club tracks. This, too, placed a significant amount of control in the Jockey Club's hands.

Theodore Roosevelt's model of the "bully pulpit" and "big stick" diplomacy actually had been in place at the Jockey Club for seven years by the time this twenty-fifth U.S. president moved into the White House in 1901. That is to say, the Jockey Club had anticipated the desire to instill bureaucratic order on all entities, a desire that characterized Roosevelt's presidency. William Robertson writes: "It was an awesome concentration of power, and the Jockey Club wielded it with gusto." Not all were in agreement with the club's policies or practices, but, unlike previous jockey clubs, this organization indicated that it was in racing to stay.[33]

Despite the power and control that the Jockey Club assumed, the sport across the United States did not fall uniformly under its control. In Chicago, the second-largest racing venue behind the Eastern tracks of New York and New Jersey, all matters pertaining to sports, politics, and corruption marched to their own beat. Ed Corrigan, as the owner of Hawthorne Race Course in Cicero, dabbled in at least the first two, if not the third. At war with a long-standing rival track owner whose Garfield Park was within Chicago's city limits, Corrigan persuaded the mayor of Chicago to shut down the Garfield track. Two hundred police officers descended on Garfield Park on September 7, 1892, and loaded bettors, racing officials, and even jockeys still wearing their racing silks into the patrol wagon for a trip to jail. One horse owner from Texas resisted arrest, killed two policemen, was fatally shot by other police, and Garfield Park closed—never to reopen.[34]

Black horsemen felt a change descending on horse racing. The change of color in the sport's prominent positions, from black to white, would occur less noticeably at Northern tracks, where whites traditionally had dominated the ranks of horse trainers and jockeys. But, at Southern and Midwestern tracks, including those in Kentucky, blacks traditionally had dominated these job categories from the slavery era on. By the end of the century, they would not.

Some racing historians have explained the displacement of black jockeys as a function of the increasing value of purse money available as the nineteenth century progressed. This explanation never accounted for the displacement of black horse trainers. Much more was responsible for this change of color in the sport's front lines, not the least the societal transitions under way at that time throughout the United States. Segregation was becoming institutionalized, and sports, including horse racing, were falling in line with the trends of larger American society.

As mentioned, Alvin Harlow wrote in *Weep No More, My Lady,* "'These new people,' meaning New Yorkers, Northerners, who have barged in and taken over much of the breeding, don't understand the Negro, say the veterans." This racist belief served generations of Southerners effectively in exploiting black labor. But the reality was that white Americans, North and South, finally had figured out "what to do with the Negro in American society," that old dilemma that Myrdal argued had plagued Americans since the end of the Civil War. The solution that whites finally hit on was to render blacks invisible by means of segregation. The U.S. Supreme Court validated segregation in 1896 with its infamous *Plessy v. Ferguson* decision. This ruling determined that "separate but equal" facilities for blacks and whites were, indeed, constitutional, as argued in the appeal. The result was the proliferation throughout the South of segregationist Jim Crow laws.[35]

Two years earlier, Congress had repealed the Enforcement Act, thus opening the way for states to disenfranchise African Americans. With blacks no longer permitted close association with whites or to possess a voice in the electoral process, it would hardly do to see African American athletes starring in sports, particularly if women were in the audience. White patrons of the sport would not have wanted their female companions making heroes of black jockeys. Isaac Murphy did not live long enough to know that no longer would a place exist for a jockey of his extraordinary talent.

In 1905, the *Washington Post* published an article titled "Negro Rider on Wane." The subheadline read: "White Jockeys' Superior Intelligence Supersedes." Here lay another slap in the face of jockeys who, like Murphy, had outridden whites in many a horse race, including the most significant in the United States. No one had spoken about relative intelligence during the 1870s and 1880s, when the black jockeys were at their peak in terms of both numbers and success. Yet, by the early years of the twentieth century, white Americans had fixed their attention on the notion of saving the United States for the sake of Anglo-Saxons. Theories of racial determinism became popular. Scientists studied the size and shape of the skulls of African Americans, claiming that they found evidence of inferiority. In the popular culture, racist ephemera began depicting African Americans as monkeys.[36]

The *Illustrated Sporting News* took up the cry that, in golf, "the disturbing race" was invading the peaceful links. "With all due respect to the great work of leading the lowly brother toward the hill-tops of industry and equality," it intoned, "there is something incongruous in the idea of the negro as a follower of golf, just as there would seem a lack of harmony if he tippled nothing but Scotch and soda, and banished the watermelon in favor of the Welsh rabbit [*sic*]." Race was seen here as defining class, a contradiction to the enviable positions that some black horsemen had held among the African American upper class in the horse-oriented society of Lexington.[37]

All throughout sports, black athletes began to take a place not on the sidelines but behind the scenes: in racing, in college football, in major league baseball, and in cycling. As tension increased, some-times blacks fought back. The news out of Kentucky in 1891 was a race war among jockeys at the Latonia Race Course: white jockeys accused blacks of a conspiracy against them. As we have seen, the *Spirit*'s cor-respondent observed: "Whether or not there is . . . prejudice in the ranks of the riders, it is certain there has been altogether too much jostling and crowding." In Chicago, the word at prestigious Washington Park was that black riders had formed an organization to control all the choice mounts, thus creating racial tension and fear. This would not have raised any interest in the previous decade, for black jockeys had predominated in numbers at Southern and Midwestern tracks. White youths had not wanted to ride alongside them; the work had been considered "Negro" work. But, after riders like Murphy had developed the work from labor into a profession, white youths eyed the increased amount of money available in racing, with the result that, as the *Washington Post* wrote, "the white jockey is now crowding out the colored riders as the paleface is pressing back the red men on the plains."[38]

In 1900, the *New York Times* had reported that black riders disap-peared when "a quietly formed combination [of whites] formed in New York to shut them out." If this surprised anyone at the time, it should not have. The lynching of African Americans had reached its highest numbers during the 1890s and did not end with the turn into the twen-tieth century. Black horse trainers had disappeared from their high-profile positions, out in front of the public, for the same reasons that black jockeys had been shuffled back behind the scenes: they could no longer be seen as heroes to be cheered or applauded in full public view. Black horsemen who might have become horse trainers consequently worked as grooms; youths who might have developed into jockeys faced no greater future than that of exercise rider for morning gallops. The di-verse face of Thoroughbred racing had changed to one color—white—and the narrative of the sport would be related in white-only terms from that point until the discovery of Murphy's grave site in the 1960s.[39]

What did not change in racing was the great amount of money that continued to churn through the bookmakers in the ontrack betting enclaves known as the *betting rings*. With racing laboring under a cloud tainted by the crime and moral decline that social reformers desired so sincerely to extinguish, it was a wonder that anyone of means or social

standing participated in the sport. However, owning a racing stable has
always marked a man with the badge of success, by its showy nature and
its obvious expense placing the owner symbolically above everyone else.
Racing has fanned the flames of rich men's egos for as long as men have
seen the racing capabilities in horses. The sport of racing is in the business of selling glamour and outrageous dreams. Keene once described
the ownership of premier racehorses as "the gratification of possessing
something that you know is a little better than that possessed by any-
body else." And so racing continued its expansion as the nineteenth
century ended and the twentieth began.[40]

The Kentuckian who knew precisely how to sell the appearance
of those ethereal qualities that placed the rich above the common folk
was John Madden. There were wizards of Wall Street like James Keene,
a "man who lifts his finger and stocks obey his slightest sign," in the
words of the *New York World*. And then there was the Wizard of the
Turf, John E. Madden. Madden exclusively owned this sobriquet for
the last thirty years of his life (he died in 1929). People viewed him
as an alchemist who turned everything he touched into gold, the way
Keene did with stocks. He accomplished this with much less money
than Keene brought into racing.[41]

Madden was an extraordinary salesman of great charm that moguls like Marcus Daly or William Collins Whitney could not resist. He
completely understood why racing appealed to the very rich. He once
wrote: "Why do people race horses? Why do people play golf? Why do
people play baseball? Why do people operate theaters? To enable a rich
man to find an outlet for some of his surplus wealth. To gratify a thirst
for notoriety on the part of some 'unknown to fame.'"[42]

Madden grew up in the steel mill country of Bethlehem, Pennsylvania, learned to excel at running footraces and driving trotting horses,
and, as a young man, began selling various types and breeds of horses
at county fairs. On moving his business to Lexington at age thirty in
the early 1880s, he styled himself as a trotting-horse man. By 1894,
he began to change course, "forseeing [*sic*] that races on the flat would
soon supersede the harness events," as the *New York Times* explained the
transition. He paid $400 for a Thoroughbred yearling, trained it to race,
and shipped it—where else—to New York, where he sold it for $10,000
to Mike Dwyer.[43]

John E. Madden, known as the Wizard of the Turf, founded a
breeding farm in Lexington that he called Hamburg Place after
the horse Hamburg, whose $40,000 sale price to Marcus Daly
in 1897 enabled Madden to purchase the property. Madden
bred five winners of the Kentucky Derby and won the race
still another time with a colt he had purchased. (Courtesy of
Keeneland-Cook Collection, Keeneland Library, Lexington.)

When Madden's horse Yankee lined up against the horses of
Keene, William Collins Whitney, Perry Belmont, and other scions of
the turf for the Futurity in 1901, the *World* wrote: "John E. Madden, not
a millionaire, is the man who stands arrayed against all this great combination of wealth. . . . The aggregation of wealth represented by all the
owners engaged in the Futurity runs up into the billions." Yankee won

the Futurity in record time, and the *World* savored the moment of David defeating the Goliaths. The next day's headline announced Yankee as the winner and noted that he defeated "the High-Priced Animals of Wm. C. Whitney, Perry Belmont, Clarence H. MacKay and other Millionaire Aristocrats of the Turf." Madden was on his way to becoming a millionaire himself. On this occasion, when Madden remained a man of moderate resources, and during this age, when America stood in awe of its rising numbers of extremely wealthy men, Madden and Yankee had accomplished the extraordinary by showing their heels to the rich men. Whitney promptly purchased the horse.[44]

On Madden's death in 1929, the *Thoroughbred Record* paid him its highest compliment: "He was a natural horse-trader." Working out of Hamburg Place in Lexington and at the racetracks in New York, Madden gained the confidence of wealthy men like the Dwyers and the railroad mogul William Collins Whitney, managing the horses of the latter to great success. He also was a highly successful breeder in his own right at Hamburg Place. He bred five winners of the Kentucky Derby and won the race another time with a colt he had purchased.

The farm was renowned for its pastoral beauty, for its novel equine graveyard, and for the champion horses among its stallions and broodmares. Serenity prevailed in this place, where one writer, seeing the farm at twilight, described an ethereal scene "with fresh, soft air" to breathe as "the mists of darkness were gathering, with the afterglow rosy above them." Nearly fifty years later, a retrospective on Madden's life described his feeling for Hamburg Place as akin to that of Gerald O'Hara's for Tara in *Gone with the Wind*.[45]

The reference was slightly anachronistic—*Gone with the Wind* would not be published until 1936, seven years following Madden's death. But the residence at Hamburg held a nostalgic charm evocative of the antebellum era that framed the first portion of the novel. A house at Hamburg Place indeed held a certain charm, for people believed that Henry Clay had been married on the farm early in the nineteenth century. Like a proper patriarch of that era, Madden had built a small and isolated community within his farm. He constructed a dormitory for the youths who exercised his horses. He required them to attend school and church on the farm. The notion of an orderly life was everywhere about Hamburg Place and readily present even in the habits of its owner. The turf moguls of the Northeast and Far West were businessmen who desired to attain order in all they touched. Madden inspired them to take a closer look at his Bluegrass operation, which seemed removed from the violence and disorder ruling Kentucky.

Madden also was well known for his eccentricities. His contemporaries knew him for constructing a daily regimen built around physical exercise. Staying in peak physical shape became Madden's obsession. He epitomized the natural man that President Theodore Roosevelt idealized as the only way in which Anglo-Saxon Americans would find it possible to maintain order and hold their place in this rapidly changing republic. The president feared that white Americans were becoming too soft. Madden made certain that he, personally, was never soft in physical or mental capacities.

He swam year-round in a spring-fed pond on his property regardless of the temperature and whether ice or snow covered the ground. He exercised daily at the farm or at the New York Athletic Club. He watched his diet, did not smoke, and drank alcohol sparingly. When he advertised for help at Hamburg Place, he included an advisory concerning the healthy habits he expected of his workforce: "Coca-cola addicts need not apply." In his youth, besides experiencing success in footraces, he had played baseball and was an amateur boxing champion. As the owner of Hamburg Place, he would casually vault the fences of the farm fields. He would throw rocks on his walks to exercise the muscles in his arms. The *Illustrated Sporting News* remarked that he appeared to be within a week of a [prize] fight even during his final years and remained a perfect specimen of manhood. He complemented the nostalgia that Hamburg Place evoked for a more orderly time when men had been men, servants had been the responsibility of the landowning family, and all had been peaceful in the emerald green pastures of the Bluegrass.[46]

Madden's horse business mirrored his lifestyle. He was a back-to-nature breeder who raised his horses outside regardless of the weather. He abhorred the idea of coddling them in the barns. He believed that this produced a stronger horse; the hundreds of winners that came off Hamburg Place undoubtedly proved him right. Choosing the right bloodlines in mating his horses also accounted for the high number of winners he bred. But he had help in this—perhaps more help than the historical narrative of Thoroughbred racing has been willing to acknowledge. The mastermind behind the Wizard of the Turf was none other than Billy Walker, Isaac Murphy's onetime mentor and a black horseman now retired after a career as a jockey and a second career as a horse trainer. Walker was brilliant in his knowledge of bloodlines and worked behind the scenes as Madden's adviser. The Wizard was truly grateful and remembered Walker when writing his will. He left him a $1,000 bequest.[47]

Madden was living in the Phoenix Hotel in downtown Lexington when he purchased a son of Hanover for $1,200, naming him Hamburg. He shipped the horse to New York to race. Hamburg won twelve of sixteen races at age two and was acknowledged as the champion of his age group before Madden sold him to Marcus Daly for a price estimated at somewhere between $40,000 and $60,000. Two months later, Madden purchased 235 acres of land out Lexington's Winchester Road, naming his farm Hamburg Place in honor of the horse he had recently sold. The master salesman believed that he had found the ideal location for his business; behind a fast trotter, Hamburg Place was within fifteen minutes of the Phoenix Hotel.[48]

"I wanted a place near town so, if I had a customer, I could get him out there before he changed his mind," Madden said. One success led to another; twelve years later, his farm had expanded to two thousand acres. The farm expanded because Madden knew precisely how to sell a notion of horse ownership as well as how to sell horses. He was a man of the new era that was descending on the sport, a man who realized that many more people in addition to the New York elites were coming into racing by way of Bluegrass Kentucky.[49]

Madden's fame as a horseman expanded each year of his career. People saw him as a gentleman of the old school who maintained patriarchal order on his farm, providing for his help in the way of education and religion. His well-known obsession with physical fitness evoked the physically fit cavalier of those lost times when Americans relied more on their knowledge of horses than on the oppressive presence of urban machinery. Success breeds success in the horse business, and Madden's success, combined with his unquestioned reputation for honesty, helped draw the increasing attention of outsiders to central Kentucky.

The Bruce brothers had worked hard through marketing to restore to the sport the notion that the best racehorses in the United States, horses like Longfellow and Asteroid, could be bred and raised only in Kentucky. Robert Aitcheson Alexander, Dan Swigert, John and Josephine Clay, old John Harper, Isaac Murphy, and Major Barak Thomas had helped boost this idea through their individual success—success that implied that Kentuckians possessed a unique knowledge of horses. Madden took all these notions to another level.

Madden's popularity and success grew at a time when racing most needed the image of this man. He helped shape notions of Bluegrass Kentucky even as the reformers closed in on the sport of horse racing, surrounding it like a tightening noose while trying to shut it down across the United States. Madden, although a great gambler, imposed on those harmful images that had tainted the sport a greater notion of the self-made man. The image he projected was one of the natural man, one who brought orderly control to his Bluegrass farm in a notoriously violent, lawless state.

chapter SEVEN

The Idea of Horse Country Reclaimed

John Madden's rise to national prominence occurred during a time when plantation literature experienced renewed popularity. This genre of fiction had existed at least since the 1830s but was sweeping the country once more beginning in the 1880s and into the twentieth century. Writers of plantation fiction extolled an antebellum South that was to a great extent imaginary. The picture that emerged was a vision of gentle twilight washing across the wide verandas of old mansions where sweet magnolias bloomed in perpetuity. Servants hovered discreetly in the shadows of stone columns on these moss-covered porticos, poised to fill the white folks' glasses. Life seemed so orderly and romantic for these cavaliers and Southern ladies. Perhaps, in this picture, a well-bred horse stood nearby. Or at least, in the imagination, you could hear a Thoroughbred neighing in the distance.[1]

A great many Americans of the early twentieth century actually had convinced themselves that life might be better lived in terms of this fanciful past portrayed as the Old South. The North had spent decades resenting the Southern states for their folly in bringing on the Civil War. But, by the end of the nineteenth century, it had changed its mind. Northerners were becoming increasingly enamored of the old slaveholding South. The plantation genre of popular writing transported them into this lost and fanciful past.

Certainly, no one could forget that the war had been the bloodiest one ever fought on American soil. Considering that some 2.5 million men fought on the Union side and another 750,000–1.25 million on the Confederate side, a generation of children had come of age in families that likely included at least one ex-soldier. And, since 600,000–700,000 men either were killed during the fighting or died of war-related injuries or illnesses, many of these families would have suffered the loss of a relative. Despite these former divisions among Americans, the populations of North and South were beginning to express forgiveness as the old soldiers began dying off and a new generation matured. Among those soldiers still living, Union veterans marched alongside former Confederate enemies at reunions.[2]

These early-twentieth-century Americans took up a practice that William Taylor had seen in the regional beliefs prevalent in the North and the South before the war. He concluded that these beliefs had the power to make myths and that the literature of the antebellum era reflected these myths. He saw Northerners as highly dissatisfied with their rapidly changing world and, consequently, looking for an escape. He wrote: "Northerners soon found much to criticize in the grasping, soulless world of business and the kind of man—the style of life—which this world seemed to be generating." According to Taylor's theory, imagined days from an orderly, more pleasant past offered an escape from rapidly changing times.[3]

Much the same process appeared to be transpiring in the literature popular during the early twentieth century, as David Blight has argued. The popularity of plantation literature lay in the escape it offered its readers into a more pleasant past depicted in the lifestyle of the antebellum South. Blight notes that the 1890s and the early years of the twentieth century saw small family businesses fail and the gap widen between the superwealthy and the rest of Americans. Immigrants began arriving in great waves, unsettling native-born Americans, who perceived this influx of foreigners as threatening to the American way of life. "The age of machines, rapid urbanization, and labor unrest produced a huge audience for a literature of escape into a pre–Civil War, exotic South," Blight writes. He finds it significant that Northerners embraced this notion of an idealized South when, for decades, the South, in the general estimation of the Northern population, had existed in a benighted condition.[4]

Simultaneously with this popular literary wave, Bluegrass Kentucky began to swap the remnants of its Western identity for stereotypes identifying it with the South. Kentucky's history as a former slaveholding state enabled this transition that took place within the national imagination. Plantation literature made it easy for Americans to associate all former slave states with the Confederate South. No longer did Americans need to grasp the political and social nuances that had distinguished the border state of Kentucky from the South. Bluegrass Kentucky became the South, its geographic proximity to the South assisting this transition. Travelers from the North found the Bluegrass more accessible than the Deep South. They imagined that they caught glimpses of the Old South in Bluegrass architecture and lifestyle. Bluegrass Kentucky, with its slaveholding history, its large homes, and its pastures filled with horses, evolved as the Near South and, thus, as representative of the Old South.

Americans embraced this popular plantation literature at the same time as they began to accept the growing popularity of the Lost Cause, the name given to an idealized form of Civil War memory. A groundswell of this reconstructed memory began sweeping the United States during the 1890s and continued strong into the early twentieth century. The myth that it created united people from all regions, North and South, in embracing the notion that perhaps the Old South had got it right after all—that perhaps the Civil War really had been fought to defend a lifestyle of high ideals and to preserve the Constitution, rather than in defense of slavery. Southerners had been reciting Lost Cause ideology from the time they had lost the war, attempting to explain the war to the North in these terms. This clever notion allowed the South to save face in its failed attempt at secession. Northerners had never bought into this idea—at least not until late in the nineteenth century, when racism had reached a high pitch, immigrants were arriving in increasing numbers, life seemed out of control, and white Americans feared that their way of life was endangered. As an antidote, they looked back fondly to an imagined past. They found this past in the Lost Cause. And they found it in plantation fiction.

William Ward has characterized such writing as being in the "Genteel Tradition." Like Taylor and Blight, he has told how this popular literary genre obscured the harshness of daily life. Of its readers he writes: "It was not that they were ignorant of murder, violence, rape, arson, embezzlement, and perversion. They preferred drawing rooms and garden houses to mining and mill towns. When they read, they preferred men and women in their aspiring moments to characters weighed down by trouble and futility."[5]

Within this framework, Bluegrass Kentucky experienced a rebirth as the Old South of literature and imagination. Moreover, plantation literature painted the region as something entirely different from the violent Kentucky that most Americans had read about in newspapers. A much more pleasing image of horse country emerged. "The Kentuckians are undoubtedly the finest people in the States. . . . In some respects they are the finest white people in the world. They carry about them an atmosphere of manners and breeding," wrote the *Kentucky Farmer and Breeder*, following in the pattern that plantation literature had set. This reconstructed picture of the Bluegrass began to work a change of mind with those turf moguls who had formerly believed it too unstable for capital investment. As a result, the horse business tagged along for what turned out to be a highly productive ride.[6]

Kentucky authors who linked the Bluegrass with this imagined Old South achieved wide national acclaim. Foremost among these were James Lane Allen, Annie Fellows Johnston, and John Fox Jr. So many people read these three that the Southern identity they bestowed on Kentucky clearly resonated with a readership eager to embrace the Old South.

This imaginative leap linking Bluegrass Kentucky to the Old South tied up numerous loose ends for those both within the state and outside its borders, for confusion about the entire state's identity had existed since long before the Civil War. Kentucky never had been entirely of the South—or entirely of the North. It had been a slaveholding state that identified with the South in some situations but not all. For example, and in contrast to the Deep South, Kentucky was a border state generally characterized by farms typically smaller than the vast cotton and sugar plantations of the deeper South. It fell somewhere between the geographic, ideological, and economic characteristics that had differentiated North from South. Bluegrass Kentucky, situated in the central portion of the state, had been caught between both worlds—until Allen, Johnston, and Fox placed it directly within the context of the Old South for their turn-of-the-century readers.

These writers peopled those of their works about the Bluegrass with kindly Confederate-supporting colonels, loyal slaves, and massive, columned mansions that bespoke a social power and grace originating in a timeless connection to the land. None of them cast the typical Bluegrass landowner in the likeness of old John Harper, whose eccentric, wild appearance had more clearly suggested a rough-and-ready frontier type. Authors working in this genre reified an exotic country of the imagination, a sweet country where all knew their proper place.

Johnston wrote a series of children's books, beginning in 1895 with *The Little Colonel*; the series made her a best-selling author by the turn of the century. Johnston was not a native Kentuckian but had grown up in nearby Indiana and moved to Peewee Valley, near Louisville, as an adult. *The Little Colonel* grew into a series of twelve additional volumes that sold more than 1 million copies during Johnston's lifetime.[7]

The Little Colonel series, set in post–Civil War Kentucky, featured a "little colonel" who was a young girl five years old named Lloyd Sherman whose grandfather, one Colonel Lloyd, sported a beard shaped in the Kentucky colonel's stereotypical goatee. He had disowned a daughter who had married a Yankee. The depiction of Kentucky in this series helped reinforce in the national imagination the notion that Kentucky existed as a holdover from older times, a gentle place where violence did not intrude. Anne Elizabeth Marshall has written: "The white characters, around whom Johnston's stories revolve, present an . . . appealing picture of graceful gentility as they lead lives of wealth and privilege." She also writes: "They enjoy a gentle existence buffered from insecurities by a stable social arrangement that entails powerful yet chivalrous men, and well-behaved maternal women. Most importantly, however, this safe, unburdened order rests upon the deference and servitude of faithful, contented African Americans."[8]

Allen's writings portrayed Kentucky in similar organic, orderly, and picturesque terms. Allen was a native Kentuckian, a graduate of Transylvania University who had moved to New York City. He took with him nostalgic and fanciful visions of his home state, an idealized picture that ignored the reality of a violent, lawless Bluegrass straddling the border between North and South. He wrote about a region enveloped in the smooth shadow of the gentle moon at midnight and kissed by the soft breeze of a gentle wind on the green leaves of magnificent shade trees covering plantation-like homesteads. His readers would have interpreted this as Southern.

In *Two Kentucky Gentlemen of the Old School,* Allen described a social order "which had bloomed in rank perfection over the bluegrass plains of Kentucky during the final decades of the old regime." He told how the inhabitants "had spent the most nearly idyllic life, on account of the beauty of the climate, the richness of the land, the spacious comfort of their homes, the efficiency of their negroes, the characteristic contentedness of their dispositions. In reality they were not farmers, but rural, idle gentlemen of easy fortunes whose slaves did their farming for them." The story concerned an antebellum planter, Colonel Romulus Fields, and his faithful former slave, Peter Cotton, who remained with his old master after the war. Together, they expressed displeasure with their present circumstances and worried about the future. Peter Cotton expressed a longing to return to the security of the old ways—slavery. He seemed lost in his new freedom, just as Colonel Fields appeared unable to adapt to the new order of the world. Their familiar world had belonged to a timeless past that they both found more agreeable.[9]

Not all Allen's works were fiction, at least not in the truest sense. For *Century* magazine, he wrote an article titled "Homesteads of the Blue-Grass" in which he anticipated the coming to the Bluegrass of numbers of wealthy men from outside the state. In the 1892 article he predicted: "One can foresee the yet distant time when this will become the region of splendid homes and estates that will nourish a taste for outdoor sports and offer an escape from the too-wearying cities. . . . A powerful and ever-growing interest is that of the horse, racer or trotter. He brings into the State his amazing capital, his types of men. Year after year he buys farms, and lays out tracks, and builds stables, and edits journals, and turns agriculture into grazing."[10]

Allen promised the industrialist that he would discover in the Bluegrass a pleasant escape or at least a respite from the cares of big-city life, with "no huge mills and gleaming forges, no din of factories and throb of mines." He described the Kentucky lifestyle as life lived according to gentry-class traditions transplanted from antebellum Virginia, where "in no other material aspect did they embody the history of descent so sturdily as in the building of homes," and where could be found "the English love of lawns . . . the English fondness for a mansion half hidden with evergreens and creepers and shrubbery, to be approached by a leafy avenue, a secluded gateway, and a graveled drive."

207

"On and on, and on you go," he continued, "seeing only the repetition of field and meadow, wood and lawn, a winding stream . . . a stone wall . . . a race-track . . . and . . . houses that crown very simply and naturally the entire picture of material prosperity . . . [with] a front portico with Doric, Ionic, or Corinthian columns; for your typical Kentuckian likes to go into his house through a classic entrance." Of this typical Kentuckian, he wrote: "After supper on summer evenings, nothing fills him with serener comfort than to tilt his chair back against a classic support, as he smokes a pipe and argues on the immortality of a pedigree."[11]

John Fox Jr. was better known for fictional works set in the mountains of eastern Kentucky. In fact, according to Ward, he was the first author "of any consequence to write seriously and sympathetically of the Kentucky mountaineers in their natural habitat, though he himself was born in Bourbon County in the heart of the Bluegrass country." Allen's work on the genteel Bluegrass actually had inspired Fox to tackle the intriguing stereotypes of the "two Kentuckys"—the backwardness of the mountain people and their environment contrasted with the perceived gentility and Southern mannerisms of the Bluegrass region. In his most famous work to address these conflicting images, *The Little Shepherd of Kingdom Come,* he wove a story that showed the Bluegrass ways prevailing over those of the mountains.[12]

The effect of these writers and their literary genre on the horse industry should not be underestimated. It extended into other literary realms, for the metamorphosis of Bluegrass identity to Southern also could be seen in the sporting periodicals of the day. Kentucky horsemen traveling to Northeastern tracks no longer were considered to be of the West, as the *Spirit of the Times* and *Turf, Field and Farm* had identified them for nearly thirty years after the Civil War. When Woodford Clay, the owner of Runnymede Farm in Bourbon County, went to New York in 1903, the *Morning Telegraph* determined that he had "cavalier written all over him." It described him as "a clean-cut, upright, athletic looking young fellow [recall Madden's obsessive athleticism here]" and wrote that he "would seem to you to be the beau ideal of the young Southerner of good birth." It was clear that New Yorkers had been reading all the right periodicals and books.[13]

As central Kentucky began shedding its Western identity for stereotypes marking the region as Southern, the Bluegrass horse business began to strike gold. Two changes opened wide the veins of this gold mine for the horse industry. First, the state's notorious reputation for lawlessness shifted away from the Bluegrass to eastern Kentucky. Second, capitalists from outside the state began investing in greater numbers in rural property surrounding Lexington. As the marketing literature of the era revealed, no less than the wealthy moguls of the Northeastern turf were beginning to buy into the notion that the Near South of the Bluegrass region would provide them with an escape from the harshness of their urban world.

Thoroughbred racehorse owners across the United States, always looking for that competitive edge, became fixed on the notion that in Bluegrass farmland lay a dual reward. Their horses would benefit from the mineral-rich *Poa pratensis* and limestone-infused springwater. The owners themselves would benefit from experiencing the lifestyle of a Southern country squire. Readers of popular fiction could only read about this imagined Southern lifestyle, but the very rich could afford to buy it. Bluegrass farm property no longer seemed an unsuitable investment in an unstable land. The prospect for expansion in Kentucky's horse industry lay tantalizingly close, more than three decades after Alexander and the Bruce brothers had envisioned this growth. The *Kentucky Farmer and Breeder* observed: "Breeders throughout America are coming every day to a truer realization of the fact that here and here alone can the best thoroughbreds be raised."[14]

The Bruce brothers did not live long enough to see this change. Benjamin Bruce had died in 1891. Sanders Bruce died in 1902. Sanders, in particular, had died a disappointed man. He had enjoyed prosperity during the 1880s and early 1890s, despite a fire early in the 1880s that destroyed the contents of the New York offices of *Turf, Field and Farm*. The fire nearly forced him to stop completion of volume 5 of the *American Stud Book*. His problems escalated with the Panic of 1893. He struggled to keep the *American Stud Book* and *Turf, Field and Farm* alive. However, he became embroiled in a quarrel with the newly formed Jockey Club over rights to the stud book. The quarrel turned into a lawsuit that nearly ruined him financially. A lower court found in his favor. The powerful Jockey Club appealed. Public sentiment in the world of Thoroughbred racing favored Bruce as the David going up against the Goliath of New York's turf moguls. The parties settled out of court, with the Jockey Club purchasing all rights to the *American Stud Book* for $35,000. Thereafter, the name of the Jockey Club replaced that of Sanders Bruce beneath the title.[15]

The acquisition of the *American Stud Book* placed the Jockey Club in a tremendously powerful position, with all this power situated in the Northeast. With control of the stud book, the Jockey Club held the keys to the kingdom of the turf since no breeder would be able to register a Thoroughbred in North America without its approval. This gave the Jockey Club the power to bar the horses of anyone it deemed in violation of rules—or held in disfavor. It could do this because no horse was recognized as Thoroughbred, and, therefore, eligible to race, unless the Jockey Club had accepted it into its official registry.

Prior to this consolidation, Kentucky horsemen at least had the option of selecting from two registries. They could choose either Bruce's *American Stud Book* or the Jockey Club's registry. Most people soon realized, however, that they would need to pay double fees and register with both if their horses were to race in Kentucky *and* New York. The New York tracks required Jockey Club registration exclusively. Racetracks outside New York generally belonged to the rival American Turf Congress, which recognized Bruce's *American Stud Book* as well as the Jockey Club registry. But, as everyone had known since Asteroid's era, a reputation earned outside New York wasn't all that it could be unless the horse had also raced in the metropolis.

Resentment over the Jockey Club's control of the New York tracks was no minor matter, as some of the racing periodicals had suggested. "Even the members of the Jockey Club cannot be allowed to claim the whole earth for the purpose of rendering its racing clubs tributary to their demands," the *Canadian Sportsman* editorialized during the years when Bruce's *American Stud Book* coexisted with the Jockey Club registry. "Certainly . . . it looks as if they demand the right to step in and dictate to the editor and proprietor of the *American Stud Book*, not only how he shall run his business, but insist upon it being done just as their lordly will dictates! It may be that the swell Eastern turf magnates believe in their divine right to rule everything from Maine to California." And perhaps they did. Bruce reprinted this editorial in *Turf, Field and Farm*.[16]

For years after Bruce settled his lawsuit with the Jockey Club, tension continued to exist between Kentucky and the New York power structure over equine pedigrees. In 1902, an article in the *Lexington Leader* pleaded with the Jockey Club to open a branch office in the Bluegrass for the registration of horses. Kentuckians complained in 1906 over the matter of "a disposition on the part of certain Eastern turf journals to criticize the methods of our Kentucky breeders in keeping their records as inaccurate and careless." Within this complaint lay an underlying concern that leaders of the turf in New York held the power to reject pedigrees and foal registrations submitted from Kentucky breeders. Kentuckians considered this a real possibility, for, when the great stallion Lexington had stood at the zenith of his career, accusations had arisen that he was not, in fact, of the bloodlines said to be his parentage. The power to control Thoroughbred bloodlines definitely had shifted to New York. In light of the way control of the sport had gone, Robert Aitcheson Alexander's dismissal of "some New Yorkers" when referring to Travers and his group in 1865 seemed like an error in estimation that would haunt Bluegrass Kentucky forever.[17]

Kentucky was beginning to garner an increasing measure of power in the sport, despite the ongoing controversy over the maintenance of bloodlines records. Some seventy miles west of Lexington in Louisville, a change in ownership of Churchill Downs portended a higher profile for this regional racecourse. An impresario named Matt Winn took over the struggling track the year that Sanders Bruce died. Winn began promoting the Kentucky Derby as something more than a regional race, an event greater than the race of the West, as New York papers called it. He said that he had watched the inaugural derby in 1875 as a thirteen-year-old seated in his father's wagon parked in the infield. Although he might not have seen the possibilities at the time, his vision for the derby was to work in synergy with the outside capitalists' expanding investment in the Bluegrass.[18]

Increasing numbers of Americans did, in fact, begin paying attention to the Kentucky Derby, as a result of a fortunate set of circumstances surrounding the race. In 1913, a long-shot winner named Donerail broke the track record and paid an eye-catching $184.90 on a $2 bet. The resulting newspaper headlines grabbed everyone's attention. The following year, the derby received considerably more headlines when Old Rosebud shattered Donerail's recent track record, winning the race in two minutes and four and four-fifths seconds. In 1915, Regret became the first filly (and only one of three in total) to win the race. This, too, resulted in numerous attention-grabbing headlines in newspapers throughout the country. The headlines seemed bolder, larger than real life, for a New York society figure, Harry Payne Whitney, owned the filly. Regret gave the Derby sex appeal with her defeat of the males, and Whitney gave the Derby the cachet of his wealth.

Legend tells how men at Whitney's farm rang a large bell outdoors in honor of Regret winning the race: a bell ringing that resounded with this new combination of Northeastern money and Bluegrass horses. This story implied incorrectly, however, that Regret was foaled and raised in Kentucky. Actually, she was a product of Whitney's farm in New Jersey. Whitney did not transfer his breeding operations to the Bluegrass until after her birth. By that time, he, like a growing number of turfmen, had accepted the notion that his horse farm belonged in the Bluegrass. Robert Aitcheson Alexander and the Bruce brothers would have heartily approved.

During the 1920s, Winn introduced the singing of "My Old Kentucky Home" prior to the running of the derby, thus firming up imagined notions of the antebellum South with the race. But this did not occur until at least a decade after the notion of a Southern identity had taken hold of Bluegrass horse country. Horse-farm country anticipated the cultural turn that the Kentucky Derby would take and saved the Kentucky horse industry in the process.[19]

The increasing appeal of Bluegrass land among these outside capitalists made all the difference for Kentucky's horse world. With each new infusion of outside wealth, the Bluegrass horse business expanded in ways that it had not done, on its own, during the latter part of the nineteenth century. The effect rippled throughout the entire community of Lexington and the surrounding towns. An infrastructure of ancillary businesses needed to support the horse business expanded with the growing number of farms. The horse business in central Kentucky increasingly entwined its fortunes with those of the local economy, which meant that more persons than just horse persons profited from this expansion. For example, the *Kentucky Farmer and Breeder* noted about horse auctions: "On the prices which obtain at them the prosperity of this community to some extent depends."[20]

This evolving trend represented a startling turnaround from the previous estimation of the Bluegrass region in the eyes of these wealthy beholders. They slowly were letting go of that concern that the Bluegrass appeared too unstable for development. With this changing state of mind, they marched to the same drumbeat as did the readers of popular literature who had come to see Kentucky in more pleasing terms. Wealthy horse owners were no different than the larger society. Plantation literature had helped resituate the Bluegrass in their imaginations as an idealized Old South that their fortunes would enable them to purchase, as though buying the lifestyle of a country squire. Meanwhile, despite the obfuscation of plantation literature, the realities of Kentucky lawlessness and violence still continued to transpire at their usual reckless pace.

No one could have disputed that violence and a blatant disregard for the rule of law continued unabated in horse country; in fact, the scale appeared larger, not only in numbers of incidents, but also in the high profile of some of the victims. The killing of the Harpers in 1871 was a high-profile incident of one kind, but the killing of Kentucky governor William Goebel in 1900 ranked on another scale entirely.

Goebel himself had not been above violence. He had killed an opponent in a duel five years before his own death, shooting an ex-Confederate on the steps of a bank in northern Kentucky. Goebel was controversial: critics portrayed him as a demagogue, while others viewed him as a much-needed reformer who had waged war against corporations during the long depression of the 1890s. Goebel's number one target had been the Louisville and Nashville Railroad (L&N), an entity that people widely accused of setting rates in a high-handed manner that placed increasing profits in the hands of the railroad owners.

Under leadership of August Belmont II, the L&N's board of directors formed a cartel of conservative Democrats. Belmont has never been accused of any knowledge of the Goebel assassination, but he reportedly handpicked a candidate to oppose Goebel at the Democratic nominating convention the previous spring. The L&N financed a hard-fought campaign against Goebel and his reformist wing of Democrats, all of whom had fallen under the spell of the populist William Jennings Bryan. When the convention opened, balloting quickly got out of hand

and grew so raucous that the Democratic state chairman started to walk off the stage. He changed his mind when a representative from eastern Kentucky threatened to shoot him if he left his post.[21]

The L&N lobby next attempted to disrupt the proceedings by sending a mob to storm the stage. In a desperate attempt to restore order, some delegates began singing songs like "My Old Kentucky Home." The ploy worked, and balloting continued, although not with a quick conclusion. Several days later, the Democrats remained split. Conservatives decided to depart for Lexington, where they nominated a former governor, John Y. Brown. Reformers steadfastly backed Goebel. Belmont's reportedly handpicked candidate, P. Wat Hardin, never made it past the start of balloting.[22]

The man who actually won the closely contested election was a Republican, William S. Taylor. Brown came in third. But, when the General Assembly, with Democrats in control, decided to investigate the election, armed protestors favoring Taylor descended on Frankfort from eastern Kentucky. "In this atmosphere on January 30, 1900, Goebel was shot," writes James C. Klotter. Taylor declared an emergency, called out the state militia, and ordered the legislature to reconvene in London. However, the Democrats refused to leave Frankfort and, while meeting secretly in a hotel, voted Goebel in as governor—shortly before he died of his wounds. "Two legislatures, two governors, and two militias vied for power, and civil war seemed possible," Klotter writes. Four months later, in May, the courts decided that the Democrats had acted legally. Taylor fled the state. James Crepps Wickliffe Beckham succeeded Goebel as governor of the state.[23]

If wealthy turfmen harbored misgivings about these developments, their actions did not reveal the level of concern that had previously dissuaded capitalists from buying Bluegrass farms. Following Belmont's relocation of Nursery Stud to Lexington in 1885, Lamon Harkness purchased Walnut Hall Farm in 1892. Harkness was a son of Stephen V. Harkness, a founder of the Standard Oil Company. The Ohioan planned to use his new Kentucky farm for breeding harness horses for racing purposes. James Keene purchased Castleton Farm that same year. Around the year 1898, William Collins Whitney took up Thoroughbred racing in a major way. John Madden became Whitney's turf consultant. In his six years on the turf until his death in 1904, Whitney won major races in North America and abroad. Beginning in 1900, he leased La Belle Farm in Lexington. However, he never planned to maintain an operation in Kentucky permanently. He intended to move his horses back to New Jersey or Long Island as soon as he found a suitable location. In addition to the racing dynasty Whitney founded, his contributions to the turf included the restoration of the Saratoga Race Course; the once-grand racetrack had declined in reputation and significance, and Whitney almost single-handedly brought it back to its former status as a fashionable destination. His son Harry Payne Whitney brought this legacy with him to Kentucky when he purchased his Bluegrass farm during the racing career of Regret.[24]

Other outsiders to begin horse-farm operations during this time included Edward R. Bradley, the owner of a fabulous gambling casino in Florida, who founded Idle Hour Farm and would breed and own four Kentucky Derby winners: Behave Yourself, Bubbling Over, Burgoo King, and Broker's Tip. Like Madden, Bradley began his working years as a steel mill laborer; later, he became a gold miner. He also became a gambler, opened his casino at Palm Beach, and garnered enormous wealth, which enabled him to buy his horse farm.

A Virginian, Arthur B. Hancock also moved to Kentucky after that operation began to eclipse the success of his father's Ellerslie Farm in Virginia. Hancock named his Kentucky farm Claiborne.

With the plutocrats and robber barons falling increasingly under the spell of the newly crafted vision of the Bluegrass as the Old South, their arrival in Kentucky brought remarkable changes to the landscape. The homes, barns, and outbuildings they constructed on their new farms soon made it clear that they would dictate the appearance of horse country. None of the locally owned operations could compete with the scale or the expense of the construction that industrial and Wall Street wealth was bringing to the Bluegrass. "The average Kentucky stock farmer is not a millionaire, nor anywhere near it," a writer for the *Illustrated Sporting News* wrote in 1903. Nonetheless, the local horsemen had been seeking such investment in their industry for decades following the war. Now it had begun to arrive, and, as the *Sporting News* observed, the average Kentucky stock farmer "welcomes the advent of the wealthy men of the North and East."[25]

Two years later, in 1905, an important book titled *Country Estates of the Blue Grass* appeared. Published privately in Lexington by its lead author, Thomas A. Knight, this work represented the first known effort to extol the pleasing qualities of horse country in book form. *Country Estates of the Blue Grass* was a collection of stories about individual horse farms, describing them in photographs as well as text. For some time, *Turf, Field and Farm* had published articles accompanied by photographs about individual horse farms, with the photographs generally focused on the farm mansions. But, in the new book, all these alluring images came to the reader assembled in one package. The effect produced was powerful.

The introduction to *Country Estates of the Blue Grass* spoke to those desirous of escaping the urban sphere: "City life with its conventionalities, with its politics, its corruption, has been tested and found wanting. It was a pretty bauble which, when punctured by the two disturbing agencies, disappointment and ill health, lost its charm. So that now, we find the tide of progress turned towards the country." The book presented Bluegrass scenes evocative of the Old South, showing African Americans engaged in farm labor. With photographs and stories like those in this book, Kentucky was slipping into the South as though it had always been there.[26]

It did not hurt the Bluegrass boosters' cause that the colonial architectural style became fashionable across the country at this time: the style, characterized in great part by white-columned porticos, evoked the Greek Revival Southern mansions of the 1830s. Many of the old residences on Kentucky farms acquired this new look, among them the main residence at Woodburn Farm, which went from Italianate to a colonnaded facade. Since these residences already were large in comparison to the average home, the addition of columns bespoke what people imagined as representative of the South.

Country estates had become a fond refuge of the nation's wealthy, as could be seen in the popularity of Newport, Rhode Island, where the rich had built luxurious "country" mansions for a retreat from urban life. With nostalgia for the Old South becoming popular, and with Kentucky looking more like the South than it ever had, the rich began to overlook their prior aversion to lawless Kentucky and began considering the Bluegrass for country estates. If any continued to see Kentucky as backward and perhaps too West to suit, *Country Estates of the Blue Grass*

The main residence at Woodburn Farm evolved from the Italianate villa to the colonnaded style during the Colonial Revival period. Sometime between 1904 and 1932, the Alexander family added porticos with colossal-order columns to the facade. During the first decade of the twenty-first century, the residence underwent a major renovation under its present owner, the former Kentucky governor Brereton Jones, whose wife, Libby, is an Alexander descendant. (Photograph by the author, 2009.)

offered this advice: "[The Bluegrass was] not the country of yesterday ... not the country where one was isolated from congenial companionship, from ease and every convenience, but the country of the Twentieth Century. The country, where one may meet cultured, well-bred friends, where one may find ease and luxury, where one may find every convenience that is found in the city." This Bluegrass that the boosters promoted to the plutocrats was a sort of New South clad in the clothes of the Old South: an antebellum South with all the modern updates.[27]

As a consequence of this Southern imagery, a new class of landowner was emerging in central Kentucky: the wealthy absentee owner whose farm typically was becoming less diversified. The primary focus of these farms transitioned almost exclusively to breeding and raising racehorses. Kentucky horsemen wooed this new class of absentee owners and profited economically from the changing landscape. The locals benefited greatly, for a new professional class of Kentuckian was emerging in the Bluegrass—that of the expert or professional horsemen who assumed management of these farms. Within this expanding universe of horse farming, a number of ancillary businesses also emerged to provide veterinary care, banking services, horse feed, shoeing, and other specialties to the farms. Business in central Kentucky was picking up. Business leaders and horsemen of the Bluegrass had worked hard since the Civil War to reach this plateau, so it might have seemed ironic that fictional literature had allowed their efforts to attain this reality.

Growth and expansion, no matter how much they are desired, do not arrive without some measure of regret, however. Bluegrass residents experienced this troublesome side of the transition. *Munsey's Magazine* might have suspected some feelings of sadness among the locals as they watched farm after farm pass to outsiders, for it noted in 1902: "Whatever of sentimental regret the Kentuckian may feel at the passing of historic estates into alien hands, he must admit that the infusion of new blood and the influx of outside capital has lent a decided impetus to stock breeding and training in the State—interests which, for various causes, had sadly declined." Savvy horsemen—you might consider them local capitalists—nonetheless recognized the value of investment coming from outside the state, seeing this as the only way to expand their own wealth. Their wealth was founded only in agriculture, an imbalance that had rendered them noncompetitive with the industrial wealth of Northeastern turfmen. *Munsey's* certainly recognized this imbalance when writing: "The newcomer, with unlimited capital at his back, has been able to accomplish in months what the Kentucky breeder, handicapped in many instances by lack of means, could scarcely have achieved in years."[28]

Sanford and Belmont had pioneered the way into Bluegrass Kentucky from New Jersey and New York. Keene had perfected the way with his highly successful Castleton Farm. Taking notice of the rising trend for New York horse owners to build their farms elsewhere, the *Brooklyn Eagle* published an article in 1902 with the headline "A Horse Owners' Exodus from Long Island Feared." The subtitle read "Will Long Island, So Long Famous as the Home of the Trotter and Runner, Lose Its Prestige?" The article told how William Collins Whitney and

August Belmont II were leading their peers to Aiken, South Carolina, for winter quarters. They were searching out more desirable land for the winter training of their racehorses in the same way they had sought out Bluegrass land for their mares and foals.[29]

A major change that these moguls brought to the Bluegrass landscape was the amalgamation of smaller farms into large estates. *Munsey's Magazine* observed these changes to the landscape and noted: "The old fashioned stock farm of a few hundred acres, from which came trotters and racers famous in the annals of track and turf, is disappearing. It is being swallowed up in the great modern estate, baronial in extent and perfect in equipment. For instance, eight of the old farms were joined to make the splendid domain of Walnut Hall, with its two thousand acres of unsurpassed land."[30]

Big characterized the great modern estates of outside investors whose ambitions were large, whose egos were larger, and whose bankrolls were largest of all. The greatest ambitions of all belonged to James Ben Ali Haggin, a native Kentuckian who, as previously noted, had gone west to work as a lawyer, then became a mining king. Haggin also had become the largest breeder of Thoroughbreds in North America with a vast stock operation in California and a much smaller farm at Elmendorf in Lexington. Eventually deciding, owing to the great cost of shipping horses east across the country, to consolidate his operations in Kentucky, he moved his stock to Elmendorf Farm in Lexington in 1898. The six thousand acres that he owned at the point of this consolidation, and another fifteen hundred acres that he leased, became home to some 800 broodmares, another 450 fillies under four years of age, and 23 stallions. "It is a gigantic plant which Mr. Haggin has established here," reported the *Kentucky Farmer and Breeder*.[31]

Haggin followed the pattern of Harkness at Walnut Hall Farm, buying up farms all around the original five hundred acres of Elmendorf. The landscape as it looked in the neighborhood of Elmendorf prior to this momentous change had been many small farms under cultivation for crops of wheat, corn, tobacco, and hemp. On each farm, the owner lived as a permanent resident. Over the next seven years, Haggin, an absentee owner whose main residence was now New York, rearranged these farms into one vast expanse of pasture through which ran many service roads. He also built numerous stock barns.[32]

"And from a series of unimproved, disconnected farms, many of them unattractive, has been evolved an estate on which a king might live and be satisfied," flowed a description in the *Kentucky Farmer and Breeder*. "Hundreds of workmen are daily adding to its improvements, yet other miles of magnificent roadway are being constructed between its stretches of beautiful pasture-land, thousands of trees are being planted, new buildings are being erected. . . ." But not all these farms that Haggin bought had been unattractive. In 1907, he acquired Hira Villa at an auction held at the front door of the Fayette County Courthouse. Hira Villa was a Thoroughbred breeding farm on the Huffman Mill Pike formerly owned by the late Major Barak Thomas. A large crowd of farmers and horseman attended the auction, at which bidding began at $100 an acre. Haggin had the funds to outbid them all, running the price up to $181.25 an acre, for a total of $17,662.50 for approximately ninety-eight acres.[33]

The final touch was the Greek Revival mansion that Haggin built for his new bride, Pearl Vorhies of Versailles, Kentucky, twenty-eight years old when she married Haggin, himself seventy-four. Haggin reportedly built the residence as a country retreat in keeping with the trend for country estates. No other horse farm in Lexington made quite the statement that this residence, named Green Hills, did concerning Bluegrass Kentucky's newly evolving Southern identity. Woodburn Stud, which recently had been remodeled with Grecian columns added to the facade, was no longer active as a horse farm by the twentieth century; thus, Green Hills took over as the representative mansion in this newly minted Southern state. The Green Hills mansion became a Bluegrass showplace, an attraction that drew the curious. Elmendorf Farm received anywhere from one hundred visitors or more every day, as the *Kentucky Farmer and Breeder* reported: "To the casual sightseer the feature of chiefest [*sic*] interest is the Haggin residence." With such a massive stone structure and Greek Revival portico to set the record straight, there could be little doubt in the popular imagination that Bluegrass Kentucky existed as a holdover from the Old South. The *Illustrated Sporting News* affirmed this notion, declaring Green Hills "the typical Southern style of residence."[34]

The Haggins visited Green Hills every autumn, traveling from New York in their private railroad car, which reached journey's end on a spur

James Ben Ali Haggin purchased Elmendorf Farm in 1897 and built this
$300,000 mansion, which he called Green Hills, for his new wife, the former
Pearl Vorhies of Versailles. The mansion was a Bluegrass showplace, its
massive structure and Greek Revival portico drawing praise as "the typical
Southern style of residence" (*Illustrated Sporting News* 2, no. 31 [December
12, 1903]: 28). The Haggins traveled every autumn from New York to visit
Elmendorf Farm and their Southern mansion. (Elmendorf Farm Photographic Collection, KUKAV-PA71M14-001, Special Collections, University
of Kentucky.)

of track close by the mansion. When in residence, they gave parties that
people of their day agreed were some of the most celebrated in central
Kentucky. They organized dinner and dancing for some 150–200 persons at these social events, with Haggin importing orchestras to Lexington. He also brought his entire domestic staff from New York when
they visited. With the Haggins, New York social life found a satellite
home in horse country. They established a cultural pattern for future
horse-farm owners.[35]

The dining room at Green Hills on Elmendorf Farm was rich in its design and appointments. (Elmendorf Farm Photographic Collection, KUKAV-PA71M14-013, Special Collections, University of Kentucky.)

The entrance hall at Green Hills on the Elmendorf Farm of James Ben Ali Haggin was ornately furnished with a marble table and a staircase leading to the second floor. (Elmendorf Farm Photographic Collection, KUKAV-PA71M14-011, Special Collections, University of Kentucky.)

Across Lexington from the Haggin estate, at another retreat along Winchester Road, Patchen Wilkes Farm, New York society amused itself in quite a different fashion—by staging a "Negro ball." The hostess for the ball was the young Mrs. Rita Hernandez Stokes, the wife of the multimillionaire Earl Dodge Stokes. She had attracted considerable attention on the horse-show circuit at Newport and Long Branch, New Jersey, where she ruled as an expert driver and rider. While riding the show circuit, she had drawn the eye of Stokes, fifteen years her senior and heir to a fortune of $11 million. Reportedly, he fell in love with her after seeing her picture displayed in the Fifth Avenue window of a photographer's studio. The two married in 1895, when she was nineteen years old. Depending on the stories, either Stokes gave Patchen Wilkes Farm to the new Mrs. Stokes, or she invested on her own initiative in this trotting-horse operation. Her Negro ball was an event steeped in the racism of the day and demonstrated how Northerners as well as Southerners viewed African Americans: as childlike, hapless, and appreciative of the patriarchal guidance the landowner offered. The Negro ball connected Kentucky with the Old South in the imaginations of landowners like the Stokeses.[36]

Rita Stokes imported friends from New York to observe the Negro ball. She also sent perfumed invitations to a Japanese man and his secretaries. He was the director general of that popular operetta *The Mikado,* which was playing in London and New York. Mrs. Stokes promised that she would prepare a Japanese dish for him during his stay at Patchen Wilkes, an indication that, like many women of her time, she viewed Asians as others incapable of fitting into Anglo-Saxon culture.[37]

As the *New York Times* reported, the Negro ball was *the* one social event that African Americans wished to attend. Mrs. Stokes had sent out two hundred invitations, and perhaps she did not send a sufficient number. The *New York Times* wrote: "Negroes from surrounding towns and cities have written asking for invitations to the ball." Stokes told the newspaper that the entertainment at the ball charmed her immensely. She held the ball inside a brick horse barn that she had gaily decorated with bunting and flags.[38]

Workers at Patchen Wilkes laid down a canvas dance floor over half the barn floor; the other half held a table said to be 110 feet long and decorated with fruit and large cakes. Mrs. Stokes employed a ca-

terer to "get up a supper such as negroes would enjoy," the *Times* reported. Highlighting the dinner menu were roast shoat and sweet potatoes,
fried fish and coffee, fruits, pickles, ice cream, and cake. "Jones's colored
band" furnished the entertainment. The evening also featured "buck
dances" and a "cake walk" with prizes for contestants.[39]

Only four years after Isaac and Lucy Murphy had celebrated their
tenth wedding anniversary with an elegant soiree described at great
length in the *Kentucky Leader*, the *New York Times* and Mrs. Stokes had
taken the African American community in Lexington back in time to
before the Civil War. The black community in the Bluegrass had reverted from dining on quails with champignons and claret to "a supper such as negroes would enjoy" and all that this implied about the
color line emerging after *Plessy v. Ferguson*. But, by the time Rita Stokes
had installed herself on her Lexington horse farm, Murphy had died,
black horsemen had disappeared almost entirely from the forefront of
Thoroughbred racing, and the color line in this sport and on Bluegrass
farms helped define how Northerners and Kentuckians were to view the
identity of central Kentucky. Across the emerald-green pastures of the
Bluegrass, the new identity was taking horse country back to notions of
slavery and a patriarchal Old South.

While Rita Stokes amused herself with her Negro ball, her husband
took his pleasure in his deepening interest in eugenics. This pseudosci-
ence was founded on speculation that the human race can be improved
by the selective breeding of only those persons sound of mind and body.
It was not unlike the practice of breeding purebred horses, and, in fact,
the mother of the Jockey Club member William Averell Harriman,
Mary Williamson Averell Harriman (the widow of the railroad tycoon
Edward Henry Harriman), purchased property on Long Island to be
used as a site for building the Eugenics Record Office, opened in 1909.
Stokes compiled his theories on eugenics in a book titled *The Right to
Be Well Born*, published in New York in 1917. In it, he discussed his
experiences as a horse breeder in Kentucky. Among his proposals was
a government registry of persons in the laboring classes. He suggested
that employers have access to genealogical records in this government
registry so that they could estimate the amount and quality of work that
laborers would be capable of undertaking.[40]

Stokes also thought that he had the answer for producing a lightweight "race" of jockeys. "All this starving, suffering and grilling these [jockey] boys undergo to keep down their weight can be avoided by breeding for smallness, strength and quick intelligence," he wrote, "and a family of jockeys can be produced who will always be fit and ready to meet any racing requirements. It is just as easy to produce the jockey of the right size, weight, and with it all, intelligence, as it is to breed ponies or half-pound chickens and the like. . . . A 'Jockey Registry' will come some day on this principle."[41]

The Stokeses had not created their Southern fancy in Lexington by constructing a Greek Revival mansion, as did the Haggins. Yet they lived the idea of the Southern landowner no less fully than had the Haggins by staging the Negro ball. The ball failed to become a Lexington tradition. It died with the marriage, Rita Stokes suing her husband for divorce in New York in 1900. When next heard from in 1911, Stokes had suffered serious injuries after arguing with two chorus girls in their apartment at Broadway and Eightieth Street in New York. The women shot at Stokes, and, almost immediately, three Japanese men ran into the apartment and attacked him using jujitsu. Stokes required surgery; a court acquitted the chorus girls. By that time, the Bluegrass appears to have moved on from recollections of Stokes and his wife as horse-farm owners in this Eden of the idyllic South.[42]

Little doubt remained, however, that wealthy outsiders were changing the farming landscape of Lexington, importing their spendthrift habits while building great manses, like Haggin's, that rose in stark contrast to what *Munsey's Magazine* called "the simpler tastes and standards of Kentucky yeomen." Toward the end of her lifetime, and on the close of the nineteenth century, Josephine Clay saved an article in her scrapbook. It told how outside millionaires were replacing Kentuckians as the owners of major horse farms in the Bluegrass. It was not unusual to read in the newspapers about the sales of farms to outsiders, such as that of Oakwood Farm to "the latest confederation of Eastern millionaires to locate in the Blue Grass region." The millionaires renamed the property Mill Stream, the renaming coming as their prerogative with the purchase of the property.[43]

Although Bluegrass residents had long desired an influx of outside capital to shore up horse breeding, some now felt conflicted about the presence of these outsiders. Haggin was not well liked. His marriage to a woman forty-six years his junior, with their engagement announced the night before the wedding, had shocked the community. He also engaged in a well-publicized boycott of the Kentucky Derby after arguing with Churchill Downs over the absence of bookmakers at the track. Horsemen in the Bluegrass and in New York accused him of ruining the public auctions by secretly running up the bidding on his own horses. Some Bluegrass residents complained that his buying up smaller farms in the neighborhood of Elmendorf took that land out of production for crops.

The community could not have it both ways, as the *Kentucky Farmer and Breeder* explained to its readership: "Not only have land owners been paid goodly sums for the six thousand acres of its expanse, but into the magnificent residence of its master have gone hundreds of thousands of dollars, into the beautiful stone fences which surround its entire area many other thousands, into its roadways amounts that would stagger if they were revealed. This money, whenever possible, has been spent here. Lexington contractors, Lexington business men have been the beneficiaries. Since the beginning of the establishment of Elmendorf the pauper list in Fayette county has been virtually abolished. Every man who wants work can find it there."[44]

The transition of border-state Kentucky into a Kentucky of the antebellum South thus had its practical advantages for the locals, besides filling the needs of wealthy outsiders. However, all was not well in the Eden of the Old South. The slipping disease of the 1890s had returned. "Stamp out this plague," pleaded the *Kentucky Farmer and Breeder* in desperation in 1906, for the incomes of all in the Bluegrass would be affected by this major economic loss. The publication insisted that someone take charge and formulate a plan whereby bacteriologists could study the malady and come up with some answers. "Raising and selling of blooded stock is one of the chief sources from which Kentucky derives her wealth. Such an industry as this should be fostered, encouraged, and protected by every possible means." The industry remained at a loss, however, to determine what caused the disease—or how to stop its spread.[45]

Bluegrass horse breeders faced 1907 with tepid hope and a great amount of concern, praying that the disease would not strike again. But it returned to bedevil breeders for the second consecutive year. Just as in 1890, people suspected that the disease was contagious. Outsiders were becoming so leery of Kentucky that few were sending horses to race at Churchill Downs, some seventy miles away in Louisville. Then, finally, someone thought he'd found the source of the disease. A scientist in Copenhagen suggested that it was caused by a bacterium, which he called "short bacillus." But nothing ever came of his conclusions. People remained mystified and at a loss about how to deal with the spontaneous abortions. They would occur again and again through the years, always affecting the Bluegrass economy. The abortions mimicked a number of diseases identified later in the twentieth and twenty-first centuries, such as mare reproductive loss syndrome. But the cause of the nineteenth-century abortions was never specifically identified.[46]

At this same time, a phenomenon posing a still greater threat was building momentum. This was the social reform movement of the 1890s, which got only stronger as the twentieth century commenced. Even as the expanding class of multimillionaires was discovering an idyllic retreat in the Bluegrass, a greater number of Americans became determined to shut down horse racing nationwide. The reformers no longer focused their energies primarily on New York. Their influence had brought antiracing legislation in New Jersey in the early 1890s, followed by more legislation in Missouri, Kansas, Tennessee, and Washington, DC. Louisiana banned racing in 1908, although the legislators almost did not get the job done. Someone there reportedly poisoned or doped the food of two state senators who favored passage of an antiracing bill. The two were quite ill when they managed to show up for the vote; their colleagues practically had to give their ayes for them in order to pass the bill, 21–19. The next track to fall to reformers was the original Santa Anita racetrack in California. The Rockingham track in Salem, Massachusetts, followed. The number of operating racetracks went from 314 in 1897 to 25 by 1908.[47]

New York had survived thus far because August Belmont II had worked in tandem with state legislators for passage of the Percy-Gray law in 1895. Belmont's supporters claimed that he saved the turf from inevitable ruin with this bill and that he also laid the foundation for an expanded breeding industry in New York. The rallying cry in attempting to defuse the reformers had long been that racing served a necessary purpose as a testing ground for the improvement of the breed; the idea was that all farmers would benefit from an improved Thoroughbred, perhaps in pulling their plows.

Organized Thoroughbred racing emerged a winner with the Percy-Gray law, which declared gambling illegal away from racetracks without specifically addressing gambling at the tracks. Belmont's detractors claimed that this bill had to do not so much with improving the breed as with consolidating control of gambling at metropolitan tracks like Morris Park (and, following 1905, Belmont Park) that Belmont and his colleagues owned and operated. The cry went up: "One law for August Belmont and another for [offtrack gambling interests]." Some have suggested that a number of the gravest scandals surrounded the enactment of this law. At the very least, it appeared to favor one segment of elite society.[48]

Belmont's influence in the legislature went only so far, however. Like everyone else involved in Thoroughbred racing, he ran headlong into a wall that would not budge in the form of New York governor Charles Evan Hughes. By 1908, Hughes had mounted an offense against the racetracks based on the idea that these venues should not enjoy special status exempting them from gambling. A man highly in tune with reformist aspirations, he cited the evils and demoralizing influence attendant on gambling. He organized church leaders and progressives to work against racetrack gambling, arguing that the New York constitution held gambling illegal and made no exception of racetracks despite the Percy-Gray law. On June 11, 1908, Hughes signed the Hart-Agnew Bill into law, and, with it, betting became illegal everywhere in New York, including at the racetracks.[49]

Racing enthusiasts discovered a loophole, however, that made oral betting possible. These bets, made by one patron with another, eliminated the bookmakers but appeared to be permissible under the new law. Consequently, the New York racetracks limped along for the next two years. In 1910, the system crashed. Hughes signed a new bill, the Agnew-Perkins legislation, that made the racetracks responsible for enforcing the Hart-Agnew antigambling law. Racing in New York shut down completely for the next two and a half years after the final race of the day at Saratoga on August 31, 1910.[50]

Belmont, never one to overlook the possibilities that might lie with his influence in the state legislature, appears to have tried his luck again in Albany. He was accused of slipping in and out of the back rooms of the state capital when the Hart-Agnew law came up for the vote. He supposedly turned up at Albany with an open pocketbook, which his accusers said he proffered to state legislators. The amount mentioned consisted of a "corruption fund" of $500,000 intended for bribes. One state senator claimed that the Jockey Club offered him a bribe of $100,000 to vote against the bill.[51]

As the chairman of the powerful Jockey Club, Belmont, and several others from that organization, had indeed walked the legislative halls. However, they insisted that their intention had been only to lobby against the bill. They swore during an investigation that the money in question had been paid out for legal expenses and publicity and "denied under oath that any of this money had been used for any but legitimate purposes." Nearly three years after the Hart-Agnew bill became law, a news item told how "the Jockey Club and its eight racing association members are completely exonerated of attempts to bribe the legislators to the end of bringing about the defeat of the Hart-Agnew anti–race track bill in 1908." Their denials brought an end to the investigation.[52]

Meantime, Kentucky horsemen were taking no chances of their sport appearing corrupt or operating in a state of disorder. Horsemen cooperated with state legislators in the passage of a Kentucky Racing Commission Act in 1906, creating an authority that would write state racing rules as well as assign noncompeting racing dates to the various tracks. Ironically, the new racing commission emerged amid accusations of ignoble activity having inspired the formation of this ruling body. According to these accusations, a powerful alliance of track operators and state government officials combined to form the commission in order to protect Churchill Downs from competition.[53]

Concern for the protection of Churchill Downs actually extended to all racing in Kentucky. An ownership group known as the Western Jockey Club, or the "Cella-Adler-Tilles gang," had attempted to open the Douglas Park Jockey Club in Louisville in direct conflict with the racing days that Churchill Downs enjoyed. Breeders in Lexington feared the infiltration of this group. According to the *Kentucky Farmer and Breeder:* "They would gradually endeavor to extend their interests, and their influence to other sections of the state. To have a sport . . . degraded through the management of such a crowd would indeed be a sorry reflection on the state. . . . We would rather see the Lexington track cut up and sold for building lots and forever lost to racing than to see this crowd get control of it."[54]

Douglas Park sued and sought an injunction against the racing commission for refusing it the race dates sought. It lost. The *Daily Racing Form* commented: "As the home of the thoroughbred it is well for Kentucky that racing in that state is to be controlled by men who have at heart the love of a high class sport for its own sake." The suspicion remained with some, however, that these same men had used their power to shut Douglas Park out of direct competition with Louisville's premier track. People believed that the state racing commission emerged, with power to award racing dates, in order to prevent simultaneous race meets, "with full power over all tracks at which running races are held," as the *Kentucky Farmer and Breeder* noted.[55]

Racing in Kentucky persevered under the authority of the Kentucky Racing Commission during these challenging times. Nonetheless, the sport suffered great losses during the blackout that extended nearly nationwide. The financial downturn in money paid to owners of winning horses at the nation's racetracks showed how much value the sport had lost from 1906 through 1911. In 1906, $5.4 million in purse money had been distributed in North America. In 1911, the figure fell to $2.3 million, with none of this money coming from New York, where tracks had closed. New York tracks went from paying out a total of $1,582,871 in purses to horse owners in 1908, to $790,650 in 1910, to nothing in 1911. Small wonder that owners like Haggin began to sell off their breeding and racing stock. Speculating that depressed prices at horse auctions would drive breeders out of the business, the *Kentucky Farmer and Breeder* noted in 1905 how "the disastrous influence of the recent legislation against racing is already felt." A racing editor for another publication predicted that, if racing ever returned on its former scale, "the process of rehabilitation will necessarily be slow in contrast to the swiftness with which values were destroyed under the blighting influences of the fanatical crusades that have been a feature of American politics of late."[56]

No one knew whether racing ever would be revived on a national scale. With this in mind, some of the wealthiest horse owners in New York had begun sending their stables to Europe to race even prior to the

The Kentucky Association track opened in Lexington in 1828 with the support of men like Henry Clay and Robert Aitcheson Alexander. The accomplished racehorse Lexington started off his career here. Before the track closed for good in 1933, Man o' War made a farewell appearance in 1920 (although he never raced in Kentucky). (Postcard from the collection of the University of Kentucky Libraries, Special Collections.)

blackout, fearing its effects. Others got out of the sport entirely, some dumping their horses at cheap prices on the South American markets. Elmendorf had been disposing of Thoroughbreds since 1908, after the Hart-Agnew bill passed. In 1909, the farm sent horses by ship to Argentina. In 1912, Haggin sent eighteen broodmares and twelve foals to sell near Berlin. Haggin, a man who had made a fortune in risky mining ventures, had come to suspect that the future of horse racing no longer stood as a solid bet.[57]

Patrons of racing in Lexington already knew what it was like to go without their sport. The Kentucky Association track had closed in 1898, not as a result of antigambling legislation, but because the track had fallen into a financial tailspin after the Panic of 1893. "The panic . . . forced many horses upon the market," the *Kentucky Farmer and Breeder* related. "Prices ran low, breeding ceased, and as a consequence stock farms were closed out, the market was glutted and in many instances horses did not bring the freight and expense bills of the sale. So demoralized were the conditions of the horse trade from 1895 to 1900 that breeding to a considerable extent was abandoned all over the country." The decline in breeding directly affected racing at the track in Lexington, and, consequently, it closed it gates. It took an outside capitalist—the Pittsburgh steel baron Sam Brown—to come up with the money needed to bring racing back to Lexington. Local horsemen did not have sufficient money among themselves.[58]

However, with Kentucky racing up and running again by 1905 and the state's first racing commission founded as a beacon of order, the sport appeared on better ground in Kentucky than anywhere else. Kentucky's patrons of racing had believed that their sport would survive nearly any threat, and even New York's *Spirit of the Times* had once remarked: "Kentucky is the last state in the Union where laws even incidentally adverse to that interest could be enacted." Churchill Downs soon found out that this was not the case. In 1907, Winn, its owner/operator, became engaged in a desperate struggle to head off reformers from shuttering his track. They had managed to bring about a ban on bookmaking that year at the Louisville track. Since this was the only form of wagering at Churchill Downs, Winn had acted quickly to find an alternative form of gambling in order to save the derby and the track. He was successful in this, tracking down four pari-mutuel machines that had been tried out, unsuccessfully, some years earlier at the track. In his memoir, he wrote that these four machines saved racing in Louisville. They accomplished at Churchill Downs what Sam Brown had when saving the sport for Lexington.[59]

In Lexington, Sam Brown was to the Kentucky Association track what Matt Winn was to Churchill Downs. Racing had returned to the Bluegrass thanks to him. However, Bluegrass horsemen never felt completely certain that their business could or would continue in the face of the nationwide antiracing sentiment and the blackout of the sport that followed. They felt that they needed state tax relief to help provide a more secure future. Toward this end, horsemen proposed a plan that would shift the greatest burden of the tax on equine stud fees to the "scrub" (non-Thoroughbred) stock of eastern Kentucky, freeing tax liability from Bluegrass Thoroughbred stock. With this proposal, not only were Bluegrass horsemen setting their horses apart from all others; they were completing whatever the plantation school of fiction might have left unfinished in nailing down the notion that the Bluegrass was, indeed, different from the feuding Eastern portion of the state, where the scrub stock could be found.[60]

The group worked quickly to deflect any criticism that its proposal favored the wealthier section of Kentucky, "the men able to own the

best stock in the state as against the less favored mountain regions."
Public perception indeed would have made it incumbent on these men
to soften the class issue at stake, for a senator from Woodford County
in the Bluegrass had gone further than they had, suggesting that the
breeding of scrub horses be prohibited in Kentucky. Bluegrass horsemen consequently formed a "Breeding Bureau" and planned to acquire
three Thoroughbred stallions to consign to those regions of Kentucky
"where the general class of horses is badly in need of improvement."
This meant the mountains.[61]

New York horsemen already had formed a similar bureau, hoping
to sway public opinion in favor of racing in their state. The *Kentucky
Farmer and Breeder* commented:

The masses of the people will not much longer accept racing purely
for its own sake with the gambling accompaniments which are
necessary to its success. . . . But if the people of the country become
educated to the fact that the thoroughbred horse is the most valuable of all breeds of horses, that the infusion of his blood can do
more to elevate the general class of horses . . . and this breed can
be kept pure and can reach its highest state of perfection only on
condition that racing be allowed and that wealthy men continue to
import the best stock of other countries in order to win the classic
events of our turf, then we have a tangible ground on which to advocate racing and on which to make an appeal for its continuance.[62]

Racing remained in the grip of the shutdown when someone, perhaps Belmont, thought it advisable to hold a dinner in New York simply
to boost the morale of horse owners who had been denied the pleasure
of their sport. Some three hundred patrons of the sport from throughout the United States convened in 1911 at the Waldorf-Astoria Hotel, where Belmont, the host of the affair, was identified as "Chairman
of the Jockey Club, which controls racing throughout the country." A
statement like that left little doubt about the wide scope of the Jockey
Club's control. Belmont announced a plan to offer the federal government six Thoroughbred stallions to use in starting a National Breeding
Bureau since breeding bureaus appeared to be the weapon of last resort
in fighting antigambling forces. Belmont told the gathering: "Uphold-

ing [racing] and doing it justice by passing intelligent criticism upon racing faults is right and we should frown upon the bigot whose gloomy pessimism would turn God's flowers of the field to a monotonous gray." Consoling one another seemed all they could do at the time.[63]

Thoroughbred racing was not going to return to New York as long as Hughes remained governor. That fact seemed certain. But, when Hughes ended his term in 1910 to assume a post as an associate justice on the U.S. Supreme Court, supporters of racing might have begun to glimpse some hope. A test case that arose in 1912 out of gambling on a steeplechase meeting at Belmont Park did, in fact, lead in a positive direction for the sport. The court found that a racing association could not be held liable for illegal gambling if it did not realize that such gambling was taking place on racetrack grounds. The court of appeals in New York dismissed an appeal filed by reform interests, with the result that racing returned May 30, 1913, to Belmont Park. Bennett Liebman, writing about racing's travails throughout the Progressive Era in New York, has posited that the courts' actions in continually stepping in to protect horse racing in that state actually rescued the sport, despite the temporary effect of repressive laws. The effect of racing's return in New York trickled down directly to the Bluegrass horse business, which had been struggling in the economic downturn resulting from nationwide progressive reform.[64]

Not all in the sport had given up hope that racing would return to New York. Following the death of William Collins Whitney in 1904, his son, Harry Payne Whitney, was the leading buyer of his horses at the dispersal held by the Fasig-Tipton Company at Madison Square Garden. The younger Whitney initially removed his father's breeding operation from La Belle Stud, leased in Lexington, to Brookdale Farm, leased in Red Bank, New Jersey. But, ten years later, he changed his mind, and he, too, began buying land near Lexington to develop into a horse farm. If he had changed his mind sooner, his Derby-winning filly Regret might have been born and raised on the Kentucky farm. Little mention was made of her New Jersey origins when the legend evolved about horsemen ringing the bell at Whitney's new Kentucky farm in honor of her winning the derby. There must have seemed no point in spoiling a good story. She was Harry Payne Whitney's horse, and he had set up a horse farm in Kentucky, if belatedly. That was all that mattered.[65]

With racing returned to New York, with the Kentucky Derby receiving national attention, and with increasing numbers of wealthy outsiders heeding the siren call of the Bluegrass region, the professional class of horsemen in central Kentucky had reason enough to laud their work in bringing the racehorse world back home to their state. In their time, in their era, they would not have thought to extend credit beyond themselves, for it had been men like them who had changed the sport from a gentlemen's pursuit into an industry that Kentucky had reclaimed from the Northeast.

With this, however, they would have overlooked the role that plantation fiction played in revising estimations of horse country to eclipse the lawlessness and violence. They also would have overlooked the role of women, for, with rare exceptions, women like Josephine Clay had been denied a visible place in racing. Thus, horsemen failed to grasp how women sympathetic to the old Confederacy of Southern states might have had the greatest success in reclaiming the horse business for the Bluegrass.

However, women assured the Old South myth a place in reconstructed history when they bronzed it and placed it in the form of a memorial to a Confederate general at the courthouse square in Lexington. It was women of the United Daughters of the Confederacy who conceived the idea and raised the money for a memorial to General John Hunt Morgan astride his favorite horse. Wives, daughters, sisters, and nieces from families associated with Thoroughbred racing or breeding stood as the driving force to bring this memorial to fruition. And it was General Morgan's memorial that stood as proof to Northerners that Bluegrass horse country was, indeed, a place of the Old South, a place where the "mystic chords of memory" invoked a culture that bespoke the lifestyle of the Southern cavalier—the Southern colonels and their ladies—that the wealthy might acquire by purchasing Bluegrass horse farms.

And this, as Taylor and Blight have noted, was a fact that Northerners wished to know even as Lost Cause fervor swept the nation. Lexington chose for its hero an officer from the losing side, but this decision supported the horse industry. Early in the twentieth century, when Lexington's citizens, in combination with outsiders, rewrote Bluegrass history, a Confederate officer of General Morgan's notoriety represented the perfect choice.[66]

General Morgan, born in Alabama and raised in Lexington, a close friend of Sanders and Benjamin Bruce and the husband of their sister, Rebecca, had failed to make it through the war. He was shot and killed at Greeneville, Tennessee, in 1864 during an attempted escape while awaiting a court of inquiry hearing. Days earlier, he had been suspended from command of his men. The inquiry had been ordered on reports that his men had robbed and looted on their final raid through Kentucky. It was a wonder that a Bluegrass horseman had not shot Morgan first: his men burned barns at the association track and had stolen racehorses and bloodstock from Clay, Alexander, and others. Lexington residents made a habit of boarding up their houses when they learned that Morgan was headed their way. They feared him and his men.[67]

In a strange twist that demonstrated how memory can and does change history, the horse industry provided encouragement to the Daughters of the Confederacy in a campaign to erect an equestrian statue depicting Morgan. The membership list of the Lexington chapter included numerous names of women connected to the horse business. From the time a Kentucky woman had first proposed the idea for a statue of Morgan in 1908, families at the heart of the Bluegrass horse-breeding and racing business—the power structure of central Kentucky—had worked hard to see the project through to completion. This same power structure had a major voice in the crafting of the memorial. Horsemen gave final approval to the appearance of the work, in particular, the sculptor's rendering of Morgan's horse.[68]

In 1908, the same year the Daughters of the Confederacy and Lexington's horse-based power structure united to memorialize Morgan, still another sleight of hand reconstructed local history. This effort also concerned the memory of Morgan. It reached directly into Bluegrass elementary schools, where impressionable minds had begun reading about Morgan. Students had no sooner begun their assigned history textbook for that year—*The Story of the Great Republic*—than someone discovered that the book contained an unflattering description of Morgan and his men: as a horse thief who had taken valuable Thoroughbreds from local farms, precisely how numerous Bluegrass residents had viewed him during the war.

Schools superintendent M. A. Cassidy pulled the textbooks from the schools. He demanded that the publisher, located in Ohio, correct the "error" immediately. One would not have expected a Republican newspaper to rise in support of this action to tidy up memory of the Confederate side in the Civil War, but that is exactly what occurred. The *Lexington Leader* defended Morgan's good name to the community, a signal that Lexington's embrace of the Lost Cause myth had become bipartisan. This represented a novel turnaround from during and after the actual war. Cassidy, operating from his position of power and backed by no less than the Republican newspaper, forced the publisher to reprint the offending pages.[69]

When students returned to their classrooms following the Christmas break, they resumed reading *The Story of the Great Republic*, but with the Morgan corrections now in place. Over the holidays, Morgan had metamorphosed from a horse thief into a man of ideals supporting a noble cause. Consequently, the younger generation received a reconstructed version of the Bluegrass as many wanted to believe it had existed during the Civil War. These children no doubt carried this version of local history into adulthood and might have taught it to their children, as well.

Cleansing the Morgan legend was extremely important, for the Confederate memorial going up at the courthouse lionized the once-feared Morgan into a local hero representing Southern ideals. It would not have done for textbooks to tell one story and the memorial another. The Confederate memorial effort in Lexington mirrored a phenomenon taking place in cities and towns throughout the South, and the purpose was everywhere the same. Monuments rose to "mold history into its rightful pattern," as Kirk Savage has written. The monuments told a revised story of the South that connoted ideals of order, white supremacy, and the lifestyle of a country squire removed from urban cares. In the heart of the Bluegrass, for the benefit of the horse industry, this mattered far more than whether the locals had written their history accurately. But, as Gary Gallagher and Alan Nolan have pointed out: "The victim of the Lost Cause has been history, for which the legend has been substituted in national memory."[70]

Still another twist occurred in the sculptor's rendition of the horse that Morgan sat astride. The general's favorite battle mount had been a mare named Black Bess, given him by Willa Viley, noted horse breeder of Woodford County. The Texas sculptor Pompeii Coppini was fully

The bronze statue memorializing General John Hunt
Morgan, CSA, in Lexington is iconic but confusing
because, during the Civil War, Kentucky remained loyal to
the United States. (Photograph by the author, 2009.)

aware of this. However, he announced publicly that he planned to de-
pict Morgan's horse as a stallion—in order to create the picture of power
that he perceived could come only from a male horse. The outcome was
ironic, but it also was quite fitting. This story, after all, was about power
and who held the power needed to change local history. The Morgan
memorial never really was about one man. It was all about who held
the reins of power in Lexington and which version of history those in
control wanted told. Local families in the horse business, their interests

united with the fortunes of outside capitalists who wanted to see the Bluegrass as the well-ordered, antebellum South, had much at stake in seeing central Kentucky certified as Southern in the form of a bronze memorial.

The *Lexington Leader* reported on the preparations for the unveiling of the Morgan memorial in October 18, 1911, noting in an accompanying story that James Ben Ali Haggin and his wife had arrived from the East Coast to spend time at Green Hills. Meantime, workmen completed excavation for the foundation on which the Morgan memorial would be placed.[71]

Not all the news stories concerned the memorial. The racing blackout continued to occupy a good amount of column space in local newspapers. One news story concerned Richard Croker, a former New York politician prominent in horse racing, and his thoughts on the great number of large racing stables that had been shipped to Europe owing to the blackout in New York. "This will not help the thousands of men thrown out of work," Croker declared. In other news concerning the horse business, the *Leader*'s rival, the *Lexington Herald*, praised the Kentucky capitalists John C. C. Mayo and Johnson Newlon Camden Jr. (later to operate Runnymede Farm) for their work in interesting Eastern capitalists in encouraging railroads to connect in eastern Kentucky with the Consolidation Coal Company. But the greatest number of newspaper articles focused on the parade and ceremonies planned for the unveiling of the Morgan memorial. The *Herald* noted in a headline, "Federal Soldiers Invited to Parade," that is, the parade to honor this Confederate raider turned hero. As an editorial in the *Herald* intoned: "Men who wore the gray, and men who wore the blue, march together today as the sons of a common mother, brothers in blood, companions in arms fighting for a common cause, the future of the state, and of the nation that is one and indissoluble." North and South had come a long way in this border state, particularly in this bronze memorial that the racehorse community inspired the Daughters of the Confederacy to erect.[72]

One more headline left little doubt about the real inspiration behind the work of the Daughters, the horse business in Kentucky, and the soldiers in blue and gray who would join hands in the parade to march for their common cause. "Eminent Leaders of 'Lost Cause' Arrive," announced the *Herald* on the day of the unveiling. Bluegrass Kentucky had joined in this ideology sweeping the country, and the Bluegrass would benefit financially.[73]

A month earlier, Churchill Downs had sent over twelve pari-mutuel machines from Louisville to be used during the fall meeting at the Kentucky Association track. Racing in Kentucky had staved off the reformers, racing in Lexington had clarified its position on "clean sport" by following Matt Winn's lead in adopting pari-mutuel machines, and the slant of the sun falling across the bronze equestrian statue of Confederate neohero John Hunt Morgan stood as unassailable proof that Bluegrass horse country stood on the side of the Old South and the moral values that the old cavaliers had espoused. Capitalists would have no problem accepting this new image of the Bluegrass when racing began to return across the United States, restoring Kentucky-bred Thoroughbreds and horse-farm land to their position as commodities of rising value.[74]

Kentucky horsemen would lament that Bruce had surrendered rights to the stud book for a mere $35,000 court settlement reached in his standoff with the Jockey Club. Still, Bluegrass Kentucky possessed far greater wealth in the region's land and in its horsemen's knowledge of how to breed and raise a fast horse. John Madden knew this better than anyone, and he continued to work his magic with horses, bringing New York capitalists like the Whitneys, father and son, to his door. Madden persevered through the two dark years of shuttered racing and realized the payoff, seeing not only Old Rosebud but also other horses he'd bred (Sir Barton [the first American Triple Crown winner], Paul Jones, Zeb, and Flying Ebony) or owned (Plaudit) win the Kentucky Derby. This Irish-American turned Kentuckian ruled as America's leading breeder for eleven years. This marked a position of real power in American horse racing that outsiders could not take away.

From Alexander to Madden, from Asteroid and Kentucky to Old Rosebud, Regret, Man o' War, and the vast numbers of fast horses to follow, the Bluegrass had managed to hold its own in a power play for control of the sport. It had seemed certain in the years following the Civil War that agricultural wealth could not stand on equal terms with industrial wealth. However, central Kentucky possessed riches in the water, the grass, and the land that myth had gilded and then polished to a high sheen so that they spoke to the egos of rich men. These agricultural riches, once thought to pale in the face of industrial wealth, instead took Bluegrass land and the region's horses onto the world stage in the twentieth century.

Notes

Introduction

1. Michael Kammen, *Mystic Chords of Memory: The Transformation of Tradition in American Culture* (New York: Knopf, 1991).

2. "The Value of Horses to Kentucky's Economy," *Equine Disease Quarterly* 19, no. 1 (January 2010): 5. Economic figures supplied by the Kentucky Equine Education Project. See www.horseswork.com.

3. Anne Elizabeth Marshall, "'A Strange Conclusion to a Triumphant War': Memory, Identity and the Creation of a Confederate Kentucky" (Ph.D. diss., University of Georgia, 2004).

4. E. Merton Coulter, *Civil War and Readjustment in Kentucky* (1926; reprint, Gloucester, MA: P. Smith, 1966).

5. Luke Edward Harlow, "From Border South to Solid South: Religion, Race and the Making of Confederate Kentucky, 1830–1880" (Ph.D. diss., Rice University, 2009).

1. The Fast Track into the Future

1. Descriptions of Kentucky and Asteroid are taken from "Notes by Harry Worcester Smith, Lordvale Library, 1930, to accompany the Race Horses of America First Number by Edward Troye (1808–1874)," 1867, Keeneland Library, Lexington; and also from the illustration of Kentucky accompanying "Kentucky," *Turf, Field and Farm* 5, no. 16 (October 19, 1867): 241–42.

2. "Revival of Racing at the North," *Spirit of the Times* 29, no. 30 (September 3, 1859): 355; Melvin L. Adelman, *A Sporting Time: New York City and the Rise of Modern Athletics, 1820–70* (Urbana: University of Illinois Press,

1986), 75–78. Adelman also notes: "The creation of racing stables by wealthy New Yorkers in the 1870s was a product of personal and social factors. . . . Status considerations also motivated this group. The ownership of thoroughbreds continued to serve as a vehicle for proclaiming, buttressing, and integrating the horsemen's elite status" (83). As for the reason that New York racing had collapsed by 1845, he points to "the deterioration of the breeding industry in the North": "The breeding industry had never really recovered from . . . the economic depression of 1837 and was in a state of collapse by the mid-nineteenth century. In 1850 only a single thoroughbred stallion was in service on Long Island, once an active breeding area" (78).

3. H. G. Crickmore (*Racing Calendars, 1861, 1862, 1863, 1864, 1865* [New York: printed privately by W. C. Whitney, 1901], 18) notes that the spring race meeting at Lexington appeared to have been abandoned on the second day, June 4, 1861, "by reasons of the war, Lexington being the scene on several occasions of active hostilities." Only one race occurred on that second day of the meet.

4. The racing activities reported in the text were taken from the charts of race results printed in Crickmore, *Racing Calendars*, e.g., 46, 58–59. For wartime theft or impressments of horses, see "Kentucky's Thoroughbred Industry," *Kentucky Farmer and Breeder* 3, no. 10 (March 9, 1906), 2. Adelman quotes the *New York Herald* in stating: "[The war] raging in the South, and extending to some regions of the Western states has deprived owners of racing stock there of their usual fields of turf operation, and consequently induces them to come North." He adds: "To maintain their investment, southern breeders began racing their horses at Saratoga and Paterson, New Jersey; and they became even more dependent on the revitalized northern turf in the postwar years" (*Sporting Time*, 82). See also Edward Hotaling, *They're Off! Horse Racing at Saratoga* (Syracuse, NY: Syracuse University Press, 1995), 40.

5. Hotaling, *They're Off!* 41, 74.

6. Lizzie W., a filly owned by a Kentuckian, Dr. Weldon, and ridden by a one-eyed runaway slave, Sewell, won the first race at Saratoga Springs on August 3, 1863. See Crickmore, *Racing Calendars*, 58. For more on Sewell, see Edward Hotaling, *The Great Black Jockeys: The Lives and Times of the Men Who Dominated America's First National Sport* (Rocklin, CA: Prima, 1999), 4, 177–79, 191. Northerners were bound under the Fugitive Slave Act and the Compromise of 1850 to return runaway slaves to their Southern owners, but the U.S. Army found a way around this during the war by declaring the runaways contraband and, therefore, exempted from the requirement that they be returned. For more on Saratoga, see Landon Manning, *The Noble Animals: Tales of the Saratoga Turf* (N.p.: privately printed, 1973), 62. This history of Saratoga is informative for its treatment of trotting-horse racing as well as Thoroughbred racing. Manning quotes the *Daily Saratogian* editor's comment about the

success of the trotting races, published shortly before twenty thousand soldiers would die at the Battle of Antietam on September 17, 1862: "But the country is engaged in a tremendous civil war. And yet Saratoga prospers and is now verging towards one of the best seasons she has ever enjoyed. Is not this gratifying? We think so, for it establishes the fact that wealth and fashion in the land, recreation, pleasure and wealth will be annually sought at their favorite resort" (62). Gustavus Myers (*History of the Great American Fortunes* [New York: Random House, 1936], 294) also noted the reluctance of the North's propertied elite class to join the war as soldiers: "With few exceptions, the propertied classes of the North loved comfort and power too well to look tranquilly upon any move to force them to enlist. . . . The Draft Act was so amended that it allowed men of property to escape being conscripted into the army by permitting them to buy substitutes."

7. "Kentucky" (n. 1 above), 241.

8. Ibid.

9. Manning, *Noble Animals*, 62–63.

10. "The Stealing and Recovery of Asteroid," *Spirit of the Times* 11, no. 12 (November 19, 1864): 185; "Rebel Outrages by Guerrillas in Kentucky," *Spirit of the Times* 11, no. 11 (November 12, 1864): 169.

11. Hamilton Busbey, "The Running Turf in America," *Harper's New Monthly* 41 (July 1870): 294.

12. "The American Jockey Club Races," *Turf, Field and Farm* 3, no. 12 (September 22, 1866): 184.

13. For a helpful article detailing the development of sports journalism during the nineteenth century, see John Rickards Betts, "Sporting Journalism in Nineteenth-Century America," *American Quarterly* 5, no. 1 (Spring 1953): 39–56.

14. As far back as 1847, people had referred to the village of Saratoga Springs as "The Springs," and it was the *New York Times* that, in 1865, referred to it as "the queen of watering places." See Manning, *Noble Animals*, 11, 58.

15. Hotaling, *They're Off!* 42.

16. "Betting at Cincinnati—the Saratoga Cup," *Wilkes' Spirit of the Times* 12, no. 18 (July 1, 1865): 281.

17. "The New Era of the Turf," *Turf, Field and Farm* 4, no. 23 (June 8, 1867): 360.

18. "The Turf for 1868," *Turf, Field and Farm* 6, no. 10 (March 7, 1868): 152.

19. Adelman suggests that, by this time, racing had "achieved a degree of fashion and respectability heretofore unknown in New York" (*Sporting Time*, 81). Men like Travers and Jerome brought not only money but also style to the sport. Myers recounted how capitalists made tremendous fortunes during the Civil War, often not in the most respectable manner: "They unloaded upon the Government at ten times the cost of manufacture quantities of munitions

of war—munitions so frequently worthless that they often had to be thrown away after purchase. They supplied shoddy uniforms and blankets and wretched shoes; food of so deleterious a quality that it was a fertile case of epidemics" (*Great American Fortunes*, 291–92).

20. John Dizikes, *Sportsmen and Gamesmen* (Columbia: University of Missouri Press, 2002), 35–36; Lyman Horace Weeks, ed., *The American Turf: An Historical Account of Racing in the United States* (New York: Historical Co., 1898), 36–37; Adelman, *Sporting Time*, 78–79.

21. Weeks, ed., *American Turf*, 40.

22. David Black, *The King of Fifth Avenue: The Fortunes of August Belmont* (New York: Dial, 1981), 283–85; Adelman, *Sporting Time*, 80.

23. Mark D. Hirsch (*William C. Whitney: Modern Warwick* [New York: Dodd, Mead, 1948], 24, 43) mentions fortunes made in industry and speculation during the Civil War and afterward, when "a scramble for wealth" occurred. "Wartime contracts, speculation, and inflation had created numerous fortunes," he wrote, adding: "Neither panics nor depressions could dislodge the Stock Exchange as a dispenser of fortunes." On the Kentucky-Asteroid rivalry as directly contributing to the revival of the sport in the North, see Charles E. Trevathan, *The American Thoroughbred* (New York: Macmillan, 1905), 328.

24. "Racing Problem of the Season," *Turf, Field and Farm* 1, no. 1 (August 5, 1865): 16; *Turf, Field and Farm* 6, no. 22 (May 26, 1868): 344.

25. "Asteroid and Kentucky," *Wilkes' Spirit of the Times* 12, no. 18 (July 1, 1865): 281.

26. Ibid.; "The Racing Problem of the Season," *Wilkes' Spirit of the Times* 12, no. 19 (July 8, 1865): 296.

27. "The Racing Problem of the Season" (n. 26 above), 296.

28. "Mr. Alexander's Proposition," *Turf, Field and Farm* 1, no. 1 (August 5, 1865): 16; "Dear Spirit," *Wilkes' Spirit of the Times* 12, no. 21 (July 22, 1865): 326.

29. "The Racing Problem," *Turf, Field and Farm* 1, no. 4 (August 26, 1865): 57; "Asteroid and Kentucky," *Turf, Field and Farm* 1, no. 3 (August 19, 1865): 33–34.

30. "Racing Problem of the Season" (n. 24 above), 16.

31. "Fair Play" to the Editor, *Turf, Field and Farm* 1, no. 1 (August 5, 1865): 16.

32. "The Racing Problem," *Wilkes' Spirit of the Times* 12, no. 21 (July 22, 1865): 329.

33. "Second Day's Race: Kentucky Wins the Cup," *Turf, Field and Farm* 1, no. 2 (August 12, 1865): 27.

34. Adelman, *Sporting Time*, 37. For an excellent study of these North-South races, see Nancy L. Struna, "The North-South Races: American Thoroughbred Racing in Transition, 1823–1850," *Journal of Sport History* 8, no. 2

(Summer 1981): 28–57. See also John Eisenberg, *The Great Match Race* (Boston: Houghton Mifflin, 2006).

35. Adelman, *Sporting Time*, 31–35; Struna, "North-South Races," 49–50.

36. John Dizikes, *Yankee Doodle Dandy* (New Haven, CT: Yale University Press, 2000), 13–14; "Revival of Racing at the North" (n. 2 above), 355.

37. Dizikes, *Yankee Doodle Dandy*.

38. "The Turf: Spring Meetings at Philadelphia, New-York and Boston," *New York Times*, June 23, 1862.

39. Ibid.

40. "Revival of Racing at the North" (n. 2 above).

41. Peter d'A. Jones (*America's Wealth: The Economic History of an Open Society* [New York: Macmillan, 1963]) notes: "With the Civil War out of the way, the northern and western economy boomed. Its gigantic growth was based on vast supplies of raw materials and means of power" (337). Elsewhere he writes: "The wealth of the pre–Civil War market had been overwhelmingly agricultural, though the nation did witness a manufacturing breakthrough in the textile industry. . . . Continued extension of the market after the war through the westward movement, transcontinental railroads, population increase and immigration . . . brought an irreversible alteration in the productive balance of the economy. Agriculture became the hand-maiden of manufacturing industry" (172).

42. Hotaling, *They're Off!* 56.

43. Adelman, *Sporting Time*, 22.

44. Hotaling, *They're Off!* 45.

45. Ibid., 52.

46. "Woodburn," *Kentucky Gazette* (Lexington), September 1, 1866, 2; "Agricultural Resources of Kentucky," *Turf, Field and Farm* 1, no. 10 (October 7, 1865): 149. For more on Woodlawn, see Dennis Domer, "Inventing the Horse Farm," *Kentucky Humanities*, October 2005, 3–12.

47. "Saratoga—Week after the Races," *Turf, Field and Farm* 3, no. 8 (August 25, 1866): 115.

48. For background on the Alexander family, see William Preston Mangum II, *A Kingdom for the Horse* (Louisville: Harmony House, 1999). J. A. Estes ("Woodburn!" *Keeneland Magazine*, Spring 1940, 10) wrote that Woodburn "achieved distinction as a producer of Alderney, Ayrshire, Durham, and Shorthorn cattle, Southdown sheep, Shetland ponies, and Standardbred and Thoroughbred horses." He added: "But it was in the production of Thoroughbred horses that Woodburn had its most remarkable success."

49. Trevathan (*American Thoroughbred*, 328) included Norfolk in his suggestion that a rivalry among the sons of Lexington fueled the revival of Northern racing. However, Norfolk had been sent to California after 1863 and, subsequently, raced exclusively in that state.

50. Hamilton Busbey, *Recollections of Men and Horses* (New York: Dodd, Mead, 1907), 105.

51. *Woodburn Stud Farm, 1864,* records of Woodburn Farm, Woodford County, KY, copy in possession of the author and given to her by the late Dr. A. J. Alexander. This particular farm catalog belonged to Dan Swigert, the manager of Woodburn Farm, and contained his notations.

52. For information on the ownership of Nebula, see Mangum, *Kingdom for the Horse,* 50.

53. "The Woodburn Stud Farm," *Porter's Spirit of the Times* 2, no. 47 (July 25, 1857): 325.

54. Ibid.

55. Dan M. Bowmar III, *Giants of the Turf: The Alexanders, the Belmonts, James R. Keene, the Whitneys* (Lexington: Blood-Horse, 1960), 15.

56. On the first raid at Woodburn, see, e.g., *Woodford Sun* (Versailles, KY), January 30, 1902.

57. R. A. Alexander to Henry Deedes, March 4, 1865, quoted in Bowmar, *Giants of the Turf,* 20.

58. Ibid.

59. Ibid.

60. "Proposed Sale of Mr. Alexander's Horses," *Wilkes' Spirit of the Times* 12, no. 7 (April 15, 1865): 105. On the number of horses sent away from Woodburn Farm during the war, see "Racing Problem of the Season" (n. 24 above), 16.

61. "Kentucky" (n. 1 above), 241.

62. "Jerome Park Course and Stud," *Wilkes' Spirit of the Times* 16, no. 8 (April 20, 1867): 119.

2. The Greening of the Bluegrass

1. Frank Ettensohn, interview by Maryjean Wall, Lexington, October 2, 2007. See also Frank R. Ettensohn, "Horses, Kentucky Bluegrass, and the Origin of Upper Ordovician, Trenton-Age Carbonate Reservoir and Source Rocks in East-Central United States" (paper presented at the annual meeting of the American Association of Petroleum Geologists, Eastern Section, Lexington, September 2007), and "Evidence and Implications of Possible Far-Field Responses to Taconian Orogeny: Middle-Late Ordovician Lexington Platform and Sebree Trough, East-Central United States," *Southeastern Geology* 41 (2002): 1–36; and "Agricultural Resources of Kentucky" (n. 46, chap. 1, above), 149.

2. Thomas D. Clark, *Agrarian Kentucky* (Lexington: University Press of Kentucky, 1977), 5–6 (quoting Shaler); "The Thoroughbred Horse," *Kentucky Live Stock Record* 1, no. 2 (February 12, 1875): 24 (quoting the *London Daily*

Telegraph); Karl B. Raitz, *The Kentucky Bluegrass: A Regional Profile and Guide* (Chapel Hill: University of North Carolina Department of Geography, 1980), 1.

3. "Story of Lexington," *Lexington Transcript,* October 20, 1889, 1.

4. R. Gerald Alvey, *Kentucky Bluegrass Country* (Jackson: University Press of Mississippi, 1992), 6.

5. The revival of horse breeding on Tennessee plantations supports Jon Wiener's argument that white elites in postwar Alabama retained control of the land despite Reconstruction and the emancipation of blacks. See Jonathan M. Wiener, *Social Origins of the New South: Alabama, 1860–1885* (Baton Rouge: Louisiana State University Press, 1978).

6. Ridley W. Wills II, *The History of Belle Meade: Mansion, Plantation, and Stud* (Nashville: Vanderbilt University Press, 1991), 163, 208–10, 196–97.

7. Ibid., 69.

8. Ibid., 117.

9. Robert Aitcheson Alexander to Alexander John Alexander, July 8, 1864, and June 3, 1865, Woodburn Farm Collection, box 4, folder 11 (1860–1865), Kentucky Historical Society, Frankfort.

10. "Kentucky Stud Farm Association," *Lexington Observer and Reporter,* March 17, 1866; "Charter: An Act to Incorporate the Kentucky Stud Farm Association," *Turf, Field and Farm* 2, no. 11 (March 17, 1866): 164; "Visit to Kentucky," *Turf, Field and Farm* 3, no. 8 (August 25, 1866): 118.

11. "Kentucky Stud Farm Association" (n. 10 above).

12. Ibid.

13. Randolph Hollingsworth, *Lexington: Queen of the Bluegrass* (Charleston, SC: Arcadia, 2004), 113; John Hervey, *Racing in America, 1665–1865,* vol. 2 (New York: Jockey Club, 1944), 344–45; "The Racers of Kentucky," *Wilkes' Spirit of the Times* 10, no. 18 (July 2, 1864): 281; Hollingsworth, *Lexington,* 113.

14. Edwin G. Burrows and Mike Wallace, *Gotham: A History of New York City to 1898* (New York: Oxford University Press, 1999), 906. Thomas N. Conway made this remark in his role as an envoy commissioned by the New York City Chamber of Commerce.

15. Marion B. Lucas, *A History of Blacks in Kentucky: From Slavery to Segregation, 1760–1891* (Frankfort: Kentucky Historical Society, 2003), 195; William W. Freehling, *The South vs. the South: How Anti-Confederate Southerners Shaped the Course of the Civil War* (New York: Oxford University Press, 2001), 69.

16. Hollingsworth, *Lexington,* 115, 44; Lucas, *Blacks in Kentucky,* 178, 194–95.

17. *Turf, Field and Farm* 1, no. 3 (August 19, 1865): 40; Peter C. Smith and Karl B. Raitz, "Negro Hamlets and Agricultural Estates in Kentucky's Inner Bluegrass," *Geographical Review* 64, no. 2 (1974): 217–34.

18. Burrows and Wallace, *Gotham,* 906.

19. "Agricultural Resources of Kentucky" (n. 46, chap. 1, above), 149.

20. Ibid.; Smith and Raitz, "Negro Hamlets," 226; Thomas D. Clark, *A History of Kentucky* (Ashland, KY: J. Stuart Foundation, 1992), 62.

21. Lucas, *Blacks in Kentucky*, 274; Smith and Raitz, "Negro Hamlets"; "Letter from Kentucky," *Turf, Field and Farm* 5, no. 10 (September 7, 1867): 151.

22. "Labor for the Planting States," *Turf, Field and Farm* 5, no. 4 (July 27, 1867): 54. Chinese laborers began arriving in the United States in great numbers during the mid-nineteenth century and soon became stereotyped and racialized, according to Robert G. Lee, who argues that these racial stereotypes suited the needs of the dominant, white culture. The notion of the Chinese immigrant laborer as a "coolie" came about "as the U.S. working class was formed in the 1870s and 1880s" (*Orientals: Asian Americans in Popular Culture* [Philadelphia: Temple University Press, 1999], 9). Ronald T. Takaki also has argued that Chinese immigrant labor was racialized, noting that, like Indians and blacks, "the Chinese were 'not white'" (*Iron Cages: Race and Culture in Nineteenth-Century America* [New York: Knopf, 1979], 220).

23. "The Five Races of Man," *Turf, Field and Farm* 5, no. 25 (December 21, 1867): 392. The idea of races created separately as distinct and unequal originated with the American school of ethnology during the 1830s and 1840s. Arguments designed to counter abolitionists included those made by "scientists" who insisted on the plural origins of mankind—the polygenecists whose theories abounded during the 1850s. As George M. Frederickson has written, these arguments suited the desire of Southern slaveholders to place blacks on the lowest rung of creation, thus justifying slavery (*The Black Image in the White Mind* [New York: Harper Torchbooks, 1971], 74–90). The popular thinking, which persisted long after the Civil War, was that blacks were physically, intellectually, and temperamentally different from whites.

24. "A Good Place for Colored Folks," *Tri-Weekly Kentucky Yeoman* (Frankfort), October 7, 1871. An essayist named Henry A. Scomp was still advocating colonization—in 1889. See Frederickson, *Black Image*, 267.

25. The initial notice of the death of Robert Aitcheson Alexander can be found in *Turf, Field and Farm* 5, no. 23 (December 7, 1867): 360. A lengthy obituary appeared in *Turf, Field and Farm* 5, no. 24 (December 14, 1867): 369. Another obituary appeared in *Wilkes' Spirit of the Times* 17, no. 16 (December 7, 1867): 293.

26. Abram S. Hewitt, "Daniel Swigert," *Thoroughbred Record* 211, no. 2 (January 9, 1980): 112–14.

27. Adelman, noting that around this time all sports began to witness the increased participation of a professional class, writes: "The middle class provided the organizational leadership" (*Sporting Time*, 8).

28. "The American Stud Book and Its Founder," *Thoroughbred Record* 107, no. 11 (March 17, 1928): 397.

29. Ibid.

30. Ibid. On the Bruce family and John Hunt Morgan, see also James A. Ramage, *Rebel Raider: The Life of General John Hunt Morgan* (Lexington: University Press of Kentucky, 1986).

31. "The American Stud Book and Its Founder" (n. 28 above), 398.

32. "Prospectus of the Turf, Field, and Farm," *Turf, Field and Farm* 1, no. 2 (August 12, 1865): 31.

33. Jennifer Biesel, "The American Upper Class and the American Horse Industry from 1865–1929" (Ph.D. diss., Middle Tennessee State University, 2005), 529, 145.

34. The article "Lexington" (*Wilkes' Spirit of the Times* 9, no. 18 [January 2, 1864]: 281) announced: "The most famous horse as a racer and progenitor of noble stock that America ever produced, will hereafter be kept as a private stallion. This coming season he will serve a very limited number of mares, besides those of his owner; but after that he will be retained exclusively for Mr. Alexander's stud."

35. "Preakness Stud Farm," *Turf, Field and Farm* 3, no. 3 (July 21, 1866): 41.

36. Ibid.

37. "The Preakness Stud," *Turf, Field and Farm* 4, no. 22 (June 1, 1867): 339.

38. Black, *King of Fifth Avenue*, 283–85.

39. "Belmont's Race Horses," *Brooklyn Eagle*, April 6, 1890, 12.

40. Black, *King of Fifth Avenue*, 283–85.

41. "Gath Talks Horse," *Brooklyn Eagle*, August 3, 1879, 4.

42. Biesel, "American Horse Industry," 49–73. For the purchase of Jerome Edgar, see Hotaling, *They're Off!* 44; "Stallions for 1866," *Turf, Field and Farm* 2, no. 5 (February 3, 1866): 68; and *Turf, Field and Farm* 2, no. 18 (April 28, 1866): 274.

43. "Turf Associations and Agricultural Societies," *Turf, Field and Farm* 1, no. 9 (September 30, 1865): 136.

44. Custer's articles on horse racing for *Turf, Field and Farm* have been collected in Brian W. Dippie, ed., *Nomad: George A. Custer in* Turf, Field and Farm (Austin: University of Texas Press, 1980).

45. Elizabeth B. Custer, *Tenting on the Plains; or, General Custer in Kansas and Texas* (New York: Harper & Bros., 1895; reprint, Norman: University of Oklahoma Press, 1994), 250, 216; *Turf, Field and Farm* 13, no. 2 (July 14, 1871): 25; *Turf, Field and Farm* 13, no. 22 (December 1, 1871): 337; Alvey, *Kentucky Bluegrass Country*, 131. Custer correctly identified the most popular conversation topic in the Bluegrass. Alvey quotes an earlier visitor to central Kentucky: "One drops into horse talk immediately on alighting from the train at Lexington, and does not emerge from it again till he takes his departure. It is the one subject always in order" (ibid.).

46. "Nomad in the Blue Grass Country—the Famous Breeding Studs," *Turf, Field and Farm* 13, no. 22 (December 1, 1871): 337.

47. Ibid.

48. Ibid.

49. Ibid.

50. Ibid.

51. Ibid.

52. Ansel Williamson and Brown Dick are shown with Asteroid in Genevieve Baird Lacer, *Edward Troye: Painter of Thoroughbred Stories* (Louisville: Harmony House, 2006), 210.

53. "Nomad in the Blue Grass Country" (n. 46 above).

54. Lucas Brodhead to A. J. Alexander, December 1, 1871, copy (courtesy A. J. Alexander) in possession of the author; "Nomad in the Blue Grass Country" (n. 46 above).

55. "Nomad in the Blue Grass Country" (n. 46 above).

56. Ibid.

57. Ibid.

3. A Killing Spree and a Hanging Tree

1. W. S. Vosburgh, *Racing in America, 1866–1921* (New York: Scribner Press, 1922), 86; Kent Hollingsworth, *The Great Ones* (Lexington: Blood-Horse, 1970), 175, and *The Kentucky Thoroughbred* (Lexington: University Press of Kentucky, 1976), 84.

2. Hollingsworth, *Kentucky Thoroughbred*, 74–75.

3. The *New York Times* (July 15, 1871, 5) gave this description of Longfellow's owner after the horse defeated Kingfisher at Saratoga: "Men rushed about with tears in their eyes, vowing that such a horse as this was never foaled. The only perfectly cool person was Longfellow's owner, old John Harper, 'Uncle John,' as he is universally called, who tottered along leaning on his cane and shouting directions to the negro boys who were grooming the victor."

4. Black, *King of Fifth Avenue*, 370–71.

5. "The Southern Outrages," *New York Times*, September 21, 1874, 3.Crime in Bluegrass Kentucky was rife before the Civil War, during the war, and for years afterward. The standard work on violence in Kentucky has been Hambleton Tapp and James C. Klotter, *Kentucky: Decades of Discord, 1865–1900* (Frankfort: Kentucky Historical Society, 1977). Klotter expanded the research and insights of this work in his *Kentucky Justice, Southern Honor, and American Manhood: Understanding the Life and Death of Richard Reid* (Baton Rouge: Louisiana State University Press, 2003). Robert M. Ireland addressed Kentucky violence in *Little Kingdoms: The Counties of Kentucky, 1850–1891* (Lexington: University Press of Kentucky, 1977), particularly in the chapter "Law and Order" (71–89). Newer work on violence in the Bluegrass includes James Michael Rhyne, "Rehearsal for Redemption: The Politics of Post-

Emancipation Violence in Kentucky's Bluegrass Region" (Ph.D. diss., University of Cincinnati, 2006); Aaron Astor, "Belated Confederates: Black Politics, Guerrilla Violence, and the Collapse of Conservative Unionism in Kentucky and Missouri, 1860–1872" (Ph.D. diss., Northwestern University, 2006); and Marshall, "'Strange Conclusion.'"

      6. "Ku Klux in Kentucky," *New York Times*, August 27, 1873, 4; "Ku Klux No Bar to Northern Settlers," *New York Daily Tribune*, May 1, 1871, 1; Lucas Brodhead to A. J. Alexander, December 19, 1870 (n. 54, chapter 2 above); Klotter, *Kentucky Justice*, 45, 53–54; Robert M. Ireland, "Homicide in Nineteenth Century Kentucky," *Register of the Kentucky Historical Society* 81, no. 2 (1983): 134. Ireland continues: "Kentucky's penchant for homicide fitted within the mainstream of the southern experience. . . . The murder rate below the Mason-Dixon line was from four to fifteen times that of above" (134).

      7. Klotter, *Kentucky Justice*, 53; Ireland, *Little Kingdoms*, 72.

      8. Klotter, *Kentucky Justice*, 53–54. Allen W. Trelease (*White Terror: The Ku Klux Klan Conspiracy and Southern Reconstruction* [Baton Rouge: Louisiana State University Press, 1971], 312) specifically identified Lexington and Frankfort as the epicenter of the most violent social chaos in Kentucky. This region, writes Trelease, paradoxically has been "more normally known for its bluegrass, thoroughbred horses, and bourbon whiskey." See also H. V. Redfield, *Homicide, North and South* (Columbus: Ohio State University Press, 1880).

      9. "Kentucky Is the Corsica of America," *New York Times*, December 26, 1878. See also Ireland, *Little Kingdoms*, 72; and "Ku Klux Outrages in Kentucky," *New York Times*, March 25, 1871, 4.

      10. Ireland, *Little Kingdoms*, 131. Klotter writes that the statistics from Redfield's 1880 *Homicide, North and South* appeared two years later in the *Nation* (35 [November 23, 1882]: 442), "giving them additional national exposure" (*Kentucky Justice*, 54, 156). See also *New York Times*, December 16, 1874; and Ireland, *Little Kingdoms*, 87. For a quick read on William Goebel, see James C. Klotter, "William Goebel," in *Kentucky's Governors*, ed. Lowell H. Harrison (Lexington: University Press of Kentucky, 2004), 134–36.

      11. *Adam Harper v. J. Wallace Harper*, 1873, Scott County Order Book 32, fol. 606, microfilm reel 994563, Kentucky Department of Libraries, Frankfort. Harper's account of the night in the stable and the following morning was taken from the deposition of John Harper Sr., July 18, 1873, at the offices of Blackburn and Fryman, Versailles, KY.

      12. Ibid.

      13. Ibid., Magistrate W. A. Moore testimony.

      14. Ibid., Dr. Alfred Hurst testimony. See also ibid., "Answer" of Wallace Harper, September 4, 1872; "Slander and Murder," *Lexington Press*, March 11, 1873.

      15. *Frankfort Commonwealth*, September 15, 1871; "Memoirs of Distin-

guished Kentucky Turfmen: John Harper," *Kentucky Live Stock Record* 2, no. 4 (July 23, 1875): 57; *Harper v. Harper,* James Blackburn testimony.

16. Ibid., W. A. Moore testimony.

17. Ibid., W. S. Worsham testimony.

18. Ibid., L. H. Parrish deposition, Adam Harper testimony, Thomas Bedford testimony.

19. Ibid., Dr. William Allen testimony. Allen identified John Harper Sr. as ordering the mock lynching and said that the two black persons were put to "a pretty severe test." The incident occurred in October 1871. Dr. Hurst, in his testimony, identified it as "Ku Klux business." Another who testified, Peter Ferguson, said that he was along with the party that went to hang the "negroes." See also the *Frankfort Commonwealth,* September 15, 1871. See also *Harper v. Harper,* Thomas Bedford testimony.

20. *Harper v. Harper,* Charles Lewis testimony.

21. Ibid., Adam Harper testimony, James Blackburn testimony, Charles Lewis testimony.

22. Ibid., Charles Lewis testimony.

23. "Nomad in the Blue Grass Country" (n. 46, chap. 2, above).

24. *Harper v. Harper,* Mrs. Barbara Owsley testimony.

25. "Nomad in the Blue Grass Country" (n. 46, chap. 2, above).

26. Klotter, *Kentucky Justice,* 38–39.

27. "The Shooting of President M. Lewis Clark, Jr.," *Kentucky Live Stock Record* 10, no. 14 (October 4, 1879): 217.

28. "The Shooting of Ten Broeck," *New York Times,* August 12, 1874.

29. Klotter, *Kentucky Justice,* 46 (see generally 45–45); "Lawlessness in Kentucky," *New York Times,* December 16, 1874.

30. "Nomad in the Blue Grass" (n. 46, chap. 2, above), 337.

31. Hollingsworth, *Kentucky Thoroughbred,* 84.

32. Ibid., 85.

33. Hollingsworth, *Great Ones,* 271.

4. "All the Best Jockeys of the West Are Colored"

1. For Murphy's reference to Harrison's cabinet, see "Isaac Murphy, Biographical Sketch of the Great Lexington Jockey," *Lexington Leader,* March 20, 1889.

2. The barring of blacks from sports, and the erasing from memory of their achievements, was a phenomenon not limited to horse racing at the turn of the twentieth century. Nor was the rising racism in sports different from that occurring in the larger world. David K. Wiggins (*Glory Bound: Black Athletes in a White America* [Syracuse, NY: Syracuse University Press, 1997], 29) writes that black participants in sports indeed "were facing the same type of discrimi-

nation . . . that they were experiencing in other walks of life." The heavyweight champion John L. Sullivan announced in 1892, "I will not fight a negro," when the black boxer Peter Jackson expressed his desire to challenge Sullivan for the title. Major League baseball had been integrated from 1884 to 1888, but, in that latter year, an "unwritten rule" unfriendly to blacks came into force (see Andrew Sturgeon Nash, *Negro Firsts in Sports* [Chicago: Johnson, 1963], 55–56). In John E. Driefort, ed., *Baseball History from Outside the Lines: A Reader* (Lincoln: University of Nebraska Press, 2001), 64–65, the year 1887 is cited as "a banner year for colored talent in the white [minor] leagues." However, "troubling racial episodes, fomented mostly by white players," began occurring in that same season. Driefort quotes the *Sporting Life* of June 1, 1887: "White players dislike to play with these men."

3. The temporary banning of Murphy and the discourse on whether he drank too much followed his controversial ride aboard the champion mare Firenze at Monmouth Park in 1890. See *Kentucky Leader*, August 29, 1890, reprinting a report from the *New York Sun*.

4. Alvin F. Harlow, *Weep No More, My Lady* (New York: Whittlesey, 1942), 311.

5. Frank Borries Jr., "Ike Murphy's Grave," *Louisville Courier-Journal Magazine*, n.d. The article is filed in the Keeneland Library.

6. *Lexington Daily Leader*, February 12, 1896, February 17, 1896, and March 16, 1896; *Turf, Field and Farm* 62, no. 8 (February 21, 1896): 276.

7. A biography of Murphy that writers frequently reference is Frank Tarlton, "A Memorial," *Thoroughbred Record* 43, no. 12 (March 21, 1896): 136.

8. Mia Bay (*The White Image in the Black Mind* [New York: Oxford University Press, 2000]), while demonstrating how black intellectuals challenged notions of inferiority that had been constructed into the idea of race, also discusses Northern racism. Following the Civil War, as Bay writes, "Northern democrats railed against the dangers of race mixture . . . and warned that racial equality would lead to race mixture" (90). Gunner Myrdal (*An American Dilemma: The Negro Problem and Modern Democracy* [New York: Harper & Row, 1962]) argued that "the Negro was a thorn in [Northern] flesh, an impediment in the way of reunification of North and South" (738). His conclusion was that Northerners decided quite quickly after the war that they did not care much for blacks.

9. George C. Wright, *Racial Violence in Kentucky, 1865–1940* (Baton Rouge: Louisiana State University Press, 1996), 19, 2, 11.

10. *Woodford Weekly* (Versailles, KY), August 12, 1870, reprinting an article from the *Harrodsburg (KY) People*, cited in Aaron Astor, "No Gun, No Vote: Violence and the Fifteenth Amendment in Kentucky" (paper delivered at the annual meeting of the Southern Historical Association, Louisville, November 2009).

11. Luke E. Harlow ("Against Abolitionist Heresy: Religious and Racial Orthodoxy and the Forging of Confederate Identity in White Kentucky" [paper delivered at the annual meeting of the Southern Historical Association, Louisville, November 2009]) demonstrated how the debate became a religious one, causing antislavery—but racist—conservative Kentuckians to join together after the war with those Kentuckians who had been proslavery. See also Marshall, "'Strange Conclusion.'"

12. *New York Times*, November 6, 1871.

13. *Kentucky Gazette* (Lexington), January 25, 1873, January 8, 1873, January 29, 1873, and February 26, 1873.

14. *Kentucky Gazette* (Lexington), February 1, 1873; Tapp and Klotter, *Kentucky*, 36.

15. Myrdal, *American Dilemma*, 1012. David K. Wiggins ("Isaac Murphy: Black Hero in Nineteenth Century American Sport, 1861–1896," *Canadian Journal of the History of Sport and Physical Education* 10 [May 1979]: 31) identified the racehorse jockey as among those positions considered fit only for blacks in the years immediately following the war since it was closely associated with work done on the antebellum plantations.

16. Dale Somers, *The Rise of Sports in New Orleans, 1850–1900* (Baton Rouge: Louisiana State University Press, 1972), 96–97.

17. Ibid.

18. Wiggins, "Isaac Murphy."

19. "Racing in the West," *Spirit of the Times* 119, no. 20 (June 7, 1890): 1. For the number of black jockeys in the inaugural Kentucky Derby, see Hotaling, *Great Black Jockeys*, 229–31. As for jockeys considered as laborers, Dale Somers points out how they rarely received recognition for their athletic feats, even into the 1870s. Most riders simply were contracted to racing stables and, as such, considered among the laborers working for that stable. According to Somers: "Few achieved any measure of fame for their ability. Racing accounts seldom mentioned riders unless they suffered injury or the reporter believed the jockey's 'careless or criminality' resulted in an unnecessary defeat" (*Rise of Sports in New Orleans*, 111).

20. *Live Stock Record* 41, no. 1 (January 5, 1895): 11.

21. "Negro Jockeys Shut Out: Combination of White Riders to Bar Them from the Turf," *New York Times*, July 28, 1900, 14; "Jockey War at Chicago," *Thoroughbred Record* 52, no. 7 (August 18, 1900): 77.

22. Joe Drape, *Black Maestro: The Epic Life of an American Legend* (New York: William Morrow, 2006), 63.

23. On Eli Jordan taking America Burns and Murphy into his home, see *Kentucky Leader*, July 29, 1891, 7. James T. Williams also developed the careers of at least two other African American jockeys who followed Murphy: Pike Barnes and Tommy Britton. See *Lexington Leader*, July 5, 1901, 7.

24. Tarlton, "A Memorial," 136. Tarlton, the owner of a racing stable, a racing official at the Latonia Race Course, and "a pronounced and unwavering Republican" who served as a delegate to the Republican National Convention in 1892, was also Murphy's attorney. He wrote this biographical sketch about the jockey on Murphy's death.

25. Ibid.

26. Hotaling, *Great Black Jockeys*, 236; *Live Stock Record* 37, no. 7 (February 18, 1893): 109; Liliane Winkfield Casey, oral history taken by Maryjean Wall, Cincinnati, September 12, 2002, in possession of the author.

27. Lucas, *Blacks in Kentucky*, 185–89.

28. Wright, *Racial Violence in Kentucky*, 8.

29. Lucas, *Blacks in Kentucky*, 189; "Kentucky," *New York Daily Tribune*, May 3, 1871, 5. This *Tribune* article identified the Bourbon (aristocratic) faction of the Democratic Party in Kentucky as "the Ku-Klux gentry" and argued that these persons, who had held the immediate postwar power in state government, were responsible for thwarting legislative attempts to curb Klan activities in Kentucky.

30. *Kentucky Gazette* (Lexington), February 26, 1873. See also *Tri-Weekly Kentucky Yeoman* (Frankfort), August 31, 1871; *Woodford Weekly* (Versailles, KY), September 29, 1871; *Kentucky Gazette* (Lexington), February 26, 1873, and June 11, 1873.

31. Hotaling, *Great Black Jockeys*, 253.

32. William H. P. Robertson's *The History of Thoroughbred Racing in America* (Englewood Cliffs, NJ: Prentice-Hall, 1964) includes information on Pierre and George Lorillard (127–37) and Mike and Phil Dwyer (130–31).

33. The Dwyers, Corrigan, their betting adventures, and the Freeland–Miss Woodford races are recounted in Hotaling, *Great Black Jockeys*, 254–55. For Lucky Baldwin, see Kent Hollingsworth, "Empire of the Lucky," *Blood-Horse*, January 2, 1982, 60–63.

34. On Murphy's reputation for honesty and advice to Stoval, see Hotaling, *Great Black Jockeys*, 247. On the need for black jockeys to be completely honest, even more so than white riders, see ibid., 281.

35. "Isaac Murphy," *Kentucky Leader*, March 20, 1889.

36. *Kentucky Leader*, January 25, 1891, 5. Gerald L. Smith (*Black America Series: Lexington, Kentucky* [Charleston, SC: Arcadia, 2002], 20) identifies Mary Britton as "a highly respected teacher, writer, activist, and doctor." On the anniversary of Isaac and Lucy Murphy, see *Kentucky Leader*, January 31, 1893.

37. For a list of postbellum, nineteenth-century African Americans in business, the professions, and political careers in Lexington, see Maryjean Wall, "Kentucky's Isaac Murphy: A Legacy Interrupted" (M.A. thesis, University of Kentucky, 2003). For Murphy's quote about his profession as a jockey, see Hotaling, *Great Black Jockeys*, 275.

38. "Peter," *Turf, Field and Farm* 18, no. 26 (June 26, 1874): 446.

39. Ibid. James C. Cobb (*Away Down South: A History of Southern Identity* [Oxford: Oxford University Press, 2005], 86–87) notes how African American domestics stratified class separation and identity according to the prestige of the white families for whom they worked. Peter would be one example of this. Cobb writes: "Blacks in Charleston also knew that the fine houses south of Broad Street with their two-story columns and great spreading piazzas were such powerful symbols of a white family's historic prestige and influence that even the black servants who worked in them sometimes saw themselves as 'powers in the community.'"

40. "Peter" (n. 38 above).

41. On Haggin, see Robertson, *History of Thoroughbred Racing*, 143–47; and Cherie Suchy, "Legacy of the Land," *Thoroughbred Record* 213, no. 1 (January 7, 1981): 48–51.

42. Hollingsworth, *Great Ones*, 237.

43. Ibid.

44. "Post and Paddock," *Spirit of the Times* 119, no. 22 (June 21, 1890): 970; Walter Vosburgh's account of the race on June 25, 1890, at Sheepshead Bay, as quoted in John Hervey, "W. S. Vosburgh: An Appreciation, Written for the Jockey Club" (1935), 59–61, Keeneland Library, Lexington. On the floral horseshoe, see "What the Jockeys Said about the Suburban," *Turf, Field and Farm* 50, no. 25 (June 20, 1890): 719.

45. Ella Wheeler Wilcox, "How Salvator Won," *Spirit of the Times* 119, no. 25 (July 12, 1890): 1082.

46. Hervey, "W. S. Vosburgh," 58; Hotaling, *Great Black Jockeys*, 262–65.

47. *Kentucky Leader*, August 29, 1890.

48. Hotaling, *Great Black Jockeys*, 266–67; Betty Earle Borries, *Isaac Murphy: Kentucky's Record Jockey* (Berea, KY: Kentucke Imprints, 1988), 89–91.

49. Tarlton, "A Memorial," 136. Laura Hillenbrand (*Seabiscuit: An American Legend* [New York: Random House, 2001], 66–70) describes the rigors that jockeys endured in order to keep their weight low.

50. Borries, *Isaac Murphy*, 91; Hotaling, *Great Black Jockeys*, 268; "Was Isaac Murphy Poisoned," *Live Stock Record* 32, no. 21 (November 22, 1890): 329 (reprinting an article from the *Louisville Commercial*); *Kentucky Leader*, November 22, 1890.

51. "Negro Jockeys Shut Out," *New York Times*, July 28, 1900, 14; "Latonia," *Spirit of the Times* 122, no. 10 (September 19, 1891): 371.

52. Joel Williamson (*The Crucible of Race: Black and White Relations in the American South since Emancipation* [New York: Oxford University Press, 1984]) argues that this radical turn to greater violence originated with the Panic of 1893, a depression that lasted through that decade. According to Williamson, white men who experienced financial ruin suffered psychological effects when they were unable to provide for their families; they turned their rage against

blacks. Edward Ayers (*Vengeance and Justice: Crime and Punishment in the 19th Century American South* [New York: Oxford University Press, 1984]) saw the radical turn from a different perspective, concluding that blacks and whites of the latter part of the nineteenth century had not grown up in the close contact that characterized the slavery era—thus the violence. Interestingly, in *Kentucky Justice,* Klotter suggested that people in the commonwealth faced a choice and chose to follow the Southern path of violence. With this conclusion, he added another layer to the textured view of Kentucky's Confederate identity as associated with the violence emerging in modern times.

5. Old Money Meets the Arrivistes

1. "An Incorrigible Character," *Thoroughbred Record* 213, no. 20 (May 20, 1981): 2225. For more information on Ed Corrigan, see "Death of Edward Corrigan," *Thoroughbred Record* 100, no. 2 (July 12, 1924): 17; "Mr. Edward Corrigan," *Spirit of the Times* 140, no. 7 (August 25, 1900): 150; and Horace Wade, "Tales of the Turf," *Turf and Sport Digest* 33, no. 6 (June 1956): 20–21, 34–35.

2. Paul Boyer, *Urban Masses and Moral Order in America, 1820–1920* (Cambridge, MA: Harvard University Press, 1978), 125.

3. Ibid.

4. "An Incorrigible Character" (n. 1 above), 2225.

5. Ibid. See also Drape, *Black Maestro,* 36–37; and William Robertson and Dan Farley, eds., *Hoofprints of the Century* (Lexington: Thoroughbred Record, 1975), 124.

6. Drape, *Black Maestro,* 37.

7. Amy Gregory, "An American Sportsman," *Thoroughbred Record* 217, no. 7 (February 16, 1983): 1089–96. A frequently referenced biography of Pierre Lorillard is W. S. Vosburgh, *Cherry and Black: The Career of Mr. Pierre Lorillard on the Turf* (New York: privately published, 1916).

8. "The Blue-Grass Country," *Spirit of the Times* 23, no. 18 (December 17, 1870): 275.

9. Ibid.

10. Hollingsworth, *Great Ones,* 209; "Rancocas Stud," *Thoroughbred Record* 50, no. 5 (July 29, 1899): 55.

11. Hollingsworth, *Great Ones,* 210.

12. Gregory, "An American Sportsman," 1092; *Spirit of the Times* 101, no. 19 (June 11, 1881): 500.

13. On Lexington vs. Leamington, see Hervey, "W. S. Vosburgh," 14. On Asteroid, see "The Kentucky Association," *Thoroughbred Record* 52, no. 7 (August 18, 1900): 76.

14. "The Sons of Lexington at the Stud," *New York Sportsman,* March 1, 1879.

15. "The Blue-Grass Country" (n. 8 above), 275.

16. *Spirit of the Times* 102, no. 10 (October 8, 1881): 282.

17. "A Hint to Breeders," *Kentucky Live Stock Record* 2, no. 5 (July 30, 1875): 72.

18. Bowmar, *Giants of the Turf,* 57.

19. Some information about James R. Keene can be found in Alden Hatch and Foxhall Keene, *Full Tilt: The Sporting Memoirs of Foxhall Keene* (New York: Derrydale, 1938).

20. Mary Simon, "The Man Who Loved Racing," *Thoroughbred Times* 17, no. 33 (August 18, 2001): 26–27.

21. Ibid.

22. "Foxhall: The Winner of the Grand Prize of Paris, 1881," *Spirit of the Times* 101, no. 20 (June 18, 1881): 517.

23. A helpful article on the Dwyer brothers is Dan Mearns, "The Butchers' Dynasty," *Blood-Horse* 101, no. 17 (April 28, 1975): 1658–63.

24. Robertson, *History of Thoroughbred Racing,* 131.

25. Matt J. Winn and Frank G. Menke, *Down the Stretch* (New York: Smith & Durrell, 1945), 28–29.

26. Ibid.

27. Robertson, *History of Thoroughbred Racing,* 133–34, 136–37.

28. "Sale of Thoroughbreds," *Krik's Guide* (New York: H. G. Crickmore, 1877–1878), 182–85. On Northeastern farms limiting breeding to their own stallions, see Hewitt, "Daniel Swigert."

29. On the turf moguls sending their broodmares only to their own stallions, thus limiting traffic, see Hewitt, "Daniel Swigert," 114. On the disadvantages of breeding on land other than in the Bluegrass region, see "The Thoroughbred Horse" (n. 2, chap. 2, above), 24.

30. For the complete list of members of the Coney Island Jockey Club, see Trevathan, *American Thoroughbred,* 401.

31. For the number of foals, see "The Demand for Thoroughbreds," *Live Stock Record* 10, no. 5 (August 2, 1879): 72. For the number of breeding farms and the remark that "nearly every farmer [in Fayette County] is to some extent a breeder," see George W. Ranck, *History of Lexington, Kentucky* (Cincinnati: Robert Clarke, 1872), 135. The foals for 1870 at Woodburn are listed individually in an attachment to Lucas Brodhead to A. J. Alexander, December 19, 1870 (n. 54, chapter 2 above). The total given for the mares of James A. Grinstead is found in "The Blue-Grass Country" (n. 8 above), 275.

32. "The Stud at Rancocas," *Spirit of the Times* 100, no. 14 (November 6, 1880): 357.

33. "The Demand for Thoroughbreds" (n. 31 above), 357.

34. *Spirit of the Times* 101, no. 24 (July 16, 1881): 649; *Woodford Sun* (Ver-

sailles, KY), December 24, 1883; "Mr. Edmund Tattersall," *Spirit of the Times* 100, no. 21 (December 25, 1880): 534.

35. "Thoroughbreds in the South: Belle Meade," *Spirit of the Times* 100, no. 15 (November 13, 1880): 377–78; "Tennessee as a Breeding Region," *Spirit of the Times* 100, no. 19 (December 11, 1880): 479.

36. John Clay to Josephine Clay, June 19, 1872, box 1, item 107, Papers of Josephine Clay, Special Collections and Archives, University of Kentucky Libraries, Lexington.

37. John Clay to Josephine Clay, June 24, 1872, box 1, item 109, Papers of Josephine Clay.

38. "Interesting Letter from 'The Captain,'" *Spirit of the Times* 29, no. 15 (May 21, 1859): 174; "Ashland—John M. Clay," *Turf, Field and Farm* 66, no. 11 (March 18, 1898): 347.

39. "A Visit to the Stock Farm of John M. Clay," *Spirit of the Times* 13, no. 15 (December 9, 1865): 231. See also Henry Clay Simpson Jr., *Josephine Clay: Pioneer Horsewoman of the Bluegrass* (Prospect, KY: Harmony House, 2005), 60.

40. Maryjean Wall, "Boy's Club? Deal Her In," *Lexington Herald-Leader*, November 2, 2004, C-1.

41. The address (taken from a Josephine Clay scrapbook in possession of Henry Clay Simpson) was read to delegates of the International Council of Women at Toronto, ON, June 15, 1903, and reprinted in the *Kansas City Star*, n.d.

42. Charles B. Parmer, *For Gold and Glory* (New York: Carrick & Evans, 1939), 130–31.

43. On Belmont and his concern with the Ku Klux Klan, see Black, *King of Fifth Avenue*, 382–86.

44. Bowmar, *Giants of the Turf*, 57.

45. "Rambles in Kentucky and Tennessee," *Spirit of the Times* 111, no. 1 (January 30, 1886): 12.

46. For more on Belmont's racing stable, see Joe H. Palmer, "Maroon, Scarlet Sash," *Keeneland Magazine*, Spring 1942, 8–49.

47. *Lexington Herald*, October 16, 1904, sec. 2, pp. 5–6.

6. Winners and Losers in the Age of Reform

1. "Post and Paddock," *Spirit of the Times* 119, no. 13 (April 19, 1890): 557.

2. Wade, "Tales of the Turf," 21.

3. "Pool Rooms," *Lexington Leader*, June 14, 1892, 1; "Young Men Ruined by Pool Rooms," *Lexington Leader*, October 22, 1905, sec. 2, p. 4.

4. Richard Hofstadter (*The Age of Reform: From Bryan to F.D.R.* [New York: Knopf, 1955]) placed the origins of the Progressive Era reform movement

in the upheavals in American society that had been going on since the Civil War. New money had emerged to join or replace the old monied class; portions of the middle class were displaced. Social unrest found outlets in reform movements, in anti-Semitism, and in nativism. Boyer (*Urban Masses,* 179) argued that, by banding together in a moral-control effort, the middle class achieved a sense of greater internal order designed to overcome its feeling of increasing social isolation. Consequently, the 1890s saw intensified efforts to close saloons and clean up prostitution. Boyer overlooked the antigambling crusades that also increased in intensity at this time, but the timing of these crusades would place them on a parallel course with the antisaloon and antiprostitution efforts.

5. James Duane Bolin, *Bossism and Reform in a Southern City: Lexington, Kentucky, 1880–1940* (Lexington: University Press of Kentucky, 2000), 19.

6. Bolin, *Bossism and Reform,* 19–22, 27.

7. Ibid., 27, 21–22; "Heavy Blow to Kentucky," *Lexington Leader,* June 12, 1908, 4.

8. "The Turf for 1868" (n. 18, chap. 1, above), 152.

9. Roger Longrigg, *The History of Horse Racing* (New York: Stein & Day, 1972), 229; Busbey, "Running Turf in America," 254.

10. Busbey, "Running Turf in America," 255.

11. Somers, *Rise of Sports in New Orleans,* 108.

12. On the pari-mutuel machines brought from France, see ibid., 98.

13. "The Brooklyn, New York and Coney Island Jockey Clubs," *Kentucky Live Stock Record* 31, no. 26 (June 28, 1890): 408.

14. Lloyd Wendt and Herman Kogan, *Bet a Million! The Story of John W. Gates* (Indianapolis: Bobbs-Merrill, 1948), 10; Horace Wade, *Tales of the Turf* (New York: Vantage, 1956), 14.

15. Wade, *Tales of the Turf,* 17; "A Wise Move," *Thoroughbred Record* 62, no. 15 (October 7, 1905): 233.

16. "News of the Track and Racers," *Brooklyn Eagle,* January 19, 1891, 2. See also Robertson, *History of Thoroughbred Racing,* 175.

17. *Spirit of the Times* 119, no. 1 (January 25, 1890): 6.

18. *Spirit of the Times* 119, no. 8 (March 15, 1890): 324; *Spirit of the Times* 120, no. 22 (December 20, 1890): 845.

19. Robertson and Farley, eds., *Hoofprints of the Century,* 64; Simon, "The Man Who Loved Racing"; "Keene Sells Famous Castleton Farm," *New York Times,* November 24, 1911, 11.

20. Edward L. Bowen, *Legacies of the Turf: A Century of Great Thoroughbred Breeders,* vol. 1 (Lexington: Eclipse, 2003), 11–12.

21. Ibid., 11; Simon, "The Man Who Loved Racing."

22. Hollingsworth, *Kentucky Thoroughbred,* 60–61.

23. Ibid., 62–63.

24. Hollingsworth, *Great Ones,* 73.

25. See Altina L. Waller, *Feud: Hatfields, McCoys, and Social Change in Appalachia, 1860–1900* (Chapel Hill: University of North Carolina Press, 1988); Ronald D. Eller, *Miners, Millhands, and Mountaineers: Industrialization of the Appalachian South, 1880–1930* (Knoxville: University of Tennessee Press, 1982).

26. The Tollgate War is discussed in Tapp and Klotter, *Kentucky*, 404–9.

27. Tracy Campbell (*The Politics of Despair: Power and Resistance in the Tobacco Wars* [Lexington: University Press of Kentucky, 1993]) argues that night riders were so active in central and western Kentucky that the Black Patch War, referring to the dark-leaf tobacco grown in the western portion of the state, should have been called the *tobacco wars* to include the Bluegrass and its golden-leafed Burley tobacco. On the Elmendorf Farm fire, see "Thirty-Three Brood Mares, Eleven Colts Burn to Death," *Lexington Herald*, April 3, 1908, 1.

28. "Western Racing," *Spirit of the Times* 121, no. 2 (1891): 49.

29. Carole Case, *The Right Blood: America's Aristocrats in Thoroughbred Racing* (New Brunswick, NJ: Rutgers University Press, 2001), 9. See also Dan Mearns, "When Racing Won Its Case," *Blood-Horse* 106, no. 40 (October 11, 1980): 5748–76; and Joseph Vila, "The Men Who Support Racing," *Illustrated Sporting News* 3, no. 53 (May 14, 1904): 6–7, 24.

30. Robertson and Farley, eds., *Hoofprints of the Century*, 78–79; Mearns, "When Racing Won Its Case."

31. Mearns, "When Racing Won Its Case."

32. Ibid.

33. Robertson, *History of Thoroughbred Racing*, 175.

34. Ibid., 195. See also Drape, *Black Maestro*, 43–44.

35. Harlow, *Weep No More, My Lady*, 311.

36. "Negro Rider on Wane," *Washington Post*, August 20, 1905, 3.

37. "The Race Problem on the Golf Links," *Illustrated Sporting News* 1, no. 20 (September 26, 1903): 2.

38. *Spirit of the Times* 122, no. 10 (September 12, 1891): 371; *Washington Post*, August 20, 1905, 3.

39. "Negro Jockeys Shut Out," *New York Times*, July 29, 1900.

40. Bowen, *Legacies of the Turf*, 23.

41. John E. Madden is profiled in Ed Bowen, *Masters of the Turf: Ten Trainers Who Dominated Horse Racing's Golden Age* (Lexington: Eclipse, 2007), 113–34.

42. "History of Horse Racing Traced by Madden," from an unidentified and undated newspaper article in the Madden Family Scrapbooks, Hamburg Place Farm, Lexington.

43. Bowen, *Legacies of the Turf*, 26; "J. E. Madden Dies; Was Noted Turfman," *New York Times*, November 4, 1929, 25.

44. "Millionaires Want to Win Turf Classic," *New York World*, August 27, 1901; "John E. Madden's Yankee Wins," *New York World*, September 1, 1901.

45. "Memories of John E. Madden," *Thoroughbred Record* 110, no. 19 (November 9, 1929): 286–87; Philip Ardery, "The Wizard Was No Magician," *Spur,* January/February 1984, 58–61.

46. Kent Hollingsworth, *The Wizard of the Turf: John E. Madden of Hamburg Place* (Lexington: privately published, 1965), 12–13.

47. John E. Madden, Last Will and Testament, January 23, 1929, Will Book 15, p. 76, Fayette County Circuit Clerk, Lexington.

48. Hollingsworth, *Wizard of the Turf,* 28–29.

49. Ibid., 29.

7. The Idea of Horse Country Reclaimed

1. John Michael Vlach, *The Planter's Prospect: Privilege and Slavery in Plantation Paintings* (Chapel Hill: University of North Carolina Press, 2002), 187–88. Vlach writes: "Southern writers concentrated on rehabilitating the reputation of their native region. They focused . . . on the key elements of the old plantation legend: fine houses, courtly white gentlemen, exquisitely gowned white ladies, bountiful harvests, and contented slaves." For more on plantation literature, see Cobb, *Away Down South,* 77.

2. Statistics on Civil War armies and the dead are taken from http://www.civilwarhome.com.

3. William R. Taylor, *Cavalier and Yankee* (Cambridge, MA: Harvard University Press, 1979), 18.

4. David W. Blight, *Race and Reunion: The Civil War in American Memory* (Cambridge, MA: Belknap/Harvard University Press, 2001), 209.

5. William S. Ward, *A Literary History of Kentucky* (Knoxville: University of Tennessee Press, 1988), 37, 40.

6. "An Estimate of Kentuckians," *Kentucky Farmer and Breeder* 3, no. 40 (October 5, 1906): 12.

7. "Annie Fellow Johnston: A Short Biography," http://www.littlecolonel .com/bio.htm. For an analysis of Johnston's connecting Kentucky to a Confederate past, see Marshall, "'Strange Conclusion,'" chap. 6.

8. Marshall, "'Strange Conclusion,'" 220–21.

9. James Lane Allen, *Two Kentucky Gentlemen of the Old School* (n.p., 1888), detached from *Century Magazine,* vol. 35 (1888), Samuel Wilson Collection, Special Collections and Archives, University of Kentucky Libraries.

10. James Lane Allen, "Homesteads of the Blue-Grass," *Century Magazine* (1892), Samuel Wilson Collection.

11. Ibid.

12. Ward, *Literary History of Kentucky,* 79.

13. "Young Mr. Clay of Kentucky a Welcome Invader of the Eastern Turf," *New York Morning Telegraph,* September 13, 1903.

14. "The Kentucky Thoroughbred," *Kentucky Farmer and Breeder* 2, no. 44 (November 2, 1905): 8–9.

15. "The American Stud Book and Its Founder" (n. 28, chap. 2, above).

16. Mary Fleming, "A Pedigree by Any Other Name," *Thoroughbred of California,* April 1981, 31.

17. "Stud Book Reform," *Lexington Leader,* February 11, 1902, 7; "New Volume of Stud Book," *Kentucky Farmer and Breeder* 3, no. 3 (January 18, 1906): 9; "Lexington, Race Horse and Sire," *Kentucky Farmer and Breeder* 3, no. 16 (April 20, 1906): 2.

18. Winn and Menke, *Down the Stretch,* 4.

19. For background on the traditional singing of "My Old Kentucky Home" at the Kentucky Derby, see Vickie Mitchell, "Derby Anthem's Dark Roots," *Kentucky Derby Souvenir Magazine,* May 3, 2003, 66–68.

20. *Kentucky Farmer and Breeder* 2, no. 21 (May 25, 1905): 4.

21. Maury Klein, *History of the Louisville and Nashville Railroad* (Lexington: University Press of Kentucky, 2003), 380–86.

22. Ibid.

23. Klotter, "William Goebel." See also James C. Klotter, *William Goebel: The Politics of Wrath* (Lexington: University Press of Kentucky, 1977).

24. Bowmar, *Giants of the Turf,* 166–83.

25. Robert W. Woolley, "A Beautiful Kentucky Estate—Walnut Hall," *Illustrated Sporting News* 1, no. 2 (May 23, 1903): 11.

26. Thomas A. Knight and Nancy Lewis Greene, *Country Estates of the Blue Grass* (Lexington: privately published, 1905), 5.

27. Ibid. For more on the country house movement as it related to the horse industry, see Biesel, "American Upper Class." See also Ferdinand Lundberg, *America's 60 Families* (New York: Vanguard, 1937).

28. Leigh Gordon Giltner, "The Home of the Thoroughbred," *Munsey's Magazine,* April 1, 1902, 112.

29. "A Horse Owners' Exodus from Long Island Feared," *Brooklyn Eagle,* August 17, 1902, 9.

30. Giltner, "The Home of the Thoroughbred," 105.

31. "Mr. James B. Haggin's Great Elmendorf Estate," *Kentucky Farmer and Breeder* 2, no. 49 (December 14, 1905).

32. Ibid.

33. Ibid. See also "Hira Villa Sold," *Lexington Leader,* January 13, 1907, 2.

34. "Mr. James B. Haggin's Great Elmendorf Estate" (n. 31 above); Andres G. Leonard, "J. B. Haggin's Beautiful Kentucky Estate," *Illustrated Sporting News* 2, no. 31 (December 12, 1903): 28.

35. Maryjean Wall, "History Repeating," *Lexington Herald-Leader,* September 11, 2002, E-1.

36. "Mrs. W. E. D. Stokes Sues," *New York Times,* April 5, 1900, 7.

37. Mari Yoshihara (*Embracing the East: White Women and American Orientalism* [Oxford: Oxford University Press, 2003], 6) argues that "participation in Orientalist discourse offered many American women an effective avenue through which to become part of a dominant American ideology and to gain authority and agency which were denied to them in other realms of sociopolitical life."

38. "Mrs. Stokes's Negro Ball: How the New York Woman Entertains the Colored People on Her Kentucky Farm," *New York Times*, October 3, 1897, 3.

39. Ibid.

40. Case, *The Right Blood*, 27; William Earl Dodge Stokes, *The Right to Be Well Born; or, Horse Breeding in Its Relation to Eugenics* (New York: C. J. O'Brien, 1917).

41. Stokes, *The Right to Be Well Born*, 84.

42. "W. E. D. Stokes Dies of Pneumonia at 73," *New York Times*, May 20, 1926.

43. Simpson, *Josephine Clay*, 77; "Mill Stream," *Lexington Leader*, January 20, 1907.

44. "Mr. James B. Haggin's Great Elmendorf Estate" (n. 31 above).

45. "The Slipping Evil," *Kentucky Farmer and Breeder* 3, no. 10 (March 9, 1906): 7.

46. *Lexington Leader*, January 26, 1907. See also *Kentucky Farmer and Breeder* 4, no. 17 (April 26, 1907): 6–7.

47. Robertson, *History of Thoroughbred Racing*, 196.

48. See, e.g., Vila, "Men Who Support Racing"; Peter J. Gallie, *Ordered Liberty: A Constitutional History of New York* (New York: Fordham University Press, 1996), 162–63; Alfred Henry Lewis, "The Racing Game," *Pearson's Magazine*, July 1907, 67–78; and Bennett Liebman, "The Past as Present: The Last 'Dead Heat' in the State Senate, 100 Years Ago," *New York State Bar Association Journal* 81, no. 1 (January 2009): 33–37, and "Horseracing in New York in the Progressive Era," *Gaming Law Review and Economics: Regulation, Compliance, and Policy* 12, no. 6 (2008): 556 (quote from *New York Times*, May 22, 1904, 1).

49. Liebman, "The Past as Present"; Robertson, *History of Thoroughbred Racing*, 196.

50. Liebman, "The Past as Present"; Robertson, *History of Thoroughbred Racing*, 196.

51. "The Jockey Club Is Exonerated," *Thoroughbred Record* 73, no. 5 (February 4, 1911): 54.

52. Ibid.

53. "Keep Cella Out of Kentucky," *Kentucky Farmer and Breeder* 3, no. 8 (February 23, 1906): 10–11.

54. Ibid.; "A State Racing Commission," *Kentucky Farmer and Breeder* 3, no. 9 (March 2, 1906): 12.

55. "The Racing Commission," *Kentucky Farmer and Breeder* 3, no. 40 (October 5, 1906): 8; *Daily Racing Form* quoted in "Gratification at Racing Commission," *Kentucky Farmer and Breeder* 3, no. 13 (March 30, 1906): 11.

56. *The American Racing Manual, 1923* (Chicago: Daily Racing Form Publishing Co., 1923), 409 (chart showing annual purse distributions, 1906–1922); "Racing Statistics of the Year 1911," *The American Racing Manual, 1911* (Chicago: Daily Racing Form Publishing Co., 1911), 330; *The American Racing Manual, 1909* (Chicago: Daily Racing Form Publishing Co., 1909), 268; "Racing Statistics of the Year," *The American Racing Manual, 1910* (Chicago: Daily Racing Form Publishing Co., 1910), 324; "Disastrous Effects of Unwise Legislation," *Kentucky Farmer and Breeder* 2, no. 13 (March 30, 1905): 8.

57. *Lexington Leader,* June 4, 1909, and January 29, 1912.

58. *Kentucky Farmer and Breeder* 2, no. 18 (May 4, 1905): 7.

59. *Spirit of the Times* 121, no. 2 (January 31, 1891); Winn and Menke, *Down the Stretch,* 69–77.

60. "Live Stock Taxation," *Kentucky Farmer and Breeder* 3, no. 1 (January 4, 1906): 8–9.

61. *Kentucky Farmer and Breeder* 3, no. 1 (January 11, 1906): 8.

62. Ibid.

63. "Rich Men Who Love Horse Racing," *Thoroughbred Record* 73, no. 7 (February 18, 1911): 75.

64. Liebman, "Horseracing in New York."

65. Information on Harry Payne Whitney can be found in Bowen, *Legacies of the Turf,* esp. 53–62.

66. Taylor, *Cavalier and Yankee;* and Blight, *Race and Reunion.*

67. John E. Kleber, ed., *The Kentucky Encyclopedia* (Lexington: University Press of Kentucky, 1992), 650–51.

68. "Roll of Lexington Chapter of United Daughters of Confederacy," from charter obtained October 19, 1895, box 1, folder 4A, Richard Alexander Spurr Papers, Special Collections and Archives, University of Kentucky Libraries. Among the membership, names of families connected with Bluegrass horsemen included Mrs. W. C. P. Breckenridge, wife of W. C. P. Breckenridge; Mrs. John C. Breckenridge, wife of John C. Breckenridge; Miss N. P. Breckenridge, daughter of W. C. P. Breckenridge; Curry Breckenridge, daughter of W. C. P. Breckenridge; Mrs. James B. Clay; Mrs. A. B. Chinn; Miss Ellie Chinn; Elenor D. Breckenridge Chalkley, daughter of W. D. P. Breckenridge; Mrs. H. P. Headley; Miss Mary Viley Hawkins, granddaughter of Major John R. Viley; Mrs. S. C. Lyne; Miss Nannie Lyne, niece of Sanford Lyne; Mrs. C. H. Morgan; Louisiana B. Gibson Maxfield, daughter of Hart Gibson; Mrs. Martha R. J. Nuchols, wife of S. V. Nuchols; Mrs. W. J. Loughridge, daughter of Wm. W. Bruce, niece of Mrs. John H. Morgan; Mrs. Wickliffe Preston, wife of William Preston; and Mrs. Martinette Viley Witherspoon, daughter of War-

ren Viley. For the horsemen's approval of the statue, see "Coppini's Statue of General John Morgan Accepted" (*Lexington Herald,* May 28, 1909), which lists the names of horsemen who approved the work and also of a few who did not.

69. *Lexington Leader,* September 7, 1907, 6. See also A. C. Quinsenberry, "Morgan's Men in Ohio," *Lexington Herald,* April 5, 1908, 2. Quinsenberry's handwritten version of this story, slightly different and perhaps a first draft, can be found in 0709 Clift Microfilm, no. 691, Manuscript Collection, Kentucky Historical Society, Frankfort.

70. Kirk Savage, *Standing Soldiers, Kneeling Slaves* (Princeton, NJ: Princeton University Press, 1997), 4. Blight (*Race and Reunion,* 77–80) too discussed the Confederate memorial movement. See also Gary W. Gallagher and Alan T. Nolan, eds., *The Myth of the Lost Cause and Civil War History* (Bloomington: Indiana University Press, 2000), 14.

71. "Mr. and Mrs. J. B. Haggin Arrive" and "Morgan Statue," *Lexington Leader,* September 3, 1911.

72. "American Owners Plan to Send Their Stables to Europe," *Lexington Leader,* October 3, 1911; "Republicans Heard by Very Small Audiences; John H. Flood Tells Negro Voter Loaves and Fishes Are Not for Him," *Lexington Herald,* October 1, 1911; "A Dream Made Real," *Lexington Herald,* October 2, 1911; "Federal Soldiers Invited to Parade," *Lexington Herald,* October 13, 1911; "Morgan's Monument," *Lexington Herald,* October 18, 1911.

73. "Memorable Day in Store for Men of Deathless Sixties," *Lexington Herald,* October 18, 1911.

74. On pari-mutuel machines sent from Louisville to Lexington, see *Lexington Leader,* September 10, 1911.

Selected Bibliography

Newspapers and Periodicals Consulted

Blood-Horse
Brooklyn Eagle
Frankfort Commonwealth
Georgetown (KY) Weekly Times
Harper's New Monthly Magazine
Illustrated Sporting News
Keeneland Magazine
Kentucky Farmer and Breeder
Kentucky Gazette (Lexington)
Kentucky Leader (Lexington)
Kentucky Live Stock Record
Lexington Daily Leader
Lexington Herald
Lexington Herald-Leader
Lexington Leader
Lexington Observer and Reporter
Lexington Transcript
Live Stock Record
Munsey's Magazine

New York Daily Tribune
New York Morning Telegraph
New York Sportsman
New York Times
New York World
Pearson's Magazine
Porter's Spirit of the Times
Spirit of the Times
Spur
Thoroughbred of California
Thoroughbred Record
Tri-Weekly Kentucky Yeoman (Frankfort)
Turf and Sport Digest
Turf, Field and Farm
Washington Post
Wilkes' Spirit of the Times
Woodford Sun (Versailles, KY)
Woodford Weekly (Versailles, KY)

Manuscripts and Collections

Adam Harper v. J. Wallace Harper. 1873. Scott County Order Book 32, folio 606, microfilm reel 994563, Kentucky Department of Libraries, Frankfort.

Clay, Josephine, Papers, University of Kentucky Libraries, Special Collections and Archives.

Hervey, John. "W. S. Vosburgh: An Appreciation, Written for the Jockey Club." 1935. Keeneland Library, Lexington.

"Notes by Harry Worcester Smith, Lordvale Library, 1930, to Accompany the Race Horses of America First Number by Edward Troye (1808–1874)." 1867. Keeneland Library, Lexington.

Spurr, Richard Alexander, Papers. Special Collections, University of Kentucky.

Winkfield Casey, Liliane. Oral history taken by Maryjean Wall, Cincinnati, September 12, 2002. In possession of author.

Woodburn Stud Farm, 1864. Records of Woodburn Farm, Woodford County, KY. Copy in possession of the author and given to her by the late Dr. A. J. Alexander.

Books and Articles

Primary Sources

The American Racing Manual. Chicago: Daily Racing Form Publishing Co., various years.

Busbey, Hamilton, "The Running Turf in America." *Harper's New Monthly* 41 (July 1870): 245–55.

———. *Recollections of Men and Horses.* New York: Dodd, Mead, 1907.

Crickmore, H. G. *Racing Calendars, 1861, 1862, 1863, 1864, 1865.* New York: printed privately by W. C. Whitney, 1901.

Harrison, Lowell H., ed. *Kentucky's Governors, 1792–1985.* Lexington: University Press of Kentucky, 2004.

Hatch, Alden, and Foxhall Keene. *Full Tilt: The Sporting Memoirs of Foxhall Keene.* New York: Derrydale, 1938.

Hervey, John. *Racing in America, 1665–1865.* Vol. 2. New York: Jockey Club, 1944.

Knight, Thomas A., and Nancy Lewis Greene. *Country Estates of the Blue Grass.* Lexington: privately published, 1905.

Krik's Guide. New York: H. G. Crickmore, 1877–1878.

Lacer, Genevieve Baird. *Edward Troye: Painter of Thoroughbred Stories.* Louisville: Harmony House, 2006.

Menke, Frank G. *Down the Stretch: The Story of Colonel Matt J. Winn.* New York: Smith & Durrell, 1945.

Perrin, William Henry. *History of Fayette County, Kentucky.* Chicago: O. L. Baskin, 1882.

Ranck, George W. *History of Lexington, Kentucky.* Cincinnati: Robert Clarke, 1872.

Trevathan, Charles E. *The American Thoroughbred.* New York: Macmillan, 1905.

Vosburgh, W. S. *Cherry and Black: The Career of Mr. Pierre Lorillard on the Turf.* New York: privately published, 1916.

———. *Racing in America, 1866–1921.* New York: Scribner Press, 1922.

Weeks, Lyman Horace, ed. *The American Turf: An Historical Account of Racing in the United States.* New York: Historical Co., 1898.

Secondary Sources

Adelman, Melvin L. *A Sporting Time: New York City and the Rise of Modern Athletics, 1820–70.* Urbana: University of Illinois Press, 1986.

Alvey, R. Gerald. *Kentucky Bluegrass Country.* Jackson: University Press of Mississippi, 1992.

Astor, Aaron. "Belated Confederates: Black Politics, Guerrilla Violence, and the Collapse of Conservative Unionism in Kentucky and Missouri, 1860–1872." Ph.D. diss., Northwestern University, 2006.

———. "No Gun, No Vote: Violence and the Fifteenth Amendment in Kentucky." Paper delivered at the annual meeting of the Southern Historical Association, Louisville, November 2009.

Bay, Mia. *The White Image in the Black Mind.* New York: Oxford University Press, 2000.

Betts, John Rickards. "Sporting Journalism in Nineteenth-Century America." *American Quarterly* 5, no. 1 (Spring 1953): 39–56.

Biesel, Jennifer. "The American Upper Class and the American Horse Industry from 1865–1929." Ph.D. diss., Middle Tennessee State University, 2005.

Black, David. *The King of Fifth Avenue: The Fortunes of August Belmont.* New York: Dial, 1981.

Blight, David W. *Race and Reunion: The Civil War in American Memory.* Cambridge, MA: Belknap/Harvard University Press, 2001.

Bolin, James Duane. *Bossism and Reform in a Southern City: Lexington, Kentucky, 1880–1940.* Lexington: University Press of Kentucky, 2000.

Borries, Betty Earle. *Isaac Murphy: Kentucky's Record Jockey.* Berea, KY: Kentucke Imprints, 1988.

Bowen, Edward L. *Legacies of the Turf: A Century of Great Thoroughbred Breeders.* Vol. 1. Lexington: Eclipse, 2003.

———. *Masters of the Turf: Ten Trainers Who Dominated Horse Racing's Golden Age.* Lexington: Eclipse, 2007.

Bowmar, Dan M., III. *Giants of the Turf: The Alexanders, the Belmonts, James R. Keene, the Whitneys.* Lexington: Blood-Horse, 1960.

Boyer, Paul. *Urban Masses and Moral Order in America, 1820–1920.* Cambridge, MA: Harvard University Press, 1978.

Burrows, Edwin G., and Mike Wallace. *Gotham: A History of New York City to 1898.* New York: Oxford University Press, 1999.

Campbell, Tracy. *The Politics of Despair: Power and Resistance in the Tobacco Wars.* Lexington: University Press of Kentucky, 1993.

Case, Carole. *The Right Blood: America's Aristocrats in Thoroughbred Racing.* New Brunswick, NJ: Rutgers University Press, 2001.

Clark, Thomas D. *Agrarian Kentucky.* Lexington: University Press of Kentucky, 1977.

———. *A History of Kentucky.* Ashland, KY: J. Stuart Foundation, 1992.

Cobb, James C. *Away Down South: A History of Southern Identity.* Oxford: Oxford University Press, 2005.

Custer, Elizabeth B. *Tenting on the Plains; or, General Custer in Kansas and Texas.* New York: Harper & Bros., 1895. Reprint, Norman: University of Oklahoma Press, 1994.

Dizikes, John. *Yankee Doodle Dandy.* New Haven, CT: Yale University Press, 2000.

———. *Sportsmen and Gamesmen.* Columbia: University of Missouri Press, 2002.

Drape, Joe. *Black Maestro: The Epic Life of an American Legend.* New York: William Morrow, 2006.

Driefort, John E., ed. *Baseball History from Outside the Lines: A Reader.* Lincoln: University of Nebraska Press, 2001.

Eller, Ronald D. *Miners, Millands, and Mountaineers: Industrialization of the Appalachian South, 1880–1930.* Knoxville: University of Tennessee Press, 1982.

Ettensohn, Frank R. "Evidence and Implications of Possible Far-Field Responses to Taconian Orogeny: Middle-Late Ordovician Lexington Platform and Sebree Trough, East-Central United States." *Southeastern Geology* 41 (2002): 1–36.

———. "Horses, Kentucky Bluegrass, and the Origin of Upper Ordovician, Trenton-Age Carbonate Reservoir and Source Rocks in East-Central United States." Paper presented at the annual meeting of the American Association of Petroleum Geologists, Eastern Section, Lexington, September 2007.

Freehling, William W. *The South vs. the South: How Anti-Confederate Southerners Shaped the Course of the Civil War.* New York: Oxford University Press, 2001.

Gallie, Peter J. *Ordered Liberty: A Constitutional History of New York.* New York: Fordham University Press, 1996.

Harlow, Alvin F. *Weep No More, My Lady.* New York: Whittlesey, 1942.

Harrison, Lowell H., ed. *Kentucky's Governors, 1792–1985.* 1985. Updated ed. Lexington: University Press of Kentucky, 2004.

Hatch, Alden, and Foxhall Keene. *Full Tilt: The Sporting Memoirs of Foxhall Keene.* New York: Derrydale, 1938.

Hewett, Abram S. "Daniel Swigert." *Thoroughbred Record* 211, no. 2 (January 9, 1980), 112–14.

Hillenbrand, Laura. *Seabiscuit: An American Legend.* New York: Random House, 2001.

Hirsch, Mark D. *William C. Whitney: Modern Warwick.* New York: Dodd, Mead, 1948.

Hofstadter, Richard. *The Age of Reform: From Bryan to F.D.R.* New York: Knopf, 1955.

Hollingsworth, Kent. *The Wizard of the Turf: John E. Madden of Hamburg Place.* Lexington: privately published, 1965.

———. *The Great Ones.* Lexington: Blood-Horse, 1970.

———. *The Kentucky Thoroughbred.* Lexington: University Press of Kentucky, 1976.

Hollingsworth, Randolph. *Lexington: Queen of the Bluegrass.* Charleston, SC: Arcadia, 2004.

Hotaling, Edward. *They're Off! Horse Racing at Saratoga.* Syracuse, NY: Syracuse University Press, 1995.

———. *The Great Black Jockeys: The Lives and Times of the Men Who Dominated America's First National Sport.* Rocklin, CA: Prima, 1999.

Ireland, Robert M. *Little Kingdoms: The Counties of Kentucky, 1850–1891.* Lexington: University Press of Kentucky, 1977.

Kleber, John E., ed. *The Kentucky Encyclopedia.* Lexington: University Press of Kentucky, 1992.

Klein, Maury. *History of the Louisville and Nashville Railroad.* Lexington: University Press of Kentucky, 2003.

Klotter, James C. *William Goebel: The Politics of Wrath.* Lexington: University Press of Kentucky, 1977.

———. *Kentucky Justice, Southern Honor, and American Manhood: Understanding the Life and Death of Richard Reid.* Baton Rouge: Louisiana State University Press, 2003.

Lee, Robert G. *Orientals: Asian Americans in Popular Culture.* Philadelphia: Temple University Press, 1999.

Liebman, Bennett. "Horseracing in New York in the Progressive Era," *Gaming Law Review and Economics: Regulation, Compliance, and Policy* 12, no. 6 (2008): 550–62.

———. "The Past as Present: The Last 'Dead Heat' in the State Senate, 100 Years Ago." *New York State Bar Association Journal* 81, no. 1 (January 2009): 33–37.

Longrigg, Roger. *The History of Horse Racing.* New York: Stein & Day, 1972.

Lucas, Marion B. *A History of Blacks in Kentucky: From Slavery to Segregation, 1760–1891.* Frankfort: Kentucky Historical Society, 2003.

Lundberg, Ferdinand. *America's 60 Families.* New York: Vanguard, 1937.

Mangum, William Preston, II. *A Kingdom for the Horse.* Louisville: Harmony House, 1999.

Manning, Landon. *The Noble Animals: Tales of the Saratoga Turf.* N.p.: privately printed, 1973.

Marshall, Anne Elizabeth. "'A Strange Conclusion to a Triumphant War': Memory, Identity and the Creation of a Confederate Kentucky." Ph.D. diss., University of Georgia, 2004.

Myers, Gustavus. *History of the Great American Fortunes.* New York: Random House, 1936.

Myrdal, Gunner. *An American Dilemma: The Negro Problem and Modern Democracy.* New York: Harper & Row, 1962.

Palmer, Joe H. "Maroon, Scarlet Sash." *Keeneland Magazine,* Spring 1942, 8–11, 38–49.

Parmer, Charles B. *For Gold and Glory.* New York: Carrick & Evans, 1939.

Raitz, Karl B. *The Kentucky Bluegrass: A Regional Profile and Guide.* Chapel Hill: University of North Carolina Department of Geography, 1980.

Ramage, James A. *Rebel Raider: The Life of General John Hunt Morgan.* Lexington: University Press of Kentucky, 1986.

Rhyne, James Michael. "Rehearsal for Redemption: The Politics of Post-Emancipation Violence in Kentucky's Bluegrass Region." Ph.D. diss., University of Cincinnati, 2006.

Robertson, William H. P. *The History of Thoroughbred Racing in America.* Englewood Cliffs, NJ: Prentice-Hall, 1964.

Robertson, William H. P., and Dan Farley, eds. *Hoofprints of the Century.* Lexington: Thoroughbred Record, 1975.

Simpson, Henry Clay, Jr. *Josephine Clay: Pioneer Horsewoman of the Bluegrass.* Prospect, KY: Harmony House, 2005.

Smith, Gerald L. *Black America Series: Lexington, Kentucky.* Charleston, SC: Arcadia, 2002.

Smith, Peter C., and Karl B. Raitz. "Negro Hamlets and Agricultural Estates in Kentucky's Inner Bluegrass." *Geographical Review* 64, no. 2 (1974): 217–34.

Somers, Dale. *The Rise of Sports in New Orleans, 1850–1900.* Baton Rouge: Louisiana State University Press, 1972.

Struna, Nancy L. "The North-South Races: American Thoroughbred Racing in Transition, 1823–1850." *Journal of Sport History* 8, no. 2 (Summer 1981): 28–57.

Suchy, Cherie. "Legacy of the Land." *Thoroughbred Record,* January 7, 1981, 48–51.

Takaki, Ronald T. *Iron Cages: Race and Culture in Nineteenth-Century America.* New York: Knopf, 1979.

Tapp, Hambleton, and James C. Klotter. *Kentucky: Decades of Discord, 1865–1900.* Frankfort: Kentucky Historical Society, 1977.

Taylor, William R. *Cavalier and Yankee.* Cambridge, MA: Harvard University Press, 1979.

Trelease, Allen W. *White Terror: The Ku Klux Klan Conspiracy and Southern Reconstruction.* Baton Rouge: Louisiana State University Press, 1971.

Trevathan, Charles E. *The American Thoroughbred.* New York: Macmillan, 1905.

Vlach, John Michael. *The Planter's Prospect: Privilege and Slavery in Plantation Paintings.* Chapel Hill: University of North Carolina Press, 2002.

Wade, Horace. *Tales of the Turf.* New York: Vantage, 1956.

Wall, Maryjean. "Kentucky's Isaac Murphy: A Legacy Interrupted." M.A. thesis, University of Kentucky, 2003.

Waller, Altina L. *Feud: Hatfields, McCoys, and Social Change in Appalachia, 1860–1900.* Chapel Hill: University of North Carolina Press, 1988.

Ward, William S. *A Literary History of Kentucky.* Knoxville: University of Tennessee Press, 1988.

Wendt, Lloyd, and Herman Kogan. *Bet a Million! The Story of John W. Gates.* Indianapolis: Bobbs-Merrill, 1948.

Wiener, Jonathan M. *Social Origins of the New South: Alabama, 1860–1885.* Baton Rouge: Louisiana State University Press, 1978.

Wiggins, David K. "Isaac Murphy: Black Hero in Nineteenth Century American Sport, 1861–1896." *Canadian Journal of the History of Sport and Physical Education,* May 1979, 15–32.

———. *Glory Bound: Black Athletes in a White America.* Syracuse, NY: Syracuse University Press, 1997.

Williamson, Joel. *The Crucible of Race: Black and White Relations in the American South since Emancipation.* New York: Oxford University Press, 1984.

Wills, Ridley W., II. *The History of Belle Meade: Mansion, Plantation, and Stud.* Nashville: Vanderbilt University Press, 1991.

Winn, Matt J., and Frank G. Menke. *Down the Stretch.* New York: Smith & Durrell, 1945.

Woodward, C. Vann. *Origins of the New South, 1877–1913.* Baton Rouge: Louisiana State University Press, 1971.

———. *The Strange Career of Jim Crow.* New York: Oxford University Press, 1999.

Wright, George C. *Racial Violence in Kentucky, 1865–1940.* Baton Rouge: Louisiana State University Press, 1996.

Yoshihara, Mari. *Embracing the East: White Women and American Orientalism.* Oxford: Oxford University Press, 2003.

Young, Andrew Sturgeon Nash. *Negro Firsts in Sports.* Chicago: Johnson, 1963.

Index

Index

Index

Harper, John W. (great-nephew of John), 99–100, 102

Harper, J. Wallace, 103

Harper, "Uncle" John, 90–93, 96–101, 103, 105–9, 118, 125, 136, 142, 163–64, 169, 187, 201, 206, 252–53

Harper's magazine, 44

Harper's New Monthly Magazine, 47, 177

Harper's Weekly, 4, 23

Harriman, Edward Henry, 183, 224

Harriman, Mary Williamson Averell, 224

Harriman, William Averell, 224

Harrison, Benjamin, 110

Harry Bassett (horse), 84, 106, 136

Hart-Agnew Bill, 228–29, 231

Hawkins, Abe, 33, 127

Hawthorne Race Course, 144–45, 179, 193

Haymarket Square, 145

Hearst, George, 137

heat racing, 27

hemp, 65, 71, 95, 219

Hervey, John, 62

Himyar (horse), 183, 185

Hindoo (horse), 156–58

Hira (horse), 184

Hira Villa, 186, 220

history as memory. *See* memory as history

Hollingsworth, Kent, 137, 187

Homestake mines, 137

"Homesteads of the Blue-Grass," 207

Homicide North and South, 95

horse country. *See under* Bluegrass

horse industry, 1–3, 6, 8–12, 15, 25–26, 35, 50, 55, 57, 60, 62, 67–70, 72–75, 78–79, 84–85, 107, 134, 150, 152, 159–60, 162, 164–66, 168–69, 175, 192, 196, 199–200, 205, 208–10, 212, 215, 218, 226–27, 230, 232, 234–39, 244

hospitality, 47, 87–88

Hotaling, Edward, 15, 23

Hughes, Charles Evan, 229, 234

Hunter, John, 17, 26, 30–31, 36, 39, 42, 51, 180

iconography, 2–3, 7, 47

identity
    Southern, 3–5, 10–11, 119, 203–5, 208, 212, 220, 224, 256, 259
    Western, 4, 21–22, 30, 32, 47–48, 149, 152, 203, 208

Idle Hour Farm, 215

Ill-Used, The (horse), 151

Illustrated Sporting News, 194, 199, 215, 220–21

industrialists, 2, 6, 9, 25, 145, 174

Ingleside Stud, 164

In Old Kentucky, 166–67, 168

Iroquois, 58, 149–50, 155, 162

Italianate style, 83, 216–17

Jackson, Andrew, 57

Jackson, William, 60, 163

Jefferson, Thomas, 104

Jerome, Leonard, 17–19, 26–27, 36, 38, 41–42, 51–52, 57, 78–79, 143, 147, 151, 155–56, 160, 176–77, 245

Jerome Edgar (horse), 78, 163

Jerome Park, 19, 27, 36, 41–42, 51–52, 57, 136, 147, 150–52, 155, 160, 163, 176–77, 180

Jersey Derby, 19, 31

Jewell, James Rodes, 114

Jewell, Malcolm, 175

Jim Crow, 5, 193

Jockey Club, 69, 123, 190, 191–92, 209–11, 224, 229, 233, 240

jockey registry, 235

jockeys, 70, 109, 111, 116, 122–23, 129, 137, 140, 177–79, 192–93, 225, 256, 258. *See also* black jockeys; white jockeys

Index

Index

Quantrill, William Clarke, 50

race war, 141, 195
racial violence, 5, 91, 93, 96, 100–103,
    105, 108, 110, 118, 123, 126, 134,
    142, 169, 195, 254–55
racing
    campaign to shut down, 10, 35, 67,
        170, 227–28 (*see also* Progressive
        reformers; social reformers)
    revival in the North, 14, 26, 28, 38,
        244, 246–47
raids on horse farms, 19, 32, 49, 61, 244
railroad
    industrialists, 9, 42, 144–45, 175, 179,
        183, 188, 198, 213, 224, 239, 247
    strikes, 145, 153–54
    transportation of horses, 29–30, 45, 51,
        60, 101, 106, 147
Railroad YMCA, 133
Raitz, Karl B., 55, 64–65
Rancho del Paso, 136, 161
Reconstruction, 121–22, 249, 253
Redfield, H. V., 95, 253
red-light district, 131
Reed, Charles, 78, 163
Regret (horse), 212
Republicans, 119–20, 121
Reynolds, Mrs. Hunt, 124
Rhadamanthus (horse), 156
Rhinodyne (horse), 33
Richards, Alexander Keene, 35, 42, 46,
        61, 72, 85
Right to be Well Born, 224
Riley (horse), 143–44, 165
Robertson, William, 192
Roosevelt, Theodore, 10, 192, 199
Rothschilds, 40
Runnymede (horse), 157
Runnymede Farm, 157–59, 208, 239

Salina (horse), 137

Salvator (horse), 94, 110, 136–40
Sanford, Milton Holbrook, 52, 56, 71–72,
    75–76, 169–70, 218
Saratoga Cup, 24, 31, 33, 48, 51, 101, 106
Saratoga Race Course (and predecessor),
    8, 17–19, 23, 28–32, 39, 41–42, 48,
    52–53, 56, 78, 81, 103, 127, 152,
    157, 163, 177, 215, 228, 244–45,
    252
Saratoga Springs, 13, 17, 22–23, 25, 39,
    42, 78, 245
    as "queen of watering places," 22, 245
scale of weights, 152
Scott, Will, 100
Scythian, 46
Secretariat (horse), 162
sectional
    rivalry and animosity, 20–22, 28, 32,
        34, 37
    healing, 21
segregation, 116, 121, 127, 134, 193–94
"separate but equal" ruling, 193–94
Seventh Cavalry, 81
Sewell, 127, 244
Shaler, Nathan Southgate, 55
Sheepshead Bay, NY, 138, 160, 180
Sheridan, Phil, 144
shorthorn cattle, 84, 247
Silver Fox of Wall Street. *See* Keene,
    James R.
Simms, Willie, 113, 123
Simpson, Joseph Cairn, 72
Sir Barton (horse), 240
Sir Henry (horse), 33, 34
Skedaddle (horse), 62, 164
slaves, 42, 46, 58, 61–66, 78, 118, 120–21,
    127, 205, 207, 244, 264
slave jockeys, 36, 127
slavery
    practice of, 5, 15, 17, 63, 66, 83–84,
        100, 116, 118–21, 134, 193, 204,
        207, 224, 250, 256, 259, 264